# DONALD HEALEY

# DONALD HEALEY

## MY WORLD OF CARS

by Peter Garnier
with Brian Healey

PSL
Patrick Stephens Limited

First published in 1989

British Library Cataloguing in Publication Data

Garnier, Peter
Donald Healey: the man and his cars.
1. Racing cars. Racing. Healey, Donald,
1898-1988
I. Title II. Healey, Brian
796.7'2'0924

ISBN 1-85260-212-0

Patrick Stephens Limited is part of the Thorsons Publishing
Group, Wellingborough, Northamptonshire
NN8 2RQ, England.

Typeset by MJL Limited, Hitchin, Hertfordshire
Printed by Butler & Tanner Limited, Frome, Somerset

1  3  5  7  9  10  8  6  4  2

# Contents

# Acknowledgements

The Authors would particularly like to thank the aviation writer, Hugh Scanlon, for the time he spent checking the aircraft types and aviation history with which Donald Healey was involved during World War 1. We would like, too, to acknowledge with gratitude the help of the many others whose photographs are reproduced in this book.

They include those to whom we wrote, and received permission to use their work; and those from whom our letters were returned, marked 'Gone Away'. There is also a third category — who, through D.H.'s long life, have kindly sent him photographs of his activities, often world-wide. It is no longer possible to attribute most of these — we can but record the photographers' names with gratitude. The three categories include:

The National Motor Museum, *Autocar*, L. Klemantaski, E. Eves, G. Boyd, R. Barker, H. R. Clayton, The West Briton, D. G. Bird, ?. Logan, G. Shimon, R. Mottar, Central Press Photos, J. Wheatley, Fox Photos, *The Birmingham Post*, Warwick Photo Agency, C. Wallace, R. Roskrow, *The Western Morning News*, and F. Naylor.

And those whose contributions we can not attribute: G. Anderson, G. Bradley, W. Bode, J. Aubanel, R. Kemp, Worralls, D. and G. Fisher, R. and S. Prevost, H. Nohr, S. Aurandt, J. Jarick, M. and N. Donaldson, J. Gray, R. Harrison, P. Chesworth, E. Worswick, R. Standley, P. and J. Healey, L. King, R. and J. Streng, R. Menadue, M. Healey — and members of Healey Owners and Austin-Healey Clubs world-wide who have contributed photographs that can not always be identified.

These unattributable illustrations have been noted 'B. Healey' in the captions, coming as they do from the family's vast photographic records.

# Foreword

The world is blessed by those few who leave their mark emblazoned upon our memories. They are people who live life fully, have a dream that becomes uppermost in their thinking — a goal for their life which most of us would call a mission.

Donald Healey blessed this world; he left his mark indelibly inscribed. He truly loved life and savoured every moment. His love for cars was a passion so strong that few will ever encounter it. He had that innate feeling for what the public wants and needs. He had his visions of sporting vehicles, but unlike most mortals he was able to bring his visions to reality.

Not only did he conceptualize, he produced. Then he created desire in the rest of us for his products. He excited our imagination with world records on the salt flats, driving hour after hour across the shimmering salt at speeds higher than most could dream of attaining for an instant. He competed successfully in every major endurance race in the world. His cars were always leaders in every world-class rally through the deserts, rain forests, mountains and dust bowls. There was no challenge he would not accept, and win.

He created some of the finest sports cars ever built, and at a price all of us could afford. His influence on the automotive sporting world was heavier than many realize today, but history will prove him to be a giant in his field.

I'm proud to say that Donald Healey was one of my dearest friends. We raced the salt flats together, I tore up one of his cars during the Mexican Road Race and busted myself up pretty good at the same time. I guess we were kindred spirits, loved cars, going fast, having a good time and living life fully. After all, what more can we ask out of life?

*California, 1988*                                            CARROLL SHELBY

Donald Healey's reply to my suggestion of a biography.

D. M. HEALEY, C.B.E.

Phone: Perranporth 3521
Area Code 087257

Ans'd Sep'
19

BRIDGE HOUSE,
PERRANPORTH,
CORNWALL TR6 OES
ENGLAND.

Sept 14. 83

Dear Peter,

I arrived back yesterday from a three months stay in U.S.A to find your letter of 17th July, and today yours of 10th inst. So I apologise for not answering before but I'm sure you will understand.

I have given a lot of thought to a "life story" and appreciate your offer to help me with such a project. But really is it worth the effort for either of us?, a lot of work and a very small market for the end result, even if I you could find a publisher interested, which I very much doubt.

However, Peter, I would love to have a chat with you and will be very pleased to see you if you can make your way here, as I have just returned I am really tied up until the week after next — have some American friends over all next week and this week trying to catch up with things I have overlooked, so could we make it during the week commencing 27th?

Glad to hear you enjoyed Silverstone and still manage some fast motoring. I gave up two years ago — so much frustration in modern motoring, and I found I drove so badly —

Looking forward to seeing you. You can get me on phone lunch time or most days.

All the best
Donald

8

# Introduction

In 1983, when Donald and I had both retired to our native Cornwall, and Donald was 84, I wrote to him as strongly as I dared, suggesting that it was high time somebody wrote his biography. Books had been written about his cars, and about their achievements, including three by his elder son Geoffrey, but never one about the man himself. In his reply, dated 14 September 1983, he explained that he had just returned from his annual three-month jaunt to the States, as guest of the several Austin-Healey clubs, and he went on to say: 'I have given a lot of thought to a life story and appreciate your offer to help me with such a project. But really is it worth the effort for either of us? A lot of work and a very small market for the end result, even if you could find a publisher, which I very much doubt.' Such was his personal opinion of his long, successful and exciting life. He went on to say, slightly grudgingly it seemed, that he would be very pleased to meet and have a chat about it, and I went over to Perranporth on the 25th to join him in his little flat in his son John's house.

I explained that I had intended the book to be a biography because it left me free to say things about Donald that he could scarcely say himself. I could emphasize to the reader what he had achieved, adding my own words of praise where appropriate, to make my point. I could, in fact — using reasonable restraint — write as one of his fans, which I suppose I have been since I first saw the exciting Dolomite 8 at Perranporth in 1935. But Donald would have none of it. It was either an autobiography, or not at all. 'Leave the reader to draw his own conclusions', he said. So it became Donald's personal account of his life — successes and failures included — without pride or more than a trace of prejudice.

We would talk together each Monday morning into a tape-recorder, and I would go home to Newlyn and write the resulting copy, leaving it with him the following Monday to check through. Although advancing bravely towards 90, he was still so full of life, going off upon his three-month trips to the States in summer-time, thankful to avoid the holiday season in Cornwall, and travelling to Calino, near Brescia, each May to stay with his old friend Countess Camilla Maggi at the wondrous Casa Maggi,

## Donald Healey

For two happy years the co-author, Peter Garnier, shared a works-entered 100-Six with Jack Sears in international rallies — seen here after finishing the 1958 RAC British International Rally, and hurrying through the rocky wastes of the Gavia Pass during the 1959 Liège-Rome-Liège Rally. (*G. Boyd*).

for the annual re-enactment of the Mille Miglia, a race that had been so important to him.

One Monday he announced that, on the Wednesday, he was going into hospital to have a new lens fitted to one of his eyes. 'Then you certainly won't want to see me next Monday', I said. 'Oh yes I will', he replied. And when I turned up a week later, and walked into his little flat, he grabbed my arm and led me to the window. 'Just look out there, he said. 'Look at all the colours — I'd forgotten the world was so colourful. Can you read that notice across the road?'

It was, in fact, a particularly grey day, with a steady drizzle falling. 'No Donald', I said. 'I've seldom seen it looking so colourless. And, as for the notice, I think it says "To Let"'. It did, but in small letters which I could scarcely see. It went on to say 'By order of . . .' — clearly legible to Donald with his new eye!

Sometimes, after reading my latest instalment, he would refuse to allow me to include some revelation about the goings-on within the British motor industry. 'I told you that bit for your own information — *not* for publication', he would say. 'So-and-so's a very good friend of mine — I wouldn't hurt his feelings for the world!' Writing as his biographer I could have included such *dénouements* without losing him any friends, or harming his reputation as a kindly man. But, in its reserved, restrained autobiographical form, the story was short on new material, and becoming spineless.

There came a time when Donald would say gloomily 'The more I read of this, the more I'm convinced it isn't worth writing. As I said at the beginning, there simply isn't a story.' Slowly, as his health began to fail, he lost interest. At the end of Chapter 13, having described the return to his beloved Cornwall, with the story not all that far off completion, we regretfully agreed to call it a day, and the manuscript lay forgotten for almost three years — despite, I should add, a host of letters from his public asking 'Where's our book?'

However, before his death, aged 89, on 15 January 1988 at the Duchy Hospital in Truro, Donald expressed the wish to his second son Brian ('Bic') that the book should be completed. Autobiographical, therefore, up to and including Chapter 13, it becomes biographical from there on, the combined efforts of Bic and myself, but largely Bic.

We have not included technical details of the cars, nor was it Donald's wish that these should be included. They have been comprehensively covered in several existing books. We have concentrated upon Donald as a person, which is what we believe his vast numbers of friends world-wide would prefer.

*Newlyn, 1988*                                        PETER GARNIER

Certificate issued by the United States Auto Club following the record-breaking performance.

# United States Auto Club

## USAC

Sanction No. 56-SR-7

### Sports Commission

**CERTIFICATE OF PERFORMANCE**

*The Undersigned Certify in the name of the*
*United States Auto Club Sports Commission*
*that*

the - -

AUSTIN - HEALEY STREAMLINER:
Donald Healey, Driver
Made the following PERFORMANCE, August 21, 1956, on the Bonneville Salt
Beds, Utah, U.S.A. over a distance of 1999.17 feet.

| | Time | Speed | |
|---|---|---|---|
| North Run | 6.913 Sec. | 197.17 | M. P. H. |
| South Run | 6.711 Sec. | 203.11 | M. P. H. |
| Average | 6.812 Sec. | 200.10 | M. P. H. |
| Both runs made within one hour | | | |
| Displacement 161.274 Cu. In. | Class "D" | Supercharged. | |

*B. René Dutton*
Technical Representative

*Duane Carter*
Director of Competition

Regional Director

Chairman of the Sports Commission

August 1956: left to right: Roy Jackson-Moore, myself, George Eyston and Carroll Shelby, immediately after I had achieved a two- way speed of 203.11 m.p.h. at Bonneville, qualifying for the exclusive 200 Miles per Hour Club. (*B. Healey*).

Austin-Healey

# 1

# Horseless-carriages and flying-machines

It was around 4 a.m.; the sun, soon to turn the Bonneville Salt Flats in the Great Salt Lake Desert into a limitless expanse of white, was still no more than a glow behind the Wasatch Mountains, the State of Utah's craggy backbone, lying pink to our east. To the north, west and south, it was impossible to judge the extent of this utterly featureless landscape. Nor, when the sun came up, would it be much easier — except that the horizon would show clearly the curvature of the earth's surface; a horizon which, however fast one travels, or however far, seems unattainable. This salt desert is all that survives of an expanse of water, some 45,000 square miles in area and 4,200 feet above the sea. In winter's rains, the water lies there, waiting for the sun to evaporate it; in summer it becomes surface-parched, baking-hot, and dazzlingly, brilliantly white. For only a fortnight in the year, assuming predictable weather, it is suitable for high-speed record-breaking; and then only for an hour or two after dawn, before the wind gets up.

It was in this loneliest of places, in August 1956, that I climbed into the stark cockpit of the 250 b.h.p., supercharged Austin-Healey 100-Six 'streamliner', which had been built to better 200 m.p.h. — though as yet it had nowhere near approached this speed. I pulled the Perspex bubble over my head and set off, leaving behind me the timekeepers' hut, our tiny, personal oasis, and the mechanics with my son, Geoffrey, in charge. Uppermost in my mind were two thoughts: The 'fire-button' in the centre of the steering wheel (my hand was never far from it; the year before, I had experienced a high-speed engine blow-up and the resulting fire); and the invaluable advice given by my old friend and our *chef d'équipe*, George Eyston, who had himself set several land speed records in Utah before the war. Among other words of wisdom, he had said, 'Don't worry if you wander off the black line. Just let it pay off and make another run. If you try to pull it back on-line at high-speed, it'll flip.'

There was little, if any, impression of speed. I might have been stationary on a rolling-road, the 17-mile long, 12-inch wide, tarred guide-line seemingly wound on drums beneath me. Only when I overtook two or three other Austin-Healeys, travelling parallel to the tarred line at a respectful distance and a constant 120 m.p.h., ready to pick up the bits if anything went wrong, did I realize how fast I was going. They seemed to be going quickly enough... but backwards.

Nothing blew up; the car maintained a dead-straight course astride the line, and as the critical measured mile reeled past beneath me I was pretty certain, judging by the rev-counter, that I'd exceeded the magic 200 m.p.h. At the end of the run we replaced the wheels and tyres, and hosed-off the heavy build-up of salt inside the wheel-arches. The feelings of anxiety and apprehension turned to excitement as I headed back towards the timekeepers and our base. Not until one is back with them, and they have done their sums, does one know the true result.

Then it came... 203.06 m.p.h. I had achieved membership of the exclusive '200 m.p.h. Club', of which there were only five members at the time, including my friend Stirling Moss.

There were, of course, the very human feelings of elation that we'd achieved our target, and of relief that I hadn't joined the sad list of fatal accidents at around 200 m.p.h. on that same salt desert. There was also the sense of pride that we, as a company, and I, as the driver, had justified the faith placed in us by Castrol who, as supporters of so many record attempts in past years, had invested heavily in the venture; and by Dunlop, who had made the very special tyres with their 1 mm of rubber — and by many others, not least among whom was General Griswold, then commanding the Omaha Station of the US Strategic Air Force, and a previous Austin-Healey owner.

General Griswold had wanted me to try out a test car built in their 'Hobby shop' (a wonderful institution at some of the major USAF bases, equipped with the finest machine tools available and facilities to build almost anything they fancied). So, instead of flying to the West Coast and driving to Wendover, whose famous motel has played host to almost every record attempt at Utah since 1909, I flew direct to the General's station. They had installed, in a conventional chassis, the smallest jet aircraft engine they could find. It had neither clutch nor gears: you simply sat there, revved-up the engine with the brakes hard-on and several lusty helpers holding-back this projectile, until the word of command 'Go!' when you shot off down the runway. The acceleration was good, though not up to a good conventional sports car's; and the top speed was almost 100 m.p.h. Nothing exceptional, but it was great fun.

The tests completed, General Griswold said he'd fly me to Wendover, leading me off to the runway, where I'd expected to board a small private aircraft. Instead, and to my astonishment, he had put at my disposal a military version of the Boeing Stratocruiser, with full USAF crew — and myself as the sole passenger. 'Don't worry,' he said, 'It counts as a training flight.'

In setting up the new 200 m.p.h.-plus record I had been trying to establish a reputation — or to add to my existing one — as a builder of very fast sports cars, especially in America, where out-and-out maximum speeds seem to mean a great deal more than they do in Europe; and where, at the time, our cars were beginning to sell well. Certainly the newspapers in America carried much more comprehensive reports of our record runs than did those in Europe. And I was amused to read in one of their head-lines: 'English Grand-dad Betters 200 m.p.h. at Utah.'

I had always been deeply interested in making things go fast — not perhaps speed for its own sake (the Monte Carlo win in 1931 with the Invicta was scarcely a high-speed performance, any more than seventh place in a bare-50 m.p.h. Triumph Super Seven the previous year had been), but speed in a relative sense. This Bonneville operation was for me the culmination of all I'd been working for — the proof-of-the-pudding for all the effort we had put into the Healey car.

For the benefit of those who may care to work out my age at the time of the various incidents described in this book (and thereby gain support for the 'You're never too old to try' theory), I was born on 3 July 1898. Perranporth, where we lived, was then a beautiful little village with a small fishing fleet and three miles of sands. I was christened by a parson in Bath, whose lovely daughter Evelyn Laye was to become a famous actress. Many years later, in 1974 when I was at Buckingham Palace waiting to receive my CBE from Her Majesty The Queen, who should I see waiting

Woodbine Cottage, Perranporth — my parents' temporary home, where I was born. (*B. Healey*).

15

# Donald Healey

with me but Miss Laye, about to receive the DBE! So I went over to her and told her 'Your father christened me!'

Our stretch of coastline seemed then to act as a magnet for ships, several of which I remember being blown ashore on to the sands or rocks. Either way, they were immediately stripped of anything valuable. Some of them had interesting cargoes: two-gallon petrol cans; beeswax; barrels of pure linseed oil; cases of candles, that kept the village houses lit at night for the next four or five years; and pure rubber in its native form, being shipped to the UK for processing. The 'pirates' couldn't see much use for this (being unable even to identify it), but Father, being wiser, acquired loads of it for a song from the beachcombers and sold it very profitably. Huge barrels of wine from France came ashore on one occasion, and lay about on the shore for some time. If they didn't leak, they had to be sent to the Board of Trade, but marlinespikes soon saw to this, buckets-full finding their way into the village. The local drunks had the time of their lives, lying open-mouthed beneath their personal leaks until insensible.

16

The fishing fleet, which is now completely vanished, consisted of rowing boats with four or six oars per boat; they used to launch through the rolling surf into the smoother water beyond, returning to the beach and being hauled up by teams of horses. This would be impossible today, as the beach has completely changed, and the formation of the breakers is different. No boat could put to sea now, save in exceptionally calm weather.

At this time, when I was a boy, two inventions came my way: the surfboard, and the sand-yacht. Two friends and I decided that the latter device was not only practicable, but offered great scope for development. We built one, but entirely the wrong way round, with the single, steering wheel at the back; and two wheels at the front of the triangular frame. This has been reversed in modern designs, but ours sailed all right in its fashion, though it took a gale to shift.

My father was a Somerset man; and as the representative of a printing firm, he had called upon Sampson Mitchell, whose grocery in Perranporth sold everything necessary to life. There he had met and fallen in love with Sampson's daughter, Emmie, and married her. He took over the running of the store, eventually rebuilding it into something much grander — and, come to that, Perranporth too, for in his later role as a builder ('developer', we would call it now) he put up hundreds of houses.

Fortunately for me, Father was a speed enthusiast, insofar as he could be in those days, and, as a first class oarsman, had rowed in eights at Henley, as well as taking part in cycle races on a penny-farthing. In 1908 he bought a very handsome Panhard et Levassor, the first car, I think, in our village and something pretty special where previously the only form of transport had been horse-drawn carriages. It had a large four-cylinder engine, cast in two blocks of two cylinders each, and hot-tube ignition. This was later converted to a chain-driven Bosch magneto, which transformed the running, but was responsible for breaking his arm on one occasion when it backfired while he was cranking it.

This car had a long history. When war came, he converted it to a van to replace the horse-and-cart used for bread deliveries within a ten-mile radius of the store. After the war, I removed two of the cylinders, along with their pistons and connecting rods, blanked-off the holes in the crankcase, and used the engine to supply electricity to the store and one or two houses nearby, whose lighting had previously been by acetylene gas and, later, the gas from a very volatile petrol grade which we used to call 'Six-eighty'. This, and petrol for the car, was supplied by the iron-monger's in Truro and stored in two-gallon cans from one of the wrecks. A great many cans found their way into Father's garage this way.

Apart from the Panhard, my memories of pre-war motoring

My father, always a keen cyclist, with his penny-farthing. (*B. Healey*).

include two great cars owned by friends of my Father's who used
to visit us: a Prince Henry Vauxhall, forerunner of the immortal
30/98; and a Beeston-Humber, a large, luxurious car with the
entrance at the rear, in which, as a small boy, I was driven to London and back, my first long drive in a car. The first AA filling station we came to, possibly even the first in England, was on
Salisbury Plain. It was no more than a hut with piles of two-gallon
cans. We had to take with us sufficient fuel to get us there, carried in these same two-gallon cans, which were to continue
unchanged until replaced by the large Jerricans in the last war.
It is interesting to look back at the regulations for the first Le Mans
24-Hour Race, held in 1923. The event was then confined to
genuinely 'production' sports cars, and to make it approximate
as closely as possible to the road conditions of the day, a fairly
considerable distance had to be covered between fuel stops, based
upon the average distance apart of roadside filling stations.

The roads were narrow and winding in those pre-first-war days,
dusty in summer and muddy in winter. On the Beeston Humber
we carried four spare rims with inflated tyres already in place —
Stepneys, they were called — and we used two of these on the
journey to London, due to punctures caused by horseshoe nails.

Throughout those early years I had been keenly interested in
both cars and aeroplanes, with a strong emphasis on the latter.
To satisfy my longing to get motoring I had built what may have
been the first-ever 'beach buggy', — a crude device on four bicycle wheels one of them (removed from an early powered bicycle

I seem to have been
keen on marching,
since I was a member
of the Boys' Brigade —
a well-supported
organization, as there
was little else by way of
entertainment in the
village. (*B. Healey*).

, French I think) containing its own small motor. I spent many hours driving this on Perranporth sands. More interesting to me, though, were aeroplanes, an interest shared by my father and encouraged by the weekly arrival on Saturdays of the magazine *Flight*, by horse-drawn delivery from Truro station. With the help of this journal I gained my early knowledge of the theory of powered flight, and started my boyhood hobby building elastic-powered flying-model aeroplanes. I even made 'twin-engined' pusher models with two lengths of elastic, each running along-side a boom of the triangular, open fuselage, with the propellors at the back, either side of the rudder, and the elevator on an out-rigger in front; the wings (mounted well back) did no more than provide lift. This was called the 'canard' layout and, during recent years, it has been reintroduced on some modern jet aircraft — providing, as it does, relative freedom from stall, that bugbear of all aircraft designers and pilots.

When the time came to get down to my education in earnest, I was sent to Newquay College, now the Hotel Bristol, where they had an excellent physics department — clearly my principal sub-ject. It was not long, though, before I decided that my real future lay in the aircraft industry. From *Flight* I discovered the addresses of the three British aircraft constructors of the day, Sopwith, A.V. Roe (Avro), and Bristol and wrote to all three in my boyish fashion, asking to be admitted as a pupil. I never thought, when I received an encouraging letter from Sopwith, that my father would agree to this. However, he said that if I obtained a satisfactory pass to my early Cambridge examination, he would allow me to leave school early and become a pupil at the Sopwith Aviation Com-pany's factory, which had recently been set up in a disused roller-skating rink at Kingston-on-Thames.

With this powerful incentive, I managed to get the required pass, and in 1914 went straight from Newquay College to Kingston. The fee for pupils was around £200, a considerable sum in those days; my father had also to pay 15 shillings a week for my lodging, and Sopwith paid me 6 shillings a week, out of which I could afford to take a girlfriend to the pictures on Saturday nights, at fourpence a seat! As a father of three sons myself, I can all too well imagine the trauma all this must have caused between my parents: that I should leave home at the tender age of 16, when a world war had just started. As a devout Wesleyan Methodist — and as an insurance and, perhaps, a sop to my mother — my father had writ-ten to the Wesleyan minister at Kingston, asking him to take spe-cial care of this 'little boy' from Cornwall, who was coming to live upon the borders of the terrible Metropolis, having previously been away from home only once or twice. This feeling of remote-ness was exaggerated by the fact that Cornwall was then to us a separate country. We talked about 'going to England' as quite an

19

adventure, even when, each year, father used to take us to spend Christmas with his parents in Bath. He also asked the minister to see that I went to church on Sundays (no great hardship for me, as he had two lovely daughters).

At Sopwith's I was, of course, in my element. I worked in the toolroom, where I learned how to use machine tools. I spent many hours embellishing polished aluminium engine cowlings with those precise rows of 'twirls' (achieved by wrapping a piece of emery cloth over the end of one's thumb and twisting it against the metal). If even one twirl was out of line, or unequally spaced, back you went and started the row again. Dull though this particular task may have been (however satisfying, aesthetically, the result), I was working among aeroplanes, which I found intensely interesting. Among the complex tasks of erecting an airframe, I learned how to true up the extensive steel wire bracing by means of turnbuckles, and to rig and adjust the mainplaines.

The great ambition of us all, though, was to get to the firm's sheds at Brooklands, where the earlier Sopwith aircraft had been built and where took place the testing of all their machines. Avro, too, assembled their aeroplanes at Brooklands. After almost a year at Kingston I was transferred to the famous race track, where I worked on the Sopwith Wright, Scout, Pup, and Camel. 'Tommy' Sopwith, a rich man in his own right, had married into money, becoming even richer. In 1910, before starting work in England, he had travelled to America where he met, and flew with, Howard T. Wright, an associate of Hiram Maxim, subsequently building the Sopwith-Wright biplane under licence. Among the earliest designs of his own company was the sensational little Tabloid, the fastest biplane in the world when it flew at the end of 1913, and winner at Monaco of the Schneider Trophy the following year. He was also a notable yachtsman, building an early challenger for the America's Cup.

While at Brooklands, I was given time off to learn about the technical side of aviation at a local college. But my outstanding memories are of that wonderful little flying-man (and I emphasize that term) Harry Hawker, an airman in the truest sense, as distinct from a chauffeur of aeroplanes. A dapper little Australian (he stood only 5ft 3in) he wore the strangest of suits, with perfectly tailored jacket and waistcoat, but odd trousers which were absurdly tight round his ankles, developing into balloons farther up his legs, like full-length plus fours.

He had, I believe, learned to fly with Sopwith's. One of his stunts was to fly beneath the Byfleet Bridge, where the steep Byfleet Banking and the bridge met at the top at an angle of around 45 degrees, leaving him only a couple of feet clearance for his wingtips. He also managed to fly in through the open doors of a hangar and out the other end. Later, Hawker attempted a crossing of the Atlantic in a specially built single-engined Sopwith aircraft with his navigator Mackenzie-Grieve. They came down in the ocean, and were fortunate to be picked up.

I used to travel down from Kingston to Brooklands in a veteran Daimler lorry, carrying aircraft parts to the flight sheds. After a lot of persuasion the driver would let me take over the controls along those thinly populated, dusty Surrey roads, although I held only a motorcycle licence at the time, as the owner of a 2¾ h.p. Douglas presented by my father. I was, it seems, a spoilt child. Along with these early driving experiences I had my first flight, piloted by Harry Hawker in a primitive biplane with wide-open cockpit nacelle and two propellers, one in the wing struts on each side, chain-driven from a single, central engine. I also flew with him in a One-and-a-half Strutter, the celebrated two-seat fighter with extra pairs of centre-section struts meeting at the upper wing roots.

At the time, we were working on an interruptor gear by which a machine-gun could be fired through the rotating propeller a previous expedient being steel deflector plates at the root of each propeller blade. Amazingly, though a bullet might do little enough damage if it hit a deflector, it was very rarely that one did so. I produced drawings for an interruptor gear, a mechanical device that tripped the trigger at the appropriate moments, and the foreman made it up for me in the tool-room. But it never came to anything, as Constantinesco came along with his successful hydraulically-operated gun gear. At Brooklands, too, I was introduced to fast motoring — again by Harry, in his Gregoire car. Up to then my only experience had been on the Prince Henry Vauxhall, and an Austro-Daimler, both on the road as distinct from the track.

After the war, Sopwith re-established his aircraft manufacturing company with Harry as one of the directors. In recognition of a great aviator, he called it the H.G. Hawker Engineering Co. Ltd.

Harry carried on with a host of flying activities, racing motorcycles and AC cars as his hobby. He was killed in a Nieuport Goshawk while practising for the 1921 Aerial Derby — sadly, I believe, not by accident. He suffered from tuberculosis, incurable in those days and often fatal. Rather than become a burden to himself and others, I believe he 'flew it in'. I would not wish for anyone, on reading these words, to feel he lacked courage. He possessed all the courage in the world — which, of course, such a decision would have required. It is a principle in which I have always believed myself: that you should make your exit as soon as you start to suffer seriously, before you become a damned nuisance to anyone.

During my time with Sopwith's, my longing to become a pilot in the Royal Flying Corps grew steadily and strongly, encouraged (as was the intention) by the white feathers being handed to the young men still wearing civilian clothes. Lord Kitchener's accusing finger on the recruiting poster saying 'Your country needs YOU!' helped too — and, of course, the glamour of wearing a uniform. What finally decided me was an inspired speech by a well-known orator, Horatio Bottomley, on Fred Carno's Taggs Island on the Thames.

In order to get into the RFC it was quicker to join the infantry first, so I fudged my age and went along to enlist, being accepted in the East Surrey Regiment at Shepherd's Bush on 29 October 1915. My father thought otherwise, however. By disclosing my real age, he had my enlistment cancelled, and back I went to Sopwith's until early in 1916 when, having reached the age of military discretion, I went along to Earls Court where the RFC were recruiting. The only way I could get in was as an Air Mechanic, although I could practically fly an aeroplane, and the only way to gain quick promotion to Air Mechanic 1st Class was to pass a test, the principal qualification for which was to splice a wire rope, which I had already learned at Kingston. Much importance was attached to rigging on those early machines.

This move was, I think, one of my greatest mistakes. Had I remained with Sopwith's as a pupil I would eventually have learned to fly — it was included in the original £200 fee; and, by the end of the war, my extensive experience in building aeroplanes as designer and engineer would have been invaluable, such knowledge and expertise being very rare then. Had I stayed on with them, I believe there would have been Healey aeroplanes, instead of Healey cars. Instead, I was subjected to what seemed an unending period of day-long 'square-bashing' under selected, very tough, ex-Guards sergeant-majors — wholly unprofitably, in my view, turning us into infantrymen first.

Eventually, however, when the period of drill on the barrack square had come to an end, I gleefully started my flying training. I am told that I was very nearly unique, and quite remarkably fortunate, in thus securing RFC pilot training as an Air Mechanic — let historians make of that what they will. My first flight in uniform was at 0715 hours on 9 May 1916, in BE2c No. 4509, a conventional biplane with an RAF (Royal Aircraft Factory, Farnborough) engine. My instructor was a Captain Howell, and we flew for 33 minutes, reaching a height of 3,500 feet. I made my first solo at 0740 hours on 15 June (early in the morning, as was then general, to take advantage of smooth air conditions), and my log book reads: 'Landing bumpy, too fast'. After two and a half hours' solo, and not more than a total of nine hours' flying time, I passed the test for my Wings on 20 June 1916, and was granted Aviator's Certificate No. 3139 by the Royal Aero Club. The test was carried out at Castle Bromwich aerodrome — no more

| Date and Hour | Wind Direction and Velocity | Machine Type and No. | Passenger | Time | Height | Course | Remarks |
|---|---|---|---|---|---|---|---|
| 28/7/16.9.0 | | A.W. 6205 | nil | 20 min | 2000 | Circuits | |
| 29/7/16 6.45am | | B.E.2c.4537 | nil | 1hr.5min | 3000 | Circuits | |
| ·· -- 9.30am | ·· ·· | | ·· | 30min | 7500 | Height Test Circuits | Landing on mark. |
| 29/7/16.6.30p | | A.W.6205 | ·· | 40 min | 2000 | Circuits | |
| 30/7/16. 11.15am | | B.E.2c.4537 | ·· | 5 min | 100 | Cross Country to York | machine developed uncontrollable |
| | | | | | | | Spin + crashed into Grand Stand. |

Time in Air week ending Aug 1/16 — 2h. 40m
Time Solo — 2h. 40.
Total Time in air — 19h. 7m
Total time solo — 8h. 15.m.

*J.W.Learmount* Capt.
2.8.16.

It is with no great pride that I see, in my Log Book, the entry recording my crash into the grandstand at Doncaster racecourse (*B. Healey*).

than a large, grass playing field — in a French-built Maurice Farman Longhorn, distinguished from its more conventional stablemate, the Shorthorn, by a large elevator projecting out ahead of the pilots' seats. All that was required of me was to execute a few take-offs and landings, and figure-eights.

One morning, while building up my flying time — I recall that a total of five hours' solo was necessary before being posted to an operational squadron in France — I was making a landing approach to Doncaster race course. I ran out of engine and, though I thought I was going to make the race course all right, I stalled the machine slap into the middle of the grandstand, where a large number of infantrymen were sleeping on the seats. Fortunately I missed them all, but I was trapped in the fuselage, and the engine — a water-cooled Renault — came straight through the fuel tank behind me, drenching me in petrol. Mercifully it didn't catch fire.

That was the first of some sensational escapes during my lifetime of flying and motoring, and it shook me badly. I was given a period of sick leave, then posted to a Home Defence squadron. Our principal brief was to shoot down Zeppelins — probably the easiest and most rewarding job of the war (so we thought), provided one attacked them from above (if one was ever able to get there). They were incredibly slow and virtually unmanoeuvrable: you just had to get into position, where they couldn't see you... and 'pom-pom-pom', down they went.

We flew from Kirton-in-Lindsay, in Lincolnshire, where we were provided with all manner of gadgets to help us shoot down Zeppe-

lins. One BE2e I flew had six rockets on the interplane struts each side, fired electrically. Another device was a tubular metal chute between one's legs, through which were dropped special anti-Zeppelin bombs. Upon emerging from the bottom of the tube they were ignited, letting out a mass of wires with fish-hooks at the ends, the idea being that they would hook on to the Zeppelin's broad back, setting it ablaze. One really galling occasion to us pilots, who had been flitting round the night sky week after week, was when an artillery officer, Leefe-Robinson, came home from India in 1916, got his Wings and, on his first operational sortie, found himself with a Zeppelin as a sitting target directly beneath him. He was awarded a VC for shooting it down — and the troops weren't half angry!

There was not a great deal left of my BE2C after its unscheduled arrival in the grandstand at Doncaster. (*B. Healey*).

What eventually destroyed the Zeppelins were some fancy bullets produced for the Lewis machine-gun by three inventors. I may have got the order wrong, but there was the Brock — a pure tracer that guided one's aim; then there was the Pomeroy (of Vauxhall fame), which exploded on contact; and finally the Buckingham, an incendiary. You mixed these in the Lewis gun ammunition drums, the tracer showing you where you were shooting, the explosive making a hole if you managed to hit something solid enough to explode it, and the incendiary setting fire to the resulting release of gas.

After being posted to one or two flying schools as an instructor, including Bristol and Tadcaster, I was sent to France flying FE2b night bombers. These were armed with ex-Boer War pom-pom guns firing shells 1½ inches in diameter, fed into the breech very slowly on a belt. They proved very useful to us; we would fly into a searchlight beam, turn the nose downwards along the beam, and open fire. Even if we didn't hit the light, the crew would invariably switch it off in terror.

I knew in my heart that I would never be much good as a pilot. I was suffering from vertigo due to an inner-ear trouble. This trouble was to continue, until I had a very bad attack during the Second World War, when, as a Squadron Leader, I was in charge of the Warwick Air Training Corps. I went to the RAF ear specialist, who told me: 'When you're 50 you'll completely lose the hearing in the affected ear — and all your giddiness will vanish'. I am delighted to say that he was exactly correct; and, luckily, I have exceptional hearing in the other ear.

The end of my flying career was not long in coming, when I had to make a forced landing close behind our own lines, after what I have always assumed to have been one of our own shells had burst very close to me. I recall nothing of the incident until, upon my return to England, I was met by nurses at Nottingham station and handed a packet of cigarettes.

I was sent to the Abraham Peel mental hospital, somewhere between Leeds and Bradford, where I remained for some weeks. I was examined by several medical boards, who finally agreed that I was no longer fit for active service flying. This decision brought me no great disappointment — I had no 'guts' left by then; the incident had knocked all the courage out of me. I was invalided out of the RFC, my dreams of becoming another Harry Hawker shattered for ever. My Discharge Certificate is dated 16 November 1917, after two years, 19 days with the Colours.

After this, I was transferred to the Aeronautical Inspection Department, which meant travelling round the country visiting sub-contractors engaged on making aircraft components, and checking literally everything that went into an aeroplane, before putting my stamp of approval on it. If any component failed, there was no doubt whatever as to who had passed it; the blame was squarely mine. My experience at Sopwiths, coupled with my practical, operational flying, was invaluable, and virtually unique. I finished up in charge of inspection at a factory — originally a peacetime organ factory — making wings for Avro aeroplanes at Plymouth. There I met Kenneth Heal, the son of the chairman, who was a great wireless telegraphy enthusiast, and from whom I developed my early interest in electronics, which has remained with me right through my life: my hobby is still electronics — now involving the use, of course, of today's wonderful 'chips'.

The AID appointment provided me with a beautiful 4 horse-power Douglas motorcycle, which was more than welcome, as I was without transport at the time, having damaged my earlier Douglas beyond repair when I had charged a bank with my commanding officer on the pillion (which can't have done my RFC career much good, either). I was thus able to do a great deal more motoring than most people could do in wartime. When the war ended, I remained with the AID for another year, before deciding to return to my first love of making aeroplanes. I got in touch with Sopwiths, only to find that peace and retrenchment were causing massive cancellations of aircraft contracts. They had closed down their wartime sheds at Brooklands, later to become the famous Vickers Sheds, and had embarked as a stop-gap measure upon the production of car bodies and ABC motorcycles.

For want of something better, I returned to Perranporth and took the then famous International Correspondence Schools course in automobile engineering. At the same time, I managed to obtain the very special, and hard to get, licence to transmit radio signals. Radio transmissions, as I had learned about them in wartime, had consisted only of spark transmissions; you could transmit only dots and dashes — the Morse code, that is — and at the rate of only eight words per minute. This was soon developed into a continuous wave transmission. I became profoundly interested in this development, and I still have a newspaper cutting reporting a transmission I made of a little concert by local artists across 200 yards from my father's house to the local village hall.

Prompted by this success, I turned to the manufacture of radio receivers, coining the name 'Perraphone', and I made a few hundred of them. They were simple, and sold well; I still have one of them. This, however, was no more than a side-line; in pursuit of my main objective to become an automobile engineer, I opened a garage in Perranporth, one of my first jobs being to replace the hot-tube ignition of my father's 1907 4-cylinder Panhard et Levassor with a Bosch magneto, which completely transformed the car.

The Perraphone Radio Company's notepaper. As the telephone number, Perranporth 6, indicates, telephones were scarce in those early days. (*B. Healey*).

# 2

# Early competition days: the 1929 Monte Carlo

When you look at Perranporth today, packed with cars even out of season, it is difficult to imagine it in the days before the car arrived, when there were no more than two or three phut-phutting and quivering round the streets; often a day would pass without one's ever seeing a car. We knew each of them well: there was my father's, the doctor's big single-cylinder Rover, and a little Humberette cycle-car, owned (but never used) by Edward Opie, brother to the Cornish artist John Opie. I bought that car in the 1950s, when it was still unused!

It was like this in the early days after the First World War, before car production got under way, and before people became confident not only of the car's capabilities, but of their own. It was in this atmosphere of doubt and misgiving that I had to sell my father my absolute conviction that there would be the need for a garage in Perranporth.

To this day I shall not forget my gratitude when he agreed to the idea, allowing me to start up in the old stores premises alongside his magnificent, rebuilt emporium.

As an indication of Father's enthusiasm for the garage project, and his helpful attitude, while I began to establish my small business in the old store, he went to work supervising the building of a new garage for me, with a frontage of 50 ft. There was a serious shortage of building materials all over the country immediately after the war, especially timber. Even though everyone knew that Cornish-grown timber wasn't much good, he was so anxious to get me started that he was obliged to use it.

My tool-room experience with Sopwith's was to prove invaluable. Spare parts were hard to come by, and we had to make most of them. In my temporary premises I set up small milling and drilling machines, a grinder and a beautiful little Drummond flat-bed lathe, with about 18 inches between centres and a gap-bed that gave a swing of about 12 inches. This was pretty well the only small lathe available to garage owners at the time, and it was to become as popular in its field as the famous Drummond 'Round Bed' became among model-makers. These fairly basic machine tools were belt-driven from line-shafting, power being provided, as ever, by the now two-cylinder engine from Father's Panhard et Levassor car. As yet there were no petrol pumps, fuel being stored in the ubiquitous 2-gallon cans. It was not until we transferred, along with the tool-room, to our new purpose-built premises that the first pumps came along. By means of a simple semi-rotary hand-pump, the fuel was raised from underground storage tanks to a heavy five-gallon glass container, supported on a cast-iron pedestal which formed the upper half of the pump, and thence into the vehicle. The whole thing was crowned by a glass globe announcing 'Pratts' Spirit'.

My father had decided that there was nobody within at least ten miles of Perranporth who knew the slightest thing about a motor car, and had consulted an old friend in London. He was in consequence introduced to Alfie Easton, a very fine, old-time mechanic, who was accustomed to scraping bearings by hand and taking a week to fit a crankshaft; and he was familiar with machine tools — a fitter, we would call him today. Father persuaded him to move down to Perranporth and set-up home with his family. He worked with me for many years, right through until I sold the business in 1933. His children are all here, in Perranporth, to this day — they've become a local family.

I am indebted to Alfie in so many ways. I had never learned to drive properly: smoothly, quickly and with a sympathy for the engine and transmission. With his experience of London driving in a variety of cars, he was able to help me a lot. I had decided to go in for car-hire, and in 1921 father bought me a brand-new six-cylinder, valve-in-head Buick — one of the earliest cars to go into quantity production with overhead valves. The cylinder head was not detachable, the valves, guides and springs being inserted into sockets which were screwed into the head. It was a surprisingly modern car for its time, and had hydraulically-operated, external-contracting band brakes on all four wheels — there's a combination for you! It had detachable-rimmed, wooden-spoked artillery wheels as original equipment but I changed these for Michelin steel discs, which were fashionable at the time.

With the Buick and a BSA — a very quiet car with a sleeve-valve engine which gave good service, even when driven by the inexperienced Cornish lads I used to employ — we went into the chauffeur-driven hire business. Easton and I took turns at driving, as I was anxious to gain as much experience as I possibly could, preparatory to embarking upon my competition career, which had always been foremost in my mind.

I soon felt there was work for a charabanc — a large, open, single-deck coach with a separate side-door to each row (or 'banc') of seats. I bought an American Garford chassis and had a 25-seater body fitted by a coachbuilder in Hereford. It was the first multi-passenger vehicle I'd ever seen in England with pneumatic tyres; all others had had shallow-section, solid rubber tyres — rubber bands, more like — which were frequently slit by mounting kerbs, the resulting rubber projection making a loud 'flap...flap...flap' as the wheel revolved, audible a mile away. And, in case we needed anything between the 25-seater and the hire cars, I bought an ex-Army Fiat 13-cwt chassis with a 12-seater body. It was a fine, reliable vehicle, except for its temperamental, unpredictable main brake, which worked on a drum on the transmission drive-shaft.

During those early years my father had bought himself a large RMC 'underslung' tourer with 3.2-litre, four-cylinder, 18/20 hp engine, built by the Regal Motor Car Co. of Detroit. This company had started business in 1907, producing and selling a run of 50 cars with four-cylinder, 20 hp engines. The following year they created something of a precedent in the motor industry by taking them all back and providing their astonished owners — free — with the latest, 1908 model! Father's car was eventually to join the hire fleet.

It was due largely to the hire business that the garage survived those early post-war years. Though people were by then beginning to 'think' motor cars, ownership was still rare, especially in our remote Cornish lanes where local transport still relied on the horse-drawn wagonette or 'jingle'. The precipitous coastal areas involved as much getting-out-to-walk as they did riding — a drawback that continued through to the twenties with the early cars.

In writing of those pioneering days, some social historians — who mostly do little more than rewrite contemporary material with the advantage of hindsight — suggest that the car was the perquisite of the 'swells', leaving their readers with the impression that a sense of ill-feeling existed, born of envy. It is true that cars were owned largely by the wealthy (and those whose professions demanded their speed and convenience), but no more than were the early wireless sets, gramophones, television sets, calculators, videos and so on. It is always the better-off who provide the development — the proving-ground — for any advanced new product, until, with the bugs eliminated and production techniques perfected, the selling price comes down. With so complicated a product as the car, having so many components requiring development, it took a long time for this process to gain momentum. Those to whom cheap, reliable personal transport became available in the thirties should never forget their debt to the wealthy who so kindly provided the proving-ground.

Our hire fleet was kept busy collecting people from, and delivering them to, the GWR stations at Truro and Chacewater. The latter was the closest to Perranporth, Newquay and other resorts along our stretch of coast, where the bed and breakfast boarding-house industry was rapidly taking root and developing. The railway companies, especially our much-loved GWR, ran special, cheap holiday excursions to the Cornish Riviera from all over the country. These were the equivalent of today's package tours to foreign parts.

Having driven the holiday-makers to their hotels, we would be engaged to take them sight-seeing around Cornwall during their stay. During the peak of the summer season, we were very busy indeed. The great thing about those early cars, and their horse-drawn contemporaries, was the wonderful view of the countryside from the high seats, towering over banks and hedges.

There was an aged professor who was set upon visiting every church in England, the one on Perran sands being of great importance to him as England's oldest place of worship with four walls still standing. A preservation society was subsequently to put up a concrete building around the remains, to protect them; but in due course this collapsed and there is now virtually nothing left of St. Piran's Oratory, as it was called, from which Perranporth got its name. Pilgrims were guided to it by the ancient granite Cornish crosses along the wayside, to which we took our professor upon many pilgrimages.

Like the old Panhard, the Buick assumed all manner of duties. It was, I believe, the first car I ever drove in competition when, in around 1921-2, I entered it for a speed trial run by the Truro Motor Club on a straight stretch of road near to Perranporth. There was no trouble whatever in getting the road closed by the local Police. I stripped the car of its mudguards and windscreen, and covered the flying mile at 66 mph, which seemed like the Land Speed Record in those far-off days.

As the existing cars began to wear out, we added to the hire fleet a big 30 hp Armstrong-Siddeley, with a fine aluminium engine that looked as if it had been built for an aeroplane. It was far too big and uneconomical for use as a hire-car, so I had it converted by a local coachbuilder into an eight-seater. We also had two very handsome pre-1914 Rolls-Royces in the fleet, both 40/50s. One was a big open tourer with two 'occasional seats' (making it a seven-seater) and wooden artillery wheels; I paid about £200 for that car. The other was a large, dignified and very handsome landaulette with a beautifully made opening hood, complete with those lovely curved, exposed hinges on either quarter, over the rear compartment. The chauffeur's compartment remained closed, and was separated from the passengers by a glass division.

With the hire business fully on its feet, by 1922 I was able to attend to my interest in motor sport — my 'hobby' as it was regarded. The first car I bought expressly for the purpose was an ABC with a horizontally-opposed, air-cooled flat-twin engine. It was designed by Grenville Bradshaw and, whilst it had some interesting features, it also had some lunatic ones. Worst of all was the radiator, its shape influenced by that of the Rolls-Royce, and which contained the petrol! Among its better features was the rear

31

# Donald Healey

Not only Austin-Healey drivers suffer from hot feet! With the ABC, somewhere in Cornwall. (*B. Healey*).

axle casing, which consisted of pressed-steel cones bolted either side of the central final-drive housing, making an extremely light-weight conventional rear axle.

The engine, though, was poorly designed, with the exhaust valves overheating badly if one tried to do a speed hill-climb — or even to climb one of the observed hills in the Land's End, Exeter or Edinburgh Trials which were my principal interest at the time. Between us, though, Easton and I managed to endow it with an acceptable degree of reliability and I won several awards with it in these events. It was an encouragement, in the early twenties, to see that the great Sammy Davis was using one of these cars in sporting events; but I wanted something even more sporting and competitive.

These three trials — which feature to this day in Britain's sporting calendar — attracted numerous entries, both from private owners and from manufacturers such as Morgan, Trojan, Jowett, Morris and others. One of the test hills was Beggars Roost, later to become the name of our successive homes in Cornwall. Whilst out testing one day at Bluehills Mine, near St Agnes, I discovered a superb hill, which was an old mine cart-track. Immediately at the foot was a vicious and precipitous left-hand hairpin, and the climb up the side of the valley continued very steeply. This hill was taken up by the Motor Cycling Club as the final observed section in their Land's End Trial at Easter and, as the 'local boy', I was expected by the hundreds of locally-based spectators to make a perfect climb. I thought it would be fun to make the climb a little more 'interesting' and on the night before the event with a couple of friends, dug a ditch on the inside of the hairpin. Needless to say, many of the 'regulars' failed to negotiate this turn, although I — with the benefit of advance knowledge — made a perfect climb, to the delight of the very partisan pro-Cornish crowd.

I was introduced at about this time to Jack Sangster, who made a car called an Ariel 10, using a Swift engine — the Swift company being owned by Jack's father, Charles. The Ariel was a good little car, with its 10 hp four-cylinder, side-valve engine and a small, four-seater touring body. Jack asked me if I'd like to do a long run to demonstrate its economy and reliability. So, accompanied by an RAC observer who measured every drop of petrol that went into the tank, we drove from Land's End to John O'Groats and back, climbing Porlock, Beggars Roost and Bluehills Mine *en route*, showing that this was no easy way round. The little car was credited by the RAC with an overall fuel consumption of 52.2 mpg, and, only a year or two ago, they sent me a copy of the certificate to this effect. It was a great achievement by the car, considering that the roads were tarmacked only in very occasional parts, and the farther north you drove the worse their surfaces became. It did the Ariel sales a lot of good, especially so far as I was concerned, as in 1919 I had obtained the sole agency in Cornwall for

The Ariel 10 outside my garage in Perranporth before setting out on its long run. (*B. Healey*).

Mission complete. The Ariel 10 on the promenade at Perranporth, after averaging 20 miles per hour and 52 miles per gallon on the RAC-observed run from Land's End to John O'Groats and back. (B. Healey).

Ariel cars. In consequence (and partly for publicity reasons) I continued to drive the little Ten in long-distance reliability trials and in a few of the less demanding events at the Brooklands track.

I still hankered after something that was really suited to competitive motoring, as I was steadily becoming 'better than the car'. In 1923 I obtained an introduction to the famous Riley brothers: Victor, the managing director; Cecil, the accountant; Alan, the 'stylist' — cum-body-man; and Percy, who was responsible for the engines and later designed the famous four-cylinder Nine with its high camshafts, which (with an additional two cylinders) was developed to power the ERA racing voiturettes. In 1923, the Riley Redwinger was introduced, the Sports version a streamlined two-seater with polished aluminium body, pointed tail, and red wings and chassis-frame. It was a pretty little car with a side-valve, 1½-litre, four-cylinder engine giving 35 bhp. A top speed of 70 mph was guaranteed — and all this for a price of only £450.

I collected the car early in 1924 and immediately entered it for the Land's End Trial, starting from London on Good Friday night. On the way to the start I decided to try it out for speed on the Gossmoor, a well-known two-mile straight to the west of Bodmin, upon which local enthusiasts used to try for their maximum speeds. Many a good car, and motor-cycle too, has been blown-up on that stretch of road!

Petrol on the Redwing was carried beneath the bonnet in a cylindrical tank mounted on the bulkhead, just above the 'jump-spark' magneto, a new and special device in those days. I had worked up almost to 70 mph when there was a loud bang, as the tank went up in flames. Fortunately for me, the flames shot out of the bonnet, as one end blew out of the tank, while I shot out of the cockpit. Sadly, the car for which I had held such high hopes was burned out only ten miles from home. I towed the remains home behind the ABC, 'phoned the organizers to tell them of my change of entry, and arrived in London in good time for the start the following day — and the old ABC won another 'Gold'.

While all this was going on, I was keeping up my wartime interest in radio, which was still in its infancy in the early twenties. My brother Hugh, who never enjoyed the best of health, joined me in forming the Perraphone Radio Company, which was listed as the manufacturer of Perraphone receiving sets and loudspeakers. We made crystal sets in small numbers and they sold well. Many years later, my youngest son, John, was offered one with a trumpet speaker by an elderly gentleman who had taken it over from his father. John presented it to me on my 80th birthday, 60-odd years after we had made it. Within a short space of time I had found some suitable batteries and the set still worked. I was very proud indeed of this, and the family will keep it, though one could never claim a lot for its reception!

Hugh and I had the bright idea of transmitting from an aircraft to the ground, and we were friendly with a Captain Phillips, a

The Riley Redwinger after the fire on the way to the start of the 1924 London-Land's End Trial. I went home, collected the ABC, and won my first Gold Medal. (*B. Healey*).

Cornishman who flew with the famous Alan Cobham's Air Circus. The transmitter was installed in the aircraft at St. Austell, and I set off in the passenger seat, complete with radio. As we flew over Perranporth I had the distinction of being the first man in the county — and possibly even in the country — to talk to the ground from an aircraft; in this case, the persons on the receiving end were my wife Ivy, and my father. Though more and more people were entering the radio field, my real interest lay in cars and driving them in competition, so the Perraphone Company gradually died. When I returned to Cornwall many years later, I again turned to radio and television as a hobby.

Electricity in Cornwall in those early days was supplied by the Cornwall Power Company, but it was not the comprehensive service we enjoy today, and Perranporth was not linked to the main grid. I grabbed the opportunity provided by this opening, and set about supplying electricity to individual households by means of a generator in an outhouse — built, of course, by my father's company, which by this time had become very much involved in the growth of Perranporth. A constant supply of electricity was a boon to the local dentist, doctors and shopkeepers, and we were able to supply their needs as well as those of a few private individuals. It was not long, though, before Perranporth became linked to the mains, and in 1925 another of my brainchildren became absorbed — but to this day, I can hear the familiar chugging of the generator at 'Beggars Roost'; it scarcely ever let us down.

In the meantime I was becoming really restless, desperate to get into competition motoring at the wheel of something worthwhile. I was fortunate at this stage to lay the foundations of a lasting friendship with Gordon Parnell, a brilliant engineer who, among other achievements, had introduced the hydraulic braking system to this country from the States, as an employee of the Lockheed company on both sides of the Atlantic. He eventually became chief engineer of the Triumph company, for whom I held a dealership, and which produced in 1925 the first British car to be fitted with Lockheed internal-expanding-type hydraulic brakes. This car, successor to the first-ever Triumph car, was the 1.9-litre 13/30, which sold for £495. With the glamorous MGs dominating the British sporting scene from the very late twenties and through the thirties, it is often overlooked that the sporting Triumphs were born first. There is no better way of angering an MG enthusiast than by reminding him of this!

It was in 1924 that the foundations were laid of another long and valued friendship, with Cecil Kimber who, as managing director of William Morris's Oxford agency, Morris Garages, had been experimenting with sporting bodies on standard Morris chassis. In 1924 he had produced the MG Super Sports, by tuning the

1.8-litre Morris Oxford engine and mildly improving the handling. Prior to entering it in the Land's End Trial and showing-off this sporting newcomer to the public, he felt he should try it out on some of the West Country observed sections included in the Trial, to make certain it wouldn't let him down. So he brought it to Perranporth and asked me to take him on a conducted tour of Beggars Roost, Hustyn, Bluehills Mine and the rest. This friendship grew over the years, until his tragic death in a railway accident. Through his kindness, I used the prototype of the little MG TD Midget right through the war years, a car which was not announced until 1949.

Bournemouth Rally 1928: The start at John O'Groats (top) and the finish at Bournemouth. With Harold Jones, the Perranporth dentist we won the Premier Award in the Triumph Seven. (*B. Healey*).

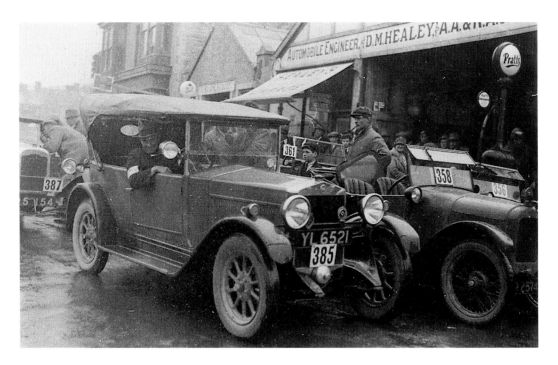

**Above** At the wheel of a Fiat during the 1926 London-Land's End Trial, with an Austin Chummy alongside and a Rover astern. The garage was an official check-point and refreshment halt. (*B. Healey*).

**Above right** 'Going foreign' for the first time. In a Triumph Seven we were entered to start the 1929 Monte Carlo Rally from Riga. (*A. Well*).

**Right** The 1929 Riga to Barcelona Rally. The Triumph Super Seven averaged 25 mph throughout the 3,000 miles, at 35 mpg, and was the smallest car to complete the course, having an engine capacity of only 850 cc. (*B. Healey*).

I drove the most unlikely-looking Triumph Seven and Super Seven family saloons in all sorts of events in this country, from local rallies, trials and speed events, to speed trials at Brooklands and the MCC's long-distance reliability trials. Though they could scarcely be regarded as 'competition' cars, they did well in the Land's End, Exeter, and Edinburgh trials, events which attracted entries of 400-plus motorcycles and cars and included a fair proportion of official, works-entered cars. Success in these events provided very valuable advertising material. Driving the far more sporting 832 cc side-valve, supercharged Super Seven two-seater (announced in 1929 at £250), I won the RAC's first British Rally outright.

In 1929, somewhat ambitiously since I had driven neither in Europe, nor on ice and snow before, I entered a little side-valve, unsupercharged Super Seven family saloon for the Monte Carlo Rally. We chose Riga as our starting point, in what was then Latvia, giving us the longest drive to the finish (not quite as unwise as it sounds, since we were given bonus marks for the extra distance covered). We went three-up in this absurd little car: my brother and Lewis Pearce ('Konky', we called him, because of his nose), a local boy who came with me on very many of my sporting events, and myself. When we reached Deutsches Krone (on the East Prussian/Polish frontier) on our way to the start, we became completely snowed-up. We were lucky enough to find Mrs Victor Bruce in a similar predicament with her Arrol-Aster. After

**Above** Monte Carlo 1929 — the weary crew at the finish consisted of myself to the left of the group and Tommy Wisdom to the right. The spare wheel mountings improved neither engine accessibility nor forward vision! (*B. Healey*).

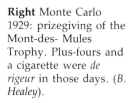

**Right** Monte Carlo 1929: prizegiving of the Mont-des- Mules Trophy. Plus-fours and a cigarette were *de rigeur* in those days. (*B. Healey*).

consultation with the local automobile club, it was decided to abandon the Riga start, using Deutsches Krone instead. We had a pleasant stay there, which we used profitably in learning how to drive on ice and snow.

We had chains, of course, but stretches of the road were dry. Chains wear out and break very quickly on dry roads, so we were constantly having to remove or replace them. We had no means of demisting the inside of the screen, other than night-lights (very short, large-diameter tallow candles in little, metal holders), one each in front of the driver and passenger. To keep the outside of the screen clear, we had a very primitive, hand-operated wind-screen wiper. As well as its three passengers, this wretched little car also carried two spare wheels and an outsize fuel tank, as well as de-ditching gear and a full tool-kit. No wonder it had its work cut out, trying to maintain the 30-plus m.p.h. scheduled average, with a flat-out speed of 45-48 on the level!

Despite all this, though, it reached the Paris control on time, and kept to schedule right down through the Alps to the Riviera, though it was getting pretty tired by then. It was the heavy traffic in the Riviera that was our undoing, and the complicated little roads through Juan-les-Pins, Fréjus and the rest. We arrived at the finish a few minutes late, and were excluded. Without its excessive burden, though, the Super Seven managed to win its class in the Mont-des-Mules speed hill-climb which took place the day after the finish.

Many years later, when my collection of trophies really had begun to assume somewhat alarming proportions, we were bur-

After we were burgled in a big way at Leamington, and so many of my trophies were never recovered, I have to confess that I lost interest in those that remained — shown here — and gradually disposed of them. (B. Healey).

## Donald Healey

**Right** Creature comforts during a control stop in the 1930 Monte Carlo Rally. Space in the Super Seven was in short supply. (*B. Healey*).

**Below** Monte Carlo 1930: first-placed British car and seventh overall, after starting from Tallinn, Estonia. My brother Hugh (extreme left) and Lewis Pearce crewed the Triumph Super Seven with me, an all-Cornish team. (*B. Healey*).

gled, the thief getting away with approximately 30 of them. The Police eventually ran him to earth, at his home, but all that remained of my share of his booty was the little cup for the Mont-des-Mules hill-climb in 1929 — the only one that wasn't silver!

We used the same unlikely little car for the Barcelona Rally that year, held in summer-time in connection with the World Fair. We again decided we needed the bonus points awarded for distance-covered, so we again chose the Riga start, farthest of all from the finish. Travelling only two-up and without the added weight of the winter equipment, we succeeded in winning the event out-right, which helped our West Country Triumph sales considera-bly. In this event, as with every other at the time, the kindness and hospitality of the national Automobile Clubs, running the con-trols, was remarkable. This was especially so in events such as the Barcelona, which allowed rest periods. At the Bucharest con-trol one of the club officials said: 'Now, you chaps, you've driven a long way. You've several hours in hand — would you like a bed? And would you like it alone, or with a companion?' Has hospi-tality ever achieved such heights?

The following year, 1930, I again drove a little Triumph Super Seven saloon in the Monte, three up. We finished seventh overall — the start of a personal 'run' on the Monte. By now I was begin-ning to get noticed, and my early associations with Riley and Invicta were being formed, which were to become very impor-tant to me later.

# 3

# Invicta, Riley, and Triumph

The first I'd heard of the Invicta was when, in 1929, the lovely Cordery sisters covered 30,000 miles in 30,000 minutes at Brooklands, for which the Company was awarded the Dewar Trophy, having already won this important award in 1927 for similar long-distance, high-speed reliability runs with a 3-litre car. The car's creator, Noel Macklin, had in 1925 conceived a type of car new to Britain, intended to combine relatively high power, and American flexibility and low-speed torque, with light weight and the highest standards of British quality. The Meadows-engined 2½-litre was the outcome. It could accelerate from an easy walking pace to 60 m.p.h. in top. The following year, 1926, the 3-litre engine was introduced, also Meadows, and marketed alongside the 2½-litre for a year, after which the 2½ was discontinued, to be replaced by the 4½-litre, again Meadows-engined. With its 85 m.p.h. maximum, which was real speed in those days, it combined the same light weight, low-speed torque and excellent acceleration. In 1930 it was joined by the very special low-chassis 100 m.p.h. S-type, the 3-litre being dropped so that the Cobham-based company could concentrate on the exciting new car.

Its specification was lavish, with dual ignition by coil and magneto, electric fuel pumps feeding from a rear-mounted 20-gallon tank, four-speed gearbox with right-hand change, and a wheel-base and track of 9 ft 10 in and 4 ft 8 in respectively. The bare chassis cost £750, a lot in those days, and the complete car with standard two-seater body was £875. Engine output has been quoted at 100 b.h.p. for the early cars, and even 140 for later versions, pulling a 3.6:1 rear axle and giving 60 m.p.h. at under 2,500 r.p.m. in top; 3,500 r.p.m. gave 25, 43 and 65 m.p.h. respectively in first, second and third gears. Handling, however, was not its strong point, despite claims to the contrary by some of today's historians, and, with the heavy, six-cylinder engine in front, and a full, 20-gallon fuel tank at the rear, one became acutely conscious of polar moments of inertia! The controls were not all that light, either, and with my light weight and somewhat small stature, when the time came to drive one I began to wonder how long I could keep pressing the clutch!

After my outright wins with the little supercharged Triumph

Super Seven, kindly loaned by my friend Gordon Parnell, in the first RAC British Rally in 1928 and in the Brighton Rally in 1929, I had gained something of a name for myself. In fact, I was sometimes overwhelmed by the publicity provided by such successes in those days — even the town band turning out to lead me through the crowded streets upon my triumphal return to Perranporth! When Noel Macklin began to seek publicity for his cars in international rallies in 1930, he approached Humphrey Symonds of *The Motor* (sadly killed in the last war) for suggestions as to who should drive for him. Humphrey searched his mind: 'I know', he said, 'there's a chap called Donald Healey — lives down in Cornwall. He's done pretty well in long-distance events recently. Why don't you have a word with him?'

The result was the loan of a high-chassis (but sporting-looking in the manner of contemporary Bentleys, Vauxhall 30/98s and others) 4½-litre Invicta, and an entry in the Alford Alpenfahrt, the first-ever (I think) Austrian Alpine Trial, scheduled for July 1930. It was a marvellous event; they had very little traffic on their roads, some superb hill-climb courses, including the Grossglockner, and an intensely enthusiastic national motor club. With my limited experience of frontiers and all the other problems of foreign travel, I set off for the start with my navigator (no compulsory co-drivers; we drove single-handed in that 1,000-odd mile event, confined to the roads of Austria). When we reached Vienna, a dream city to me, I found I was expected to carry two Austrian

July 1930: the 3-litre Invicta, heavily travel-stained after winning a Glacier Cup in the International Alfold Alpine Trial. History doesn't record what I was photographing from on-high. (*B. Healey*).

In Austria with the
3-litre Invicta and a
missing headlamp.

journalists with me in the back seats. One of them, a Professor
Wolfbauer, was the largest man I'd ever seen in my life.

The Invicta turned out to be a marvellous car, with its light
weight, tremendous torque, and acceleration better by far than
the opposition's. I had no difficulty in beating such drivers as Hans
Stuck, with his Austro-Daimler, who on more than one occasion
became Hill-Climb Champion of Europe. It was no problem to
beat the target time set for the hill-climbs, taking engine capacity
into account (and load carried!) I won the event outright, along
with a magnificent trophy, returning to England very proud of
myself, for the civic reception at Perranporth which I was secretly
growing almost to regard as my right!

Following this success, Noel Macklin developed a taste for international rallies, and once more he approached me to drive an
Invicta, this time in the Hungarian Alpine. There, again, it was
a great sporting event with lots of hill-climbs, some of them on
unmade roads. Again, I won outright. I was growing to love the
events, and the Invictas I drove. So far as the buying public was
concerned, we were ostensibly private entries, which gave added
kudos to the manufacturer and encouraged private buyers to use
their cars in competition. The manufacturers were taking a risk,
of course, as poor performances resulted in bad publicity; but it
was a risk worth taking. As for us drivers, we were essentially
amateurs, since we received no fee for driving, only our out-of-
pocket expenses being paid. Apart from that, our only real advantage was that we drove first-class, properly prepared cars — and

still the true privateers stood every chance of winning, which they frequently did. In my opinion, it was a great pity when international rallying became almost completely professional, with no hope whatever of success for private entries against the massive factory operations with teams of mechanics along the route, and piles of tyres with treads specially suited to the section ahead. It was inevitable, though: no manufacturer could afford not to cash in on the publicity.

Towards the end of 1930, Noel decided to give his splendid new low-chassis 4½-litre S-type an airing in the Monte Carlo Rally in January 1931, and he lent me a car to 'learn' and prepare. To me this car was phenomenal. It had a very light Weymann body, with slightly open joints in the timber frame, each being held in place by metal plates, the whole thing aft of the aluminium bonnet being covered with a layer of thin felt and then fabric; this construction gave the body a degree of flexibility on a none-too-rigid chassis-frame, the only components bolted firmly to the frame being the seats. It was phenomenal in other ways, too: it was far too low for the Monte, and it had far too much weight in front, unless balanced by a full fuel tank at the back, when the transition from under- to over-steer was frightening, making handling, even on a perfectly-conditioned road surface, more like driving on ice. It was fitted with a truck gearbox made by Meadows, like the engine, without synchromesh, which meant double-declutching for every gear-change. Even when learning to handle the car, I began to feel the effects of continually having to press the heavy clutch pedal.

I decided I'd concentrate on complete reliability and some degree of comfort; this was essential, as I had learned with the little Triumph. Despite the advantage of an ability to go for long periods without sleep, four days and nights awake and on the ball were too much for me. I needed a comfortable passenger seat, at least, in order to grab short periods of rest and keep myself fit for the demanding ice sections. I also fitted much larger wheels and tyres, to give us clearance over the deep-rutted snow, with cycle-type wings to clear them. I had to practise for this event, too, laying-out a dummy wiggle-woggle course, as shown in a diagram in the Regulations, which was to be held on the promenade at Monte Carlo; it consisted of a series of figure-eights, swerving between pylons, reversing into a 'garage', stopping astride a line and so on — all against the clock, making a pretty demanding test of what remained of the brakes and acceleration after the long road section.

With journalist Humphrey Symonds and Lewis Pearce as my co-drivers, we chose the Norway starting point at Stavanger, and were faced by ice and snow for probably the first 1,000 miles or so. When the roads became fairly straight in Sweden, I handed over the driving: we slid off the road, hitting the left-side rear wheel against

Donald Healey

an enormous telegraph pole that seemed to carry the entire telephonic communication between Germany and Sweden. It must have been a mighty bump, as it brought down the pole, wires and all. We pulled the car out of the ditch and discovered that the rear axle had been knocked back all of three inches on the left-hand side. This had the effect of locking-on the left-side, rear brake, which, like the rest, was rod-operated. As so often with the Monte, we were running behind schedule because of the filthy weather conditions, so time was not on our side. Also, it was necessary to get clear of the scene before Authority came along and discovered what we'd done to their communications system.

We sawed through the brake rod, releasing the brake. I tried the car, and found that it was still driveable, though I had to compensate for the newly-acquired rear-wheel steering by maintaining a degree of opposite-lock on the steering-wheel. Because I felt that I was responsible for the car and that conditions had become more than usually demanding, I drove it in all but the most straightforward, main-road, daytime sections; we went all the way to Monte Carlo in this condition. It was a lovely and memorable experience to climb over the Alps, to drive down into the beautiful, early morning sunshine of the Riviera, and along into Monte Carlo for the finish.

We had only the wiggle-woggle test to face, and I felt the car

**Above left** December 1932: preparing to leave Perranporth for Umea, and the start of the Monte Carlo Rally, in which I finished second with Montgomery. (*B. Healey*).

**Left** The 1931 Invicta's exhaust system was modified, to increase ground-clearance — to the discomfort of the rear-seat passenger. (*B. Healey*).

**Above** With Lewis Pearce (centre) and Humphrey Symons, immediately before setting out in the Invicta on the 1931 Monte Carlo. (*B. Healey*).

was capable of winning it, despite our three-wheel braking system. Also, I had practised the test every day for weeks on a little bit of quiet road at home in Cornwall. I could nearly do it with my eyes shut, and knew I was probably more familiar with it than most others. We slackened-off the right-side rear wheel brake, so that, provided I did all my braking in a straight line, all would — or should — be well. Off I went when my turn came, while Lewis timed me. 'You've done a good time', he said when it was over — and it compared well with the best I had managed during my endless practice runs.

I went to bed that night, and for some reason or other had no idea whatever that we'd any hope of winning the Rally. I didn't sleep at all well, as was so often the way after three or four nights without sleep, dosed-up with caffeine to help me stay awake. I remained in bed late to try and get some rest — until, fast asleep at last, I was woken up by a loud banging on my door. 'Come in', I shouted. In came Lewis, and told me 'You've won the Rally!' I couldn't believe it. I thought he was joking, and told him to clear off. But he insisted: 'You've *won*. . . you're the outright winner. . . get up'. It was true; and we also won the Mont-des-Mules hill-climb, following the Rally.

It was for me an unforgettable occasion; my greatest ambition had been to win the Monte, and I can't describe my joy. I telephoned my wife to come out for the celebrations. Having no passport, she approached the Home Secretary direct, who had a special passport issued because of the British success, and she came out to join in the fun and visit the Palace for the prize presentation by Prince Rainier.

Looking pristine after its travels, the Invicta lines up at the prizegiving with Ivy, Lewis Pearce and Humphrey Symonds on board. I have to confess that I regarded it as my greatest-ever win. (*B. Healey*).

In Sweden, in the 1932 Monte Carlo Rally. (*H.R. Clayton*).

I learned a tremendous amount from this event, with a powerful car on ice and snow, as distinct from the under-powered little Triumph Sevens — and a lot more about what not to do. With so little hard weather in England, one very quickly gets out of practice between Montes; when I had arrived in Sweden I had been slower even than the buses. I had had a few days to spare, though, and had spent them all on one of the ice lakes, working hard to learn how to control this none-too-easy car which, I have to say, was one of the worst I'd handled, and one which nearly killed my old friend Sammy Davis in a race at Brooklands because of its characteristics, when he cornered it too fast.

This was my start, though, with the 4½-litre '100 m.p.h.' Invicta. I drove one in the 1931 Alpine Trials, winning a Glacier Cup and putting up fastest time on the Galibier hill-climb. And in 1932 I drove one again in the Monte — a car that had previously been used as everyday transport, and had covered a considerable mileage, somewhere around 50,000, I believe. We started from Umea, in Sweden, where weather conditions were even worse than the previous year's had been. A day or two before the start we left the car overnight in an open shed, and in the morning we could move it neither backwards nor forwards. The old-fashioned oil in the back axle and gearbox had such a high freezing point that they were solid, and we had to get the local blacksmith to thaw them out with a blow-lamp. At our hotel I asked where I could get a newspaper, and they pointed out a shop across the road, As I set out to buy one, a policeman grabbed me and bundled me back into the hotel, explaining that if I went out without a

51

hat in that temperature, I'd die. The Rally itself went entirely without incident, however, and we finished second in the overall results — making up for that by again winning the Mont-des-Mules hill-climb.

Three of us were entered for the 1932 Alpine Trials, each of us winning a Glacier Cup for maximum points on a fault-free run, while I managed a new record for a climb of the Stelvio Pass. In 1933 Noel again entered me for the Monte, driving the same hard-worked car I'd driven in 1932, starting from Tallinn, in Estonia. It was not to be our year, though. In the middle of Poland an out-of-control, horse-drawn sleigh with four people in it came slew-ing at us, all over the road. I had no alternative but to take to the ditch, which was full of snow. Concealed by the snow was what must have been one of Poland's very few kilometre stones. We hit it square-on in the middle of the radiator, wrecking the car, and putting us out of the Rally.

During those years with Invicta I drove the cars in a number of lesser events, including the Paris-Nice Rally, a pleasant, sum-mer event 'par Vichy', as I recall in the regulations. It concluded with a timed climb up La Turbie hill, out of Nice; and it also included acceleration and slow-speed-in-top tests. To deal with the latter, I had fitted the car with a Clayton-Dewandre vacuum servo, attached to the clutch withdrawal mechanism. When I com-pletely closed the throttle, the increased vacuum declutched com-pletely, so that I could control the large engine, with its considerable torque, with such delicacy that I could move off gently in top gear and continue at whatever speed I wished, right down to a standstill, without touching the clutch. It was as good as today's torque-converters.

The test was so ludicrous that we could not stop laughing. One famous French driver shuffled along beside us, staring spellbound into the cockpit to see what I was up to — preparatory to lodging a protest. They then made me go out with an official observer in the passenger seat. He was dumbfounded; he watched my feet like a hawk, but he couldn't fault me. My left foot rested idly on the floor, while my right was on the throttle pedal. Convinced, finally, that the Invicta possessed low-speed torque comparable only with that of a steam engine, he gave us first prize — for the test and for the class! In retrospect, I suppose it was cheating — yet there was nothing in the regulations to prevent it. We had merely anticipated automatic transmission by a few years.

On one of the Alpine Trials I did with Invicta I had Ian Flem-ing, later of James Bond fame, among other things, with me as navigator. At the time, he was with Associated Press, and had been sent with me to report the event. On many subsequent occasions, when I used to cross the Atlantic three or four times a year in the *Queens*, we would meet and recall our rally together. We had started from Friedrichshaven, and one of the awards for a Glacier Cup was a free flight in the Graf Zeppelin. For this, we had to return to its base near Friedrichshaven for a 4 a.m. start, when there was no wind. It took 250 men to launch and land it, the only way to bring it down to earth being to fly it to within 50 feet or so of the ground and then release 250 ropes, which were grabbed by the landing party, who pulled the whole thing down on to a big, flat railway truck and made it fast. While in flight, we were able to buy postcards illustrating the Zeppelin, and already stamped and franked with its own special postmark. I bought several of these to send home to the family and, when we were flying low over the post office square in Breganz, in Austria, a bag containing our mail was jettisoned, the cards being sent on to their various destinations. Luckily, I still have one of these. Ian, as a very young man on his first foreign assignment, obtained some valuable copy from this trip; and it started in him an interest in cars that lasted right through his life, always prompting him to buy the most exotic he could find. For me the flight was not without a few misgivings, for it was the year following the tragic loss of Britain's R101 in northern France, on her flight from Cardington to India, with the loss of all but six of the 54 people on board.

Not all my Invicta drives were successful. Towards the end of my days driving for the company, when Macklin had produced the smaller, 6-cylinder, 1½-litre model, I drove one in a Belfast Rally. The car was dreadfully underpowered and it had little performance. We didn't even get to the finish. What little performance

A postcard posted from on board the Graf Zeppelin, addressed to my son Brian. I sent one to each of the boys as a souvenir of the experience. (B. Healey).

it had was obtained by transmitting its meagre 45 b.h.p. through a 6:1 final drive. To obtain a better output, and thus use an increased final-drive ratio of 5:1, the engine was subsequently given a Powerplus supercharger, but bearing life suffered. There were several RAC Rallies which I always enjoyed and in which I did well enough; but I never won with an Invicta. They were always concluded with some sort of trivial driving test, upon which the final classification depended far too much, and for which the Invicta was insufficiently compact and nimble.

My association with Invicta ended in early 1933, though I remained close friends with Noel Macklin — later Sir Noel, as the result of his magnificent work in designing for the Royal Navy that famous maid-of-all-work, the Fairmile B-Class ML, which did yeoman service throughout the war, principally in escorting coastal convoys, and which was built in considerable numbers by yards scattered far and wide. At the end of the war, scarcely surprisingly, he was appointed in charge of small craft disposals.

It was interesting, and very pleasant too, when, some 20 years later, cars bearing my name came into being and Noel's son Lance became one of my foremost drivers. And it was emphatically not through any question of nepotism!

My successes with Invicta cars seemed to mark the culmination, or very nearly so, of what I had for so long been trying to achieve. That was a close association with the motor industry, so that I could eventually get into it myself — finally to reach my ultimate objective of building a motor car of a type that I knew from experience to be what the sportsmen of the day needed. To further this end, I knew I had to have experience in international competition of the widest variety in such sporting cars. I had, as it were, sucked the Invicta dry. Although it was ideal, with modifications, for winning long-distance rallies, because of its (then) high power-to-weight ratio, I felt I needed to 'learn' one more make. Subsequently, by the way, I've discovered that the Invictas were possessed of remarkably long life. The two splendid cars I drove in the Monte, from Stavanger in 1931, Umea in 1932, and Tallinn in 1933, are still in use and must have covered phenomenal mileages in their time.

I looked around again for my final stepping-stone — a car which I knew was able to win international rallies, and which could help build-up my name and so get me closer still to the manufacturers. My usual 'subtle' method of going about this was to buy a car myself to begin with, and achieve success in competitions — and, as this often meant, achieve an entrée or, better still, the offer of a job by its manufacturer. As I have said before, I had already grown to know the famous Riley family in the days of my Redwinger in the early twenties — four brothers, each a well-qualified specialist in his own particular aspect of car manufacture. It was

Carburettor adjustment on the Riley during the 1933 International Alpine Trial, in which we finished second in our class. (*B. Healey*).

tragic that this factory, which produced so many fine cars, was to go into liquidation. But, like so many manufacturers — myself included — who were able to design an excellent car, and even produce and sell it at a price that was competitive with the products of the big manufacturers, they were good designers, good entrepreneurs — but not good accountants!

I did not even have to buy a Riley as it turned out; for the 1933 Alpine they lent me one of their little low-slung Brooklands models. It was a stark machine, with scanty protection from the mud, provided by its cycle-type wings, an extremely small windscreen, no wipers or any such concessions of that sort, and no hood of course — though we may have had to fit it with something of the sort in order to comply with the regulations. It was an entirely unsuitable car for the Alpine Rally, but with many minor modifications I was able to make it comfortable enough for me as the driver to endure the buffeting I knew I would get in that sort of event. I was still young enough to enjoy the challenge of driving in wretched conditions; the worse they became, the happier I grew, and this helped too. But except perhaps for a much later experience with a Healey Silverstone, when I had not got age on my side, this must go down as the most uncomfortable event I ever drove in. The conditions of the Rally, too, didn't help matters. It was quite different in those days from anything we know now, the roads very often being unsurfaced and the route including sections on Alpine passes that rally organizers wouldn't even consider today.

For Rileys, that particular event in 1933 was important, though. It was given far more publicity than today's events receive — this was true for most of the big events of the day, the Bentley successes at Le Mans qualifying for front-page headline treatment in some of the dailies. To make sure our performance was not over-looked, I took with me Roger Fuller, a well-known newspaper journalist, and quite a character too. Though great fun to be with, he just sat there; he didn't even want to drive, which suited me. But he got a good story, and Rileys got their publicity — we won a Glacier Cup, the premier award for a fault-free run, of which I won seven in eight pre-war Alpines.

For me it was important too — perhaps more important than the Riley brothers knew. Victor found that he had somebody who could do this sort of event, and made use of me — which was precisely what I'd wanted. I was never a true racing driver, nor even a particularly fast one. I was simply somebody who could stand long periods at the wheel, and who put success in the event as my principal objective, undaunted by discomfort and undeterred when the car went wrong and I had to get down to putting it right (a quality seldom possessed by today's great rally drivers, who have teams of factory mechanics at frequent intervals along the route). For me, though — and at the time — it was a great advantage. One of my reasons for starting my little garage business in Perranporth had been to learn the sort of things that went wrong with rally cars, and how to put them right by the roadside, without skilled, professional help.

This has always seemed to me to be the basic difference between some of the highly-qualified automobile engineers, who have achieved their learning without any real practical experience of working on cars in a garage or at the roadside, and those less qualified — like myself — who are in essence practical engineers. Some of the highly-qualified men, though first-class engineers and able to produce a superbly-designed job, have still been unable to produce a particularly good car, simply because they have had no experience of keeping it going under extreme conditions — and it is these conditions that find out the weaknesses in a design, however good it may be.

Rileys had produced a wonderful engine, and it was used very successfully in racing, both by their own drivers and private owners; and, later, in modified six-cylinder form in the ERAs, Britain's greatest contenders in the pre-war 1½-litre voiturette class. The engine was also used for many years in their production cars as sold to the public. While I worked for them, I chose events where the degree of engine-tuning required was small, but where a fairly considerable amount of work was essential on the chassis and running-gear to make the cars suitable for the big, international trials and rallies.

One of the events that stands out particularly in my memory was the 10,000-kilometre *Fahrt*, run by the Automobilclub von Deutschland in 1931, which was one of my first Riley drives. We crossed 20 frontiers in Europe in 14 days, mostly over roads that weren't really roads at all. I remember some stretches in the Balkans down into Yugoslavia where the cars were given a terrible bashing — which, of course, was excellent as a proving-ground for the manufacturers. The finish was in Berlin at the time of the Olympic Games, where the arrival of the battered, mud-stained cars was given the greatest possible exposure. On the way back to the coast, driving very gently, the crankshaft broke!

By 1933 I was covering around 20,000 miles each year in international rallies and trials, as well as in many, many lesser events at home, in cars based on the standard product, though modified in many small respects. They looked the part, though, and Riley's sales began to benefit from the publicity. One memorable day, Victor Riley telephoned to ask me if I'd come up to the Midlands, joining the company for a spell, and prepare a team of cars for the forthcoming Alpine Rally. It was just what I had wanted, what I had been working for through so many years — an entrée at last to the motor industry. What is more, I was looked after by Cecil Riley in his cottage at Barford where he welcomed me as his guest during my first-ever stay in Warwickshire, which was eventually to become my home for so many years.

One of their production sporting models was the Lynx Tourer, a very snappy little car with the 9 h.p. engine which, thanks to its hemispherical cylinder heads and short, light pushrods operated by camshafts half-way up the cylinder block, was capable of quite high revs and, in standard form, would push the car along at around 75 m.p.h. It was an extremely good car which I knew was capable of putting up high speeds on Alpine tests. I spent some weeks getting the cars ready at the factory; four were prepared — a team of three plus a spare. When the 1933 Alpine Rally came along, they justified our faith in them, two of us winning Glacier Cups — myself in the 'Brooklands' and Victor Leverett with one of the Lynxes, who had won the light car class in the 1931 Monte Carlo Rally, driving a Riley.

Though I became pretty closely involved with the Riley company, I began to wonder how long they would keep going in the face of their apparent lack of financial know-how, the cars being almost too good value-for-money. It was clear to me, though, that the strain of running my little garage business at Perranporth at the same time as maintaining my long-sought Midlands employment was proving too much. I decided to sell my own business and concentrate on the motor industry. Again, my 'solo' performances were to pay off, this time as a result of my earlier successes with the little Triumph Sevens and Super Sevens in the Monte Carlo and British rallies. In the autumn of 1933 I was summoned by Colonel Holbrook, Managing Director of Triumph at the time, who was endeavouring to build a car that would compete with the Riley Nine.

1934, and the family reunited at Perranporth during one of the infrequent spells when I wasn't away from home. Left to right: Geoff, myself, Garbo the Great Dane, Ivy, Brian and John. (*B. Healey*).

We talked, and he told me they were almost ready to go into limited production with a pretty little sports car to be called the Gloria. When he asked me to try out an early example, I had to tell him I was disappointed with it in an awful lot of respects. I told him that if it was going to compete with the Riley they'd have to get someone on to their payroll with sufficient experience to put it right. 'Well, we've got to find somebody', he said — and this was my opportunity. He offered me the job of Experimental Manager, a new title dreamed-up in order to get my knowledge and experience behind this new car, and make it really competitive. I jumped at it — though, looking back, I sometimes wonder at my infidelity to my good friends the Riley brothers. I was to become engaged upon developing a direct rival to the cars that had meant so much to me. I was intensely ambitious, though, and this, coupled with my doubts as to Riley's long-term future, decided me.

I received every possible cooperation from Holbrook's people. His General Manager Charles Ridley became a very close friend, and he and his son Jack, who was to do so well in subsequent Monte Carlos and other rallies with the cars I built, made life very pleasant for me. Having sold my business I moved my family up to Warwickshire where we set up our home. I had made up my mind that there was nowhere in Cornwall where my boys would get a good education and also develop a more mature outlook upon their future. Perranporth was a delightful village, and Cornwall a delightful county, but it was dead in those days. So up we moved to Warwickshire, and I started my career with the Triumph Company.

# 4

# The fabulous Dolomite 8

It didn't take long in 1934, my first full year with Triumph, for me to appreciate how right I'd been over my greatest ambition. For the 1934 Monte I had to prepare two Glorias which would 'get through anything'. To increase ground clearance I substituted the high, straight frame of the Southern Cross for the double-dipped, very low-slung Gloria's. And to cushion the car against road shocks, I fitted big, Extra Low Pressure 9.00 by 16 in. Dunlops, which ran at only 10-12 p.s.i. pressure, increasing the overall wheel diameter from 28 to 32 in. The combination of frame and wheels meant that we had ample clearance — the car looked as if it was on stilts! The final-drive ratio was, of course, changed to give the same set of gear ratios as with standard wheels and tyres.

I drove the car fast over every bit of rough ground I could find — along many miles of roadside grass verge, with drains and cross-gulleys, up and down kerbs, through radiator-high duckponds deep in mud, and on the soft sands at Perranporth. It would go through anything, and the transmitted shocks were greatly

Monte Carlo Rally 1934: Jack Ridley and I inspect our protection against wolves and bandits, prior to starting the event from Athens in the Triumph 10, in which Norman Black, Tommy Wisdom and I finished third overall. (*B. Healey*).

reduced. In the meantime, I had sent Jack Ridley, who was to drive the second car, over to Athens for a reconnaissance trip, driving Lord de Clifford's Lagonda which had been entered for the Athens start and needed delivering — which suited us well, as we, too, had chosen Athens. Jack reckoned we could face almost anything on the route.

When the time came, I decided there was no point in risking damage to the cars, by driving all the way, so we drove across France and Switzerland to Italy, embarking at Venice for the sea crossing to Greece. We had plenty of practice in the ice and snow we met on the way, and found the ELP tyres every bit as good as normal wheels fitted with chains. We were thankful for my decision not to drive all the way for, as we sat safely in Athens awaiting the start, other competitors came limping in with broken springs, buckled wheels, battered mudguards and even broken engine bearers.

In the event, even on the first stage from Athens to Salonika, I was completely satisfied I'd done the right thing in fitting the Dunlop tyres; I was able to get away clear of the big American cars and all the others, in the little 10 h.p. Gloria. I had as co-driver my close friend, the late Tommy Wisdom — a great person who, as I had learned to do when with him, could hand over the wheel and go straight off to sleep in the passenger seat, trusting each other to do the right thing. Not only was he a good all-round competition driver, but a respected motoring journalist too, and we competed in many, many events together, sometimes in the same car, sometimes as rivals.

Competitors in today's big-time, international rallies might consider the trials faced by their forebears. This was the main road out of Athens in 1934. (*B. Healey*).

Crossing the Straits of Messina in southern Italy before competing in the 1934 Monte Carlo Rally with Norman Black (sharing the work here) and Tommy Wisdom. We finished third overall. (*B. Healey*).

In addition to our two cars, there were five other Triumphs in the event: Major and Mrs Montague-Johnstone, from the John O'Groats start; Jack Hobbs from Umea; Edgar Kehoe from Stavanger; Margaret Allen, Mrs Eaton, and Mrs Marshall from Umea; and J. Beck and R. Tanner from Tallin. It was a source of tremendous pride for me when, some 2,400 miles and four days and nights later, all seven arrived at the finish to be classified in the results — Jack Hobbs' car with the left-side, front wheel knocked back the best part of a foot, and the dumb-iron split, as a result of hitting a car which had shot out of a farmyard without warning. Yet, in this state, he had averaged 50-odd m.p.h. for 308 miles.

The results made me even prouder. Norman, Tom Wisdom and I took third place overall, winning the small car category, in which Ridley was sixth, Beck tenth, Hobbs twelfth, Margaret Allen 26th (doing the latter part of the road section, and the 'wiggle-woggle' test on two cylinders, with a blown head gasket); the Montague-Johnstones 31st; and Kehoe 38th. And to demonstrate that my ELP tyres, set to high pressures of course, lost us nothing in manoeuvrability, I managed fastest time on the wiggle-woggle — the Coupe de Monte Carlo — which was to stand as a record for quite a time.

As the result of my first and second places with the Invicta in 1931 and 1932, and now my third place with the Triumph, I was awarded the magnificent Coupe de l'Illustration Automobile which for many years had been 'not awarded'. It remains among my few trophies that have not been stolen through the years — too big and heavy for any burglar's 'swag-bag'.

In February 1934 the residents of Perranporth gave a dinner in my honour to celebrate my winning the Coupe de l'Illustration Automobile for having finished in one or other of the first three places in the Monte Carlo Rally on three occasions. Left to right: Ivy, JF, myself, Emmie and Geoff. (*B. Healey*).

I drove Triumphs in an enormous number of events that year — every British rally that was held, the MCC's 'classic' trials, small events in France, Brooklands high-speed trials and so on; and I gained a wonderful lot of friends. The success of the cars in the Monte aroused even more interest at the factory in international rallies, and our next major outing was in the 1934 Alpine. The first time any Triumphs had competed in this event had been in 1933, when they had had a trouble-free run throughout the event, until the final afternoon when one of the drivers had crashed into an enormous rock, and was excluded. No awards were won, but this was intended only as an initial move in the development of the Gloria.

The 1934 event was run over some extremely poor roads in Yugoslavia, one-in-three gradients in Austria, timed climbs of the 9,000ft Stelvio and the Galibier, and a high-speed test over six miles of Autostrada; stricter than usual time schedules were imposed, and radiators were sealed for the whole of each day's run. The event covered 1,800 miles in six days, and all entries had to be identical in every respect to a minimum of 100 cars already sold to the public. Jack Ridley, as Competitions Manager, and I went off to do a dummy run over the route, to see whether Triumphs in standard, production form stood a chance. We reckoned they did, and six cars were entered — a team of three to compete for outright victory in the Coupe des Alpes, and three private entries to go for the Glacier Cups, the highest individual awards. All six were 1,087 c.c. Triumph Ten four-seater with two-seater hoods and the rear seats removed to make space for spares and tools.

The team cars were driven by Col. Holbrook (with Shemans, from the Experimental Shop, to look after the cars), Jack Ridley (with Sharp, also from the Experimental Shop), and Victor Leverett (team leader; ex-Riley like myself, and accompanied by W. Rolla-son, Works Manager of Coventry Radiators, whose presence would ensure nothing went wrong with the radiators; he was also an outstanding timekeeper). The three 'individual' entries were driven by Maurice Newman and Commander N.D. Holbrook, VC; Miss Joan Richmond and Mrs Gordon Simpson; and myself, with my old friend and co-driver in many events, Lewis Pearce from Perranporth.

Relaxing at Perranporth between events — left to right: Geoff, John, myself and Brian. (B. Healey).

We all arrived without incident at Nice, the starting point, and after a few days' swimming in the blue Mediterranean, submitted the cars for scrutineering. Hawk-eyed German officials sealed radiators and drain-cocks, and marked every vital part of the cars with yellow paint, so that the replacement of any part so marked meant disqualification. Everything seemed to have been marked — cylinder heads, water pumps, steering parts, road springs, dynamos, batteries, axles, the lot. Somehow, it gave one a feeling of claustrophobia — there was simply no leeway at all.

The route read like a 'Guide to the Cols', the first day's itinerary including the Col de la Cayolle, Col de Vars, Col d'Izoard, Col du Lauteret and Col de Glandon; and the second day's the Little St Bernard, Grand St Bernard, Col de Pillon and Sannen Moser. And thus it continued, with the Stelvio, among others, on day four. Though we were timed over the entire 12 miles of the Stelvio, with its 49 acute *lacets* and a great many other twists and turns, the Triumphs' set average was 35 k.p.h. and we had to keep going flat-out the whole way. Only one of us lost any marks! Joan Richmond's car had slithered straight-on at a dusty hairpin and struck the rock-face. Though neither the chassis-frame nor the front axle had been damaged, the main leaf on one front spring had been badly deformed. The girls had carried on with the speed hill-climb, and down the other side, where they had found a smithy, borrowed a hammer and anvil, and straightened the spring-leaf. Unfortunately, although they completed the whole distance to Munich, and the finish, they were excluded on the grounds that the hammer and anvil had not been carried in the car!

We drove into the lovely old city of Munich in triumphal procession, not one — save for the gallant girls — having lost a solitary mark. Behind us came the Singer team, with a loss of 28 points, then the German Adler-Trumpf-Juniors in third place. Maurice Newnham and I won Glacier Cups; it was my sixth Alpine, and I was immensely proud that I'd won a Glacier Cup in all but one.

By now, Col. Holbrook had become engrossed with the idea of building truly competitive sports cars, with particular emphasis on bridging the gap in Britain between the great Bentleys and Lagondas, and the spate of what we used to refer to unkindly as 'buzz-boxes' — the MG Midget, Singer Le Mans and others, successful though they undoubtedly were in their own particular fields. We had nothing to compete with the all-conquering 1750 and 2.3-litre Alfa Romeos, and vaguely decided to set our sights on the 2-litre class. On the day following our successful Alpine, it happened that Tommy Wisdom came to lunch with us at Triumph and we fell to discussing this exciting subject — which by now was very much occupying our minds.

It was, from memory, Tom's idea to get hold of an Alfa Romeo, strip down the engine to the last nut and bolt and inspect it, in

an effort to establish what made it such an outstandingly successful design. So far as I personally was concerned, I was not averse
to the unreasonably frowned-upon practice of copying — or let's
say seeking inspiration from — someone else's design. I consider
this to be the whole essence of being a successful motor-car
designer — the ability to select the best features from the individual designs of each of one's main rivals, and embody them
in a winning whole. Greater manufacturers than Triumph have
done this unashamedly and without being pilloried, both before
and since.

The background to the stylish and exciting straight-eight, supercharged Triumph Dolomite that resulted has always been wrapped
in mystery, so far as the public were concerned, with unfounded
tales of law suits, plagiarism and suchlike, through the years.
There was, in fact, nothing mysterious about it, the whole operation being carried out with complete co-operation from Alfa
Romeo.

Col. Holbrook (he was knighted in 1938) agreed with our
proposals to base the design on the successful 2.3-litre, straight-
eight Monza Alfa Romeo, and gave me an extremely tight budget
of £5,000 which, today, would scarcely design and build a prototype wheelbarrow. It so happened that the Hon. Brian Lewis (later
Lord Essendon, and now sadly passed away) owned, and was
racing, an almost new Monza — which, interestingly, was much
later to become the property of the Hon. Patrick Lindsay. We
bought the car, stripped the engine completely, and found it to
be in perfect condition with virtually no wear, so that, in making
production drawings, we had few problems over tolerances
(whether the sample was on the top or bottom limit, for example). We decided to keep as close to the engine design as possible, though not making an exact copy.

We were fortunate at Triumph in having what was possibly the
finest tool-room in the Midlands. They could, and did, make
everything, including motor cycles, various one-offs and, of
course, all the machining involved in our car production. We had,
too, some outstanding draughtsmen, and I chose for this job an
elderly and vastly experienced man by the name of Swettenham,
who had earlier been a personal assistant to Sir Henry Royce, and
Ken Middleton. Some of the parts posed real problems: the supercharger lobes, for example, which had to be hand-formed, and
the two-part crankshaft, machined from solid billets, which was
hand-made in two four-cylinder halves, bolted together at the
centre with the train of gears (also hand-made) running up the
centre of the block to drive the overhead camshafts. We had no
drawings from which to work — we had to make those ourselves,
and hand-make everything from them. Peter Cowley and Albert
Ludgate were responsible for the chassis.

The strikingly beautiful straight-eight, supercharged Triumph Dolomite prototype at Perranporth in 1934. (*B. Healey*).

As well as our absurdly small budget, we had an extremely tight time schedule, because we wanted to produce something outstanding pretty quickly to help push our less exotic cars, and to show people that we were really going ahead at Triumph and that our rally successes were no flash in the pan. I had Swettenham and his assistants working day and night sometimes, on the drawings of this complicated engine. In the meantime, I had set the bodywork people producing designs for the body. At this time, Walter Belgrove joined the company — not as a 'stylist', though Jack Ridley and I very soon discovered that he possessed an uncanny gift in this direction, and it was he who finished off the design started by Frank Warner. He did a lovely job of the little two-seater: it had all the poise and balance — the high-stepping look — of the foremost Italian sports cars, yet somehow it retained a character that was entirely English. We were very proud of it, and even today when I look at photographs of it, I can still feel a thrill.

With the stroke reduced from 65mm to get the engine capacity down to 1,990 cc, the dimensions worked out at 60 by 88 mm. With the blower virtually identical to that of the 2.3 Monza, we introduced a higher supercharger pressure. The output was officially 129 b.h.p. at 5,500 r.p.m., though we always reckoned it was comfortably above this figure. We eventually settled for an SU carburettor; and, thanks to the enthusiasm of all those involved, we had the first engine running in less than six months. We had machined the parts for two engines complete (eventually we built a total of six), unfortunately wrecking the crankshaft of one of them during testing, through no real fault of our own. When Mr

Rowbottom, of Rolls-Royce (who had advised us with materials in many ways from the start) had suggested lead-bronze bearings, he had omitted to warn us that it was absolutely vital to nitride the crankshaft if it were to be hard enough to run in these comparatively hard bearings. In consequence, we made an expensive mistake; but we produced a replacement and had it, along with the second of our first two (and subsequently, of course, the remaining four) nitrided by Rolls-Royce. We tried the engine on the bench and, to our delight, it ran extremely well from the start.

Earlier on, while Swettenham had been working away on his drawings, I went to Milan to discuss our activities with Alfa Romeo's chief engineer, Signor Jano, who had been responsible for the design of the Monza as well as other famous Alfas. He was perfectly agreeable and, in fact, expressed pleasure that so famous a British manufacturer as Triumph should have been inspired by his design. It should perhaps be borne in mind too that by 1933, when I visited Jano, the 2.3 straight-eight was growing a little long in the tooth as a design, so that we were not 'milking' his latest and greatest! We discussed the possibility of Alfa Romeo's building the 650 cc vertical-twin Triumph motor cycle in Milan, as a sort of quid pro quo and even of calling our beautiful car a Triumph-Alfa, though it was a Dolomite in the end.

There are those who may wonder why, if Jano had given the project his blessing, we didn't simply buy a set of production drawings from him and save ourselves considerable trouble and expense. The short answer is that, by the time I went to see him, we had already bought the car, and Swettenham was well advanced with his own drawings.

So far as the rest of the car was concerned, we used a ladder-type chassis-frame with 104-inch wheelbase, beam axles and half-elliptic leaf springs at both ends. At first we tried Alfa's own design, but found it to be a bit dicey at the rear. Although the Alfa was very rigidly controlled, the suspension was too soft, a shortcoming which they had offset by fitting very powerful, friction-type dampers, which were doing far too much of the work. Instead, we used springs with a larger number of leaves, thereby increasing the natural damping, with Hartford friction dampers all round. Although this combination gave a pretty awful, hard ride unless fully laden, it worked well and the car handled better. We were very unhappy about the brakes, too, though the aluminium, 16-inch drums looked impressive, completely filling the backs of the wheels. Initially they were powerful and immensely reassuring, but with their very narrow rubbing area the linings wore far too quickly and you simply couldn't keep them adjusted.

We approached Gordon Parnell, of Lockheed's: 'You'd do a darned sight better', he said, 'to fit a set of normal 10-inch production drums — they're wider, with a lower rubbing speed and a larger friction area.' We took his advice and it made a world of difference to the lining life, without reducing the braking effect in any way. Jack Ridley and I did extensive high-speed testing at Brooklands, with a lap at over 110 mph, and the car was obviously capable of quite extensive tuning. We were immensely and, I think, justifiably proud when we first unveiled it to the Press at the October Motor Show in 1934 — and it was greeted as a sensation. It seemed the embodiment of all that British sportsmen required, both in performance and looks. The price tag of £1,225 was high — higher in fact than the chassis price of a Rolls-Royce, and roughly the same as a 3-litre Bentley complete. It was comparable, though, with its direct rivals from Europe — and what a fabulous car you got for your money! For those, incidentally, who are interested in the full specification of this car, I can recommend *Triumph Cars* by Richard Langworth and Graham Robson (Motor Racing Publications, 1979).

In 1935 I decided to give the prototype car (ADU 4) an airing in the Monte, and set about converting it into a rally car. This meant increasing the wheel size to improve ground-clearance, fitting large-section tyres, removing the very pretty wings of the prototype and replacing them with cycle-type, carving out more room in the boot to carry chains and all the gear we needed, increasing the fuel tank capacity and mounting two spare wheels. It looked simply horrible, and my multi-leaf rear springs were really put to work, but it produced a rally car, of sorts. With Lewis Pearce as co-driver, I chose the Umea start, in Sweden. We had a very pleasant run up, doing all the practising I could on the ice lakes,

Monte Carlo Rally 1935: The Triumph Dolomite after hitting a train on a level-crossing in Denmark. We were lucky to escape unhurt, except for Lewis Pearce's loss of a tooth. (*B. Healey*).

as this car had extremely individual handling characteristics, especially on ice, and needed learning.

Throughout the small mileage we covered on the rally, it ran well and we began to feel really confident. As we approached the Danish frontier I was chatting with Lewis, following another car in the darkness to save our batteries, when suddenly and terrifyingly we heard a shrill, almighty scream. I looked at Lewis: 'The ruddy supercharger's seizing!', I said. I'd scarcely completed the words when there was a shattering crash, and we span round in a complete circle in the middle of the road.

We just sat there, dazed, but with no sense of nervous shock, nothing. We just thought 'We've hit something.' Then we heard the sound of escaping steam and, looking up from beneath the edge of the low hood, we saw the lights of a train with a long row of passengers peering out of the lit windows. It had been the train's whistle, and it had hit our right-side, front corner on an unguarded level-crossing. The driver climbed down and came over to the car, expecting to discover a tragic and bloody mess inside. But to his amazement, all he saw was the two of us, sitting there unhurt, except for the fact that Lewis had lost a tooth. We clambered out of the wreckage, which was pretty complete, feeling no sense whatever of shock, though the following day we were stiff and scarcely able to move. Eventually the police came along and arrested us according to their law, which decreed that you went promptly 'inside' until such time as you could produce proof of insurance cover — in our case to make good the damage to the locomotive, which was limited to a few paint chips on the exposed cylinder, frame and buffer. Satisfied that we hadn't inflicted too

The battered Dolomite on its journey home, as deck cargo. (*B. Healey*).

much damage to their property, they were extremely kind and courteous, cooking delightful meals and serving us wine; it was a very pleasant police station. Finally, I obtained proof from Triumph that we were properly covered, and they let us go. Then we had the depressing business of getting the wrecked car on to the boat and, sadly crestfallen, restoring to the factory the battered, unrecognizable remains of the beautiful thing into which so many hours of enthusiastic midnight oil had been poured.

To this day, I believe we could have done well. The Dolomite handled beautifully; the performance was better than that of anything I'd driven, and it was so smooth, with the little bit of a whine from the supercharger gears adding to the 'character'. It was reminiscent of the aristocratic whine from the gearbox of the great Bentleys of the 1920s. When we got back to the works I was pretty certain I'd get the sack, but by then I'd been made Technical Director and there was no question of it. Nor was there any question of abandoning active participation in competition for a while. Holbrook said immediately: 'Right! Straighten it out and get it ready for another rally.' We had also to face the decision whether or not to put the car into production, having carried out a few modifications.

In order to 'tame' the car a little, to make it better suited to rallying than to racing, I removed the blower and enlarged the cylinder bores to give us a swept volume of 2.6 litres, and fitted a normal induction system and carburettors. Oddly enough, it gave us a pretty well identical performance, as all the blower had apparently been achieving was to overcome the inadequacies of the old induction system — blowing at only seven or eight pounds, anyway, because of the poor quality of the fuel available in those days, especially in some of the more remote countries traversed on the Monte in Europe. I had friends, though, in the Esso Corporation, and they were able to provide us with a few bottles of tetra-ethyl lead, on the condition that I used rubber gloves when handling this dangerous fluid, that I would never let it out of its special lead bottles except straight into the tank, and so on. It did, however, enable us to run on the very low grades of fuel sometimes forced upon us, without damaging the engine.

In this form I drove the Dolomite in the 1936 Monte, finishing eighth and putting up the best British performance. We started from Tallinn, and had a thoroughly enjoyable event, completing the course without loss of marks, and finishing only five seconds behind the winning Ford V8. This encouraging performance, however, came too late. Triumph's fortunes were at a very low ebb, and the Dolomite was a high-grade, specialized and very costly car. We had built three cars (including my crashed Monte Carlo contender, which was successfully rebuilt), and six engines, of which the one from the crashed car had been a complete write-off, whittling the engine total to five.

In April 1935 it had been decided to discontinue production, and eventually the Dolomite production, lock-stock-and-barrel (or what remained of it) was sold to Tony Rolt, who had been racing a Gloria Southern Cross. Exactly what Rolt bought is somewhat lost in the mists of time, but from memory it consisted of two chassis, the 2.6-litre unblown engine, and the four surviving blown 2-litre units, plus spares. The price he paid for this treasure-trove, this labour-of-love, is also somewhat vague, but I'm pretty certain it was under £1,000. Tony Rolt (Major Rolt, as he was a regular soldier) kept the Dolomites for not much longer than a year,

52 years apart: the original Dolomite, at Perranporth in 1934 with me at the wheel (top) and the same car in 1986 on the identical spot: the same driver, but 52 years older! (B. Healey).

maybe 18 months, racing them regularly with some success, including fastest lap in the Leinster Trophy. Finally, he sold the cars, engines and everything pertaining to them, to Robert Arbuthnot, of High Speed Motors, after which, although they remained unmistakably Triumph Dolomites to those who had known and envied them in their heyday, they were renamed HSMs.

For the next few years the surviving cars seemed to vanish into oblivion, though one, under the HSM banner, used to appear occasionally at Prescott during the fifties. However, some 50 years after their creation, whilst attending an Austin-Healey meet in the States, I was thrilled to receive a call from a member of the staff of *Road and Track*, who told me not only that 'my' Dolomite had turned up in California, but that it had won the award for the finest British car in that most prestigious of all *concours d'élégance*, held at Pebble Beach. I was told that the car had been completely restored by Tony Merrick, of Reading, and was owned by David Cohen, who lived in South Africa. Not too happy about taking the car back to that troubled country, he brought it to England, where Tony Merrick did further work on it, before it was finally auctioned in London by Sotheby's in 1987, realizing the almost incredible sum of £150,000. The fortunate new owner is an American — a Mr Perkins, who I believe maintains a collection of supercharged cars in the UK. What became of the remaining two cars is unknown, but perhaps their present owners will feel inspired by Mr Perkins' example to restore the ageing remains of one of Britain's most exciting sports cars.

It was still left to us to produce something outstanding, and above all, something that would compete with the products of our neighbours, the Jaguar company. Here I must be allowed to dwell for awhile upon William Lyons, or 'Bill' as he always was to those of us who appreciated and loved him, later to receive a knighthood for his wonderful work. There is no doubt in my mind that he was the greatest, most inspired, single-handed small motor manufacturer there has ever been or ever will be. His conception of the first SS was truly brilliant, and I maintain that it could never have been achieved by a highly-trained, skilled specialist automobile engineer. It had to be done by a man who knew, or sensed, if you like, unerringly what the public wanted, what he himself wanted as a driver, and what would appeal through its individual styling. As well as this inspiration, Bill had an inborn artistic sense. These are the things that count in making motor cars — these, and the ability to produce them in quantity when the time comes, as inevitably it will.

Computers today may achieve their purpose in producing millions of good, look-alike, indistinguishable and undistinguished motor cars that will do their job extremely well. They know what not to do; but they certainly do not know how to make cars look different from each other. Today, when almost every car has come straight off a computer drawing-board, they have lost all their individuality — and I think one of the greatest causes of this sameness has been the loss of a distinctive radiator. They all have the 'Joe E. Brown' front, with square lamps instead of round, and they all look alike. It was the manufacturer's personal and often lovely radiator, his one wholly distinguishable trademark, that told you immediately what each car was; that and, in quantity-produced cars where specialist coachbuilders were not involved, the continuing adherence to the manufacturer's own individual style and indiosyncracies. Bill Lyons knew all about these things; each Jaguar produced during Bill's working days was unmistakeably a Jaguar. There are, of course, a few manufacturers who continue today a token adherence to their old radiator forms, sometimes in stylized, decorative form. I can think of Rolls-Royce, Bentley and Mercedes-Benz, of course, and to some extent Alfa Romeo.

While on the subject of styling, I shall never grow to like, even to accept, some of today's sporting cars (there's no such thing as a sports car as we knew it) with their spoilers and 'go-faster planks' that give them an improvement of maybe .01 drag coefficient, effective perhaps at speeds that some of them will never achieve. In many cases these are styling gimmicks, nothing more nor less. I've never been a great aerodynamicist myself, believing in the principle that if a car looks aesthetically pure and smooth, that's all one needs, and that was the thinking behind the Healeys; their performance proved us not all that far wrong. And this fuel-consumption fetish: numerous qualified engineers have told me, since I gave up the job, that by making all these minute improvements in drag coefficient, a saving of as little as a gallon of petrol in 1,000 miles is achieved. In return for this infinitesimal saving, you've got an ugly car — those hideous 'beards' in front, those horrible little ledges and spoilers at the back, the shape of the boot — they all add up to an eyesore, and at the speeds dictated by today's limits they mean virtually nothing except, as I have said, as styling quirks employed to make the product look 'different' or 'sporty'.

It was the same, I suppose, when I was young, when the 'sporty-boys' used to doll-up some very mundane little sports cars with all the paraphernalia of Le Mans: radiator and headlamp stone-guards, quick-action petrol tank and radiator filler-caps, straps over the bonnet, dummy knock-off hub-caps in the centre of bolt-on Magna wheels, and so on. But these were of their own choice; the 'personalization' of their cars, not part of the original equipment on the production model. Owners are free to do what they wish to their cars, but manufacturers should be above selling them mutton dressed as lamb, except on a genuine competition car, or one with competition potential.

# 5

# Another war, another car: Elliotts, Westlands, and Silverstones

As Technical Director of Triumph I was responsible between 1934 and 1939 for the design of all Triumph cars. We had as our Managing Director Maurice Newnham, a magnificent salesman, but a man who knew practically nothing about making motor cars. Inspired no doubt by his salesman's instincts, he told me he wanted to produce a car which would attract the public eye in the biggest possible way, both as to styling and specification. He particularly wanted us to think up something really striking in frontal treatments. He had, I think, been to some extent influenced by the American Hudson-Essex people, who had brought over a car with a curious radiator cowling made up of vertical slats and curved, horizontal ribs — a sort of bulbous, glorified stone-guard.

He explained his ideas to Walter Belgrove, who went to work and produced drawings of what was to become the very distinctive, and expensive, cast-aluminium radiator cowling on the 1.8-litre, four-cylinder and the 2-litre, six-cylinder saloons and roadsters which we had named Dolomite in continuation of our wonderful folly. They were beautifully fitted-out cars, with central chassis lubrication, screen-washers, leather upholstery, and even radio, which was available as an extra. They were not competition cars in any sense, though, being much too heavy, but they were excellent fast touring cars, and the two-seater, with its dicky-seat in the tail, was a regular winner in *concours d'élégance* events. Nor were they expensive, saloons and roadsters selling at £368 and £348 respectively — cheap, by contemporary standards. I liked the cars well enough, but being a stickler for the old-fashioned radiator, I didn't care much for the elaborate radiator casting. Belgrove had produced designs for some really beautiful, conventional front-ends.

It had been the Gloria/Vitesse/Southern Cross models that kept the wolf from the door during 1935, the year of the straight-eight Dolomite, and they carried us through to 1936, to be joined by the new Dolomites. During 1936 the car and motor cycle businesses were separated, and from 1937 onwards we built our own overhead-valve Triumph engines, instead of using the overhead inlet-valve, side exhaust Coventry-Climax units; we also fitted synchromesh gearboxes on all models. I shall never forget the debt we owed to Walter Belgrove throughout my years with Triumph. His very distinctive, individual — though never outlandish — styling gave an exclusive character to Triumph cars and, as I'm sure Bill Lyons would agree, provided healthy competition for his SS Jaguars.

So far as the competition side was concerned, I still managed to attend a few events, including the 1936 Alpine with a Southern Cross. But I was becoming too busy, too involved with the daily work at the factory, to spare much time. Anyway, by now our cars were appearing in a formidable number of events, driven by private owners. At the foot of observed sections in the MCC classic trials, and awaiting their turn at special tests during events such as the Eastbourne, Brighton, RAC and other rallies, it was a fine and encouraging experience to see our cars lined up in droves. We were not short, therefore, of the right kind of publicity.

From mid-1938 we built and sold only the Dolomites, introducing a compact 1½-litre model which sold at £313; and, in 1939, a 12 h.p. conventionally-styled sports saloon was introduced, though only a small number were built. As with Riley, the writing was on the wall.

We were badly handicapped by not having enough capital to tool-up for body production. Our bodies were made in the Dawson Car Company's coachbuilding works, which we had bought. They were coachbuilt in the traditional manner of specialist coachbuilders, with timber frames clad in shaped aluminium panels — the most expensive and, for that matter, the most time-consuming way to build a body. Also, we possessed

Awaiting the long and tiring timed climb of the Stelvio, during the 1936 International Alpine Trial, with the Triumph 14. (*B. Healey*).

Explaining the intricacies of the twin SU carburettors on the new Triumph Dolomite to 'Miss Vitesse' in 1937. The handsome, highly- polished, cast aluminium radiator grille that distinguished this successor to the straight-eight Dolomite can be clearly seen. (*Logan*).

no sound body-production engineers. And, although Belgrove produced some really lovely designs, we had just to sit sadly and admire them — we simply couldn't produce them to sell at the right price, for the market in which we were involved.

The number of man-hours required to build a coachbuilt body was fantastic, yet the cars, lovely though they were, were being sold for a ridiculous few hundred pounds. Added to our problems, of course, was the inevitable drop in sales during 1939, when the Second World War began to seem extremely likely.

There was no alternative but to go into liquidation.

Lloyds bank put in a receiver, and sold the company for an absurdly low figure to Thomas Ward, of Sheffield, who appointed me as their local General Manager, while they continued to look for a customer for the factory. Eventually they sold a portion of it to the Air Ministry at a big profit — more than they had paid for the two factories the Triumph company had originally owned — and retaining the car spares and the trading name, which they eventually sold to Standard. War came, and the Air Ministry, through Messrs H.M. Hobson, asked me to stay on as Works Manager of the factory, making Claudel-Hobson carburettors for aero engines. So far as I was concerned it was not a very interesting job, though it was, I suppose, some contribution to the war effort.

It cheered me tremendously when I heard that Laurence Pomeroy Senior, that great pioneer Vauxhall designer, was to be Director of the factory: I enjoyed working with him, and together we built a unique test house for the carburettors. At the same time, I was asked to take a commission in the RAFVR as a part-time officer in the Air Training Corps. I found this work very interesting, as I worked mostly with local RAF stations as liaison officer, arranging flying programmes for the Cadets. I put all my spare time into this, and was eventually promoted to Squadron Leader and given charge of the Warwickshire Wing.

It was a great shock to me when Laurence Pomeroy died; I lost interest in producing carburettors and felt I could make a greater contribution to the war effort by using my knowledge of vehicles, so I joined the Humber Car Company on the fighting vehicle side, which, with my RAF work, kept me fully occupied. During my time with Humber I met Ben Bowden and 'Sammy' Sampietro. Ben was their chief body draughtsmen and Sammy, an Italian who had been released from internment because of his valuable engineering skills and the work he had done pre-war at the Talbot works, was one of their chassis designers.

Later, when the end of the war began to seem likely, the idea of building sporting cars grew stronger and stronger in my mind, and I discussed the possibility with Ben and Sammy. We made plans for the day when we would be free to have a go at it.

During the war it was my wife who had all the headaches; in the early days she had to cope with a family of three growing boys, Geoffrey, Brian and John, and the problems of feeding them on the meagre rations. I evacuated them to Cornwall in the first year of war, when everybody was forecasting terrifying air raids, and Geoff, who was determined to become an engineer, studied engineering at the Camborne School of Mines. After a year of this, they decided to return to the Midlands, while Geoff, feeling he would be of more use to the country as a qualified engineer than in the forces — at least until he had got his Higher National Certificate in Engineering — joined the Coventry engineering company of Cornercroft as an apprentice, studying for his exams at the same time. Brian remained at school until 17, when he left to join the Royal Navy as an Able Seaman, and John went to Southampton University, learning to fly with the University Air Squadron.

At the family home in Leamington we had an air-raid shelter dug out beneath the kitchen floor, with 18 in. of solid concrete on top and access through a trap-door, down a ladder. Because the shelter floor was below the water-table, the first thing we had to do was switch on the pump to clear the foot or so of water on the floor. Geoffrey, Brian and John were still at home in 1941 at the time of the serious Coventry raids, so we had five bunks down there, and as soon as the sirens sounded, my wife would muster the boys and herd them down into the shelter for the night. She always went off to sleep first; the boys, who were not all that keen on their damp bunks, would wait until she was firmly asleep, then troop upstairs again to bed — then they'd get up in the morning, make the breakfast, and take their mother a cup of tea — still sleeping soundly in the shelter! This happened scores of times.

The laws about misuse of petrol were extremely strict — it was more than life was worth to drive out to the pub. If it happened to be on your route home from work, you could stop for a pint — even so, you'd have a job to convince the Law that you were on your way home at 9.30 in the evening. So we bought bicycles to get to the Crown, and later, the Lord Leicester in Warwick, where most of us used to gather after work. One evening, while crossing the canal bridge between Warwick and Leamington, Ivy parted company with her bicycle, and I remember with shame calling out to her: 'Come on, you old stupid — get back on again — you're embarrassing me!'

Having qualified in Engineering, Geoff obtained a commission in the Army and was posted to the Middle East, where he soon achieved the rank of Captain. John, the youngest, joined the RAF and started his Pilot's training during the last year of the war; but it was Brian who was our greatest anxiety, for he was drafted to a 'Woolworth Carrier' — a cargo vessel converted to carry aircraft — and spent much of his wartime service in the appalling and perilous Russian convoys. All this was no small worry to my wife,

The Healey family at war, with the boys representing all three services. Left to right: Ivy, John, Geoff, Brian and myself, together during a chance coincidence of leaves at home in Leamington Spa in 1944. (*B. Healey*).

for we never knew where Brian was. John did not finish his Pilot's training, because the RAF closed down on training when hostilities ended. He was moved to the Physical Training Section for training as a PT instructor. During this time he hurt his back, however, and was invalided out of the Service with a life pension.

V-Day was memorable for us. I was on duty at a local RAF station and, among other frivolities, I tried to drive my Sunbeam-Talbot up the steps of the Officers' Mess, losing the two front wings on the way. It was unwise of me, in retrospect, to treat the car in such a manner — it was the only example of that model ever to be fitted with independent front suspension, cannibalised in my spare time from a Volkswagen. Interesting though it was, it was not a great success, as I had overlooked the fact that a whippy chassis-frame could never allow the i.f.s. to do its job properly. What an incredible relief it was, though, for us and for other fortunate parents, to have survived the war with our family still intact.

The war at last over, Bowden, Sampietro and I really got down to work on the design of my new sports car. They were still at Humbers, but we worked in the evenings and at weekends, and somehow managed to get the work done. We were designing a car which, as our principal objective, would offer direct competition to the pre-war 2-litre 328 BMW, by far the best small sports car of its time. We completed our designs before we even knew where we were going to look for the engine I had envisaged.

Just before the war, Riley — who, like Triumph, had gone into liquidation — had been bought by Lord Nuffield, of Morris Motors. They had just produced a new 2.4-litre, four-cylinder engine of very advanced design with hemispherical cylinder-heads and developing just over 100 b.h.p. This was the minimum output we regarded as necessary. Victor Riley was still in charge at Riley and, after many talks together, he agreed to supply me with these engines as soon as stocks became available. This could have taken a very long time, as rigid material controls were in force, and the change-over from wartime production was slow.

Good friend that he was, Victor found me an engine, gearbox and rear axle from some secret store, and I was in business. I left Humber to get on with the job, my chief problem being to find somewhere to build the prototype chassis. An old friend and Triumph co-director, Wally Allen, owned a works in Warwick making cement-mixers, and he personally offered me the use of one of his sheds. Permits for steel had to be obtained from the Ministry of Supply; we had no background of pre-war production, and it was extremely difficult to convince them that we really intended to build cars with an export potential, this being their principal condition for allocating us the materials we required.

Riley's Supply Manager, Jack Tatton, was a tremendous help;

thanks to his influence with the MOS. I obtained a permit to purchase steel to build a very limited number of cars. These permits continued for a few years after the war: every nut and bolt we purchased had to be covered by a Permit Number. But at last I had a shed, some steel, an excellent power unit, and a transmission; all I needed now was the help to hand-build the first prototype chassis, so I enlisted one of the McClure boys, son of the Riley works manager.

With the help of the cement-mixer machine-tools, we eventually completed the first chassis. When my son Geoffrey was on leave from the Army, he would give a hand, as did numerous friends in the RAF. Many tracings of our drawings were done by girls in the WAAF, who were stationed nearby. At this time I had no name for the car. My first thought was 'Invicta', as they were by then out of business, but Earl Fitzwilliam, who owned the name, would not part with it (it was eventually to be revived as the unsuccessful Black Prince). I tried to recall all the noteworthy wartime names, even Winston Churchill, and practically settled upon 'Crusader'. I went to my old friend Victor Riley for his advice. He looked at all my suggestions, and then said: 'What's wrong with your own name? — it sounds all right, and you already have a good record as a sports car designer' So the car became the Healey 2.4-litre.

The chassis was easy for Sammy and me to construct ourselves, but the body was a different matter. Ben Bowden had designed a very advanced shape, but how could we get it made? It had to be coachbuilt, with a wooden frame, panelled in aluminium. The old, respected coachbuilding companies had not yet restarted after the war, so again Riley came to the rescue, agreeing to build the first body in their body experimental department. It is difficult to set a value on my lasting friendship with the Riley brothers, which started so many years before, when I look back on those early Healey years. By this time I had run out of money — I had used up all my own, and Father, as usual, had contributed more than he could really afford. So I had to form a company, and the Donald Healey Motor Company was formed in 1946, with a capital of £50,000. The subscribers included James Watt, who had been with me at Triumph before the war and who, after a fine war record in the RAF, joined us as Sales Director; he became an invaluable part of the company when we had some cars to sell.

Riley made a start on the open, touring body, but because of changes within the Morris group had to drop it half-way through. I was fortunate to find a company who, having been in aircraft production during the war, were anxious to get into car body building. They were the Westland Engineering Company of Hereford, owned by Peter Shelton. They took over the half-finished, Riley-built prototype, and eventually completed the first Healey car.

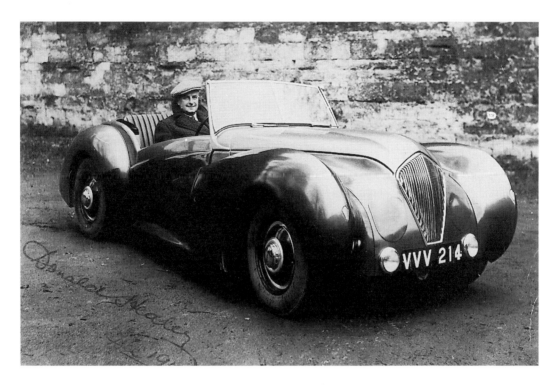

Here, again, my RAF connections came to our assistance and, with the Commanding Officer's permission, I was able to use the runways at RAF Honiley, only five miles from Warwick. The main runway was just long enough for us to reach 100 m.p.h., followed by a bit of a dice at the end to get on to the perimeter track and reduce speed. I did a lot of testing there, and soon discovered all the mistakes we had made.

Sammy's advanced trailing-link independent front suspension was too soft, the brakes were not compatible with the speed of the car, and the synthetic rubber tyres were not yet suited to speeds of over 100 m.p.h. In the meantime, we were getting on with the saloon model. I had found a firm of shop-fitters in Reading, who too had been busy on aircraft components during the war and were also keen to get into car body production. Their name was Elliots of Reading, and the first saloon model was always known as the Healey Elliot. The saloon body was originally made with magnesium-alloy panels on an ash frame — beautifully made by the craftsmen at Reading. We gave them a production order, and their managing director became a director of the Donald Healey Motor Co.

In the meantime, I did a considerable amount of testing with a loaded chassis, though this was not until after the original open car prototype had been completed. Beyond needing suspension-rate changes, the car behaved exactly as we had hoped, and its

The prototype Westland Roadster. On the production versions, the head-lamps were incorporated in the wings, instead of low-down in the valance as shown here. (*B. Healey*).

81

Donald Healey

Lockheed did us proud, with an Elliott saloon dominating their front-cover advertisement for the 24 January 1947 issue of *The Autocar*. (*The Autocar*).

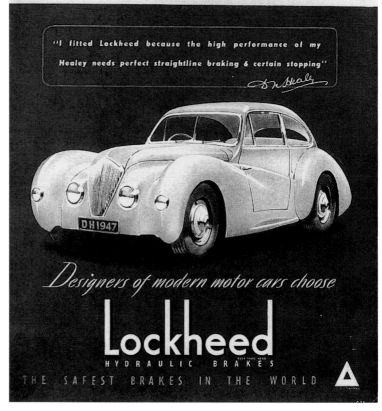

The Autocar

FOUNDED 1895     LARGEST CIRCULATION

6ᴰ

"I fitted Lockheed because the high performance of my Healey needs perfect straightline braking & certain stopping"

*Designers of modern motor cars choose*

Lockheed

HYDRAULIC BRAKES

THE SAFEST BRAKES IN THE WORLD

This 1947 Elliott-bodied 2.4-litre Saloon is now in the National Motor Museum at Beaulieu. The sales lads at our Warwick headquarters allowed £15 for this car against a new Mini Traveller, and we restored it. (*National Motor Museum*).

performance astonished everyone. It was quite a novelty in those days to drive a car weighing only 23 cwt, and with 104 b.h.p. under the bonnet. But although it was generously tyred, we had continuing problems with the synthetic rubber tyres, which threw-off chunks of tread at speeds over 100 m.p.h.

The open car, which became known as the Healey Westland, was exhibited to the Press on 6 January 1946: we invited *The Autocar* and Kay Petre, motoring correspondent of the *Daily Sketch* at the time. It was not only the prototype, but the only example in existence. It bore the chassis number 1501 (for absolutely no reason that I can recall), and the registration number was VVV 214, because we happened to have a stock of the letter 'V' and a few odds and ends in the way of numbers. Since our catalogue listed two types, and we had no examples of the saloon, we produced a heavily retouched photograph of a model, which seemed to convince everybody. So far as we were concerned, the enthusiastic reception given to the cars by the Press was nothing short of embarrassing — and even that is an understatement; we were completely overcome by it.

These two models were in production between October 1946 and October 1950, using the A-Type chassis for the first six months, followed by the B-Type, though in all essentials the two chassis were the same, proving to be a very successful design. They were built up into a light and strong box-section using 18-gauge sheet steel, running from front to rear wheel-arches and strongly braced in front and at the centre. Sammy's trailing-link i.f.s. gave a considerable wheel movement, without any change in castor or camber angles, the arms pivoting on substantial, aircraft specification ball and roller bearings in housings bolted to the chassis-frame — it proved a very costly design to produce! Wheels were steel disc, with Lockheed hydraulic brakes using 11-inch drums at the front and 10-inch at the rear. We produced an extremely precise steering mechanism by transmitting steering box movements to the wheels through a swivelling plate and link-rods. Rear suspension was by coil springs, fitted above the Riley 3.5 to 1 spiral-bevel axle, which was located by a torque-tube and track rod; we used Girling lever-arm dampers. The output of the standard Riley engine, with its twin camshafts and pushrods and twin horizontal SU carburettors, was raised to 104 b.h.p. at 4,500 r.p.m. largely by the use of an improved flow exhaust system, with a compression ratio of 6.8 to 1. With the standard Riley gearbox and axle ratio, it gave a speed of 22 m.p.h. per 1,000 r.p.m. in top.

The only changes to the A-Type chassis, in producing the B-Type, were to fit an adjustable steering column and a single 12-volt battery in the boot, instead of the twin 6-volt, and to place the petrol pumps in the boot instead of on the engine bulkhead as previously. On the introduction of this chassis, the production

Donald Healey

of Elliott saloons became double that of Westland tourers, and in the autumn of 1950 we produced the C-Type chassis with modification to the front suspension.

Running concurrently with the Elliott and Westland was the Silverstone, which had been introduced in July 1949 and which was to become the first production Healey costing less than £1,000 (omitting purchase tax, of course).

It was an open two-seater, lacking much in the way of creature comforts, and built for maximum performance on the existing chassis. The engine was moved back 8 in., an anti-roll bar was fitted, together with stiffer rear springs, and 5.50 by 15 tyres replaced the 5.75 by 15s. The body was a single stressed-skin alloy sheet, with cycle wings front and rear, which were easily removed for competition work. A full-width windscreen that could be lowered into the scuttle was an unusual feature, and we even offered a hood. We managed to effect economies in weight, and the car turned the scales at 18.5 cwt, providing a comfortable 100-plus mph. The spare wheel served as a bumper, housed in a horizontal slot in the tail.

With Ian Appleyard as my co-driver I entered a car in the 1949 Alpine Rally, and we were successful in winning our class and being placed second overall. We could, I believe, have obtained a *Coupe des Alpes* for a penalty-free run, had we not been delayed

**Left** With Geoff, I returned to competitive motoring, driving a Westland Roadster in the 1948 Mille Miglia. We finishing ninth overall and second in the unlimited sports car class. (*B. Healey*).

**Below left** Elliott saloon and Westland Roadster. (*The Autocar*).

**Below** Competition debut for the Healey Silverstone was in the 1949 International Alpine Rally, in which Ian Appleyard and I won our class and finished second overall, after being delayed at a level-crossing, which cost us one vital penalty point. (*B. Healey*).

With Louis Chiron and Tommy Wisdom before the 1949 *Daily Express* Trophy Race at Silverstone — in which the Silverstones won the Team Prize on their debut.

at a level-crossing. We did manage to drive the car under the barrier, but the delay cost us a vital two minutes. Well satisfied with the car's performance in its competition début, we entered three for the BRDC International Trophy meeting at Silverstone, and engaged three well-known drivers: Louis Chiron, Tony Rolt and Tom Wisdom. The new XK120 Jaguars dominated the race, but with the retirement of one of these, we won the *Daily Express* Team Award.

The Silverstone proved reliable, safe and easy to maintain, and many famous names in motor racing made their début at the wheel of this model. Among them were grand prix driver Tony Brooks, rally and race driver Peter Riley, who still competes with an Austin-Healey 3000 in a variety of events; and last, but not least, the privateers Charles Mortimer, Edgar Wadsworth and John Buncombe. Briggs Cunningham, that great American sportsman in so many fields, bought an early Silverstone, shipped it out aboard the *Queen Mary*, and fitted a 5½-litre Cadillac engine, racing the car very successfully in the States.

We built 106 Silverstones in all, and many of these are still in use in the States, Australia, Germany and Denmark; and a Brazilian entered his for the Mille Miglia rerun of 1986.

While on the subject of the early days of Healey cars, I must pay a special tribute to Gerry Coker. He joined me after we'd done the original Healey, which, attractive though it was, and a great credit to Ben Bowden, lacked the ultimate beauty, the flair and sporting appearance that I'd been looking for. It was not until we reached the Austin-Healey stage that I was able to give Gerry a completely free hand to interpret my ideas, and he put up some really beautiful designs. From these he made clay models, and together we discussed them and pulled them about until we had got exactly what I was looking for. I don't know of any stylist who could have produced a better-looking job. Apart from that, he was such a wonderful worker, and such a joy to work with. He would really try to understand what I wanted, and would always get it right. He stayed with me right through the Austin-Healey years, and on into the Sprite.

The Sprite was to prove a rather difficult brief from Sir Leonard Lord, in that he wanted us to produce the cheapest possible sports car, using very simple tooling. Doing my best to carry out his wishes, I had the idea of making the front and rear panels out of the same pressings. After many, many attempts, however, Gerry had to give this up and we produced a different front-end.

Geoff and Bic drove a Cadillac-engined Silverstone in the West Cornwall MC's popular Trengwainton Hill-climb, which followed the Land's End Trial on Easter Monday. (*B. Healey*).

Although everybody had a good laugh at the 'Bug-eye' when it first appeared (or the 'Frog-eye', as it was called in Britain), it had not been Gerry's idea to put the headlamps where they were. We had panelled them flat into the bonnet, with a simple mechanical actuator to raise them; this was perfectly satisfactory, and would have added probably no more than £1 to the price of each car. However, Sir Leonard said he didn't want the added complication and expense, and told us to fit ordinary lamps. We were left with the pressings, and had no choice but to fit the lamps on top.

As things turned out, the car had a real character of its own and sold very well in America — not only because it was a small car, and handy, but because it was thought 'cute'. It is interesting that when MG took over the Sprite's body design to make it the Midget (the 'Spridget'), they decided to give it a conventional front-end, despite Sir Leonard's original dictum. Although at this period we had been selling 1,500 Sprites a week in America, this figure dropped immediately the combined MG and Austin-Healey cars were announced; and, although we then had two distinct marques, and two separate selling organizations, we never sold as many per week as we had of the old 'Bug-eye'. But I am anticipating myself — the Sprite came later.

After Gerry Coker left me, he went to the Ford company of America, where he became a senior executive, doing some excellent work for Ford. I still see him regularly at Austin-Healey Club meetings in the States, and it is always a very great pleasure to me to see my old friend who put that final flair into the cars.

The Mk. 1 Sprite on its introduction to the Press in 1958.

# 6

# For export only: the Nash-Healey

At this early stage in the affairs of the Donald Healey Motor Company, there occurred one of the major stepping-stones in my life — probably the greatest and most far-reaching of them all — for which I shall never cease to be grateful. Without it there would almost certainly have been an end to Healey cars. Because of the appeal held by my cars in the States, I was crossing the Atlantic fairly frequently — as I was to do, three or four times a year, for the next 25 years or so, in one or other of the *Queens*, or the *France* or *United States*. During one of these crossings, incidentally, we were called on deck to witness what was perhaps the unique spectacle of the *United States* on one side, and the *Queen Elizabeth* on the other, passing us on a reciprocal course.

In December 1949, during one of my early crossings, I noticed a man taking a lot of shots on deck with a small, 35 mm hand-camera fitted with two lenses. I'd seen stereo cameras before, of course, but never one so compact. I got into conversation with him, and it turned out to be a brand-new model, very appropriately called the 'Realist', and I asked whether he had any results with him which I could inspect. The outcome was a visit to his stateroom that evening, when he introduced himself: 'I'm George Mason; I'm President of the Nash Kelvinator Corporation.' I remember clearly my reply: 'Well, I'm Donald Healey; I'm President of the smallest motor manufacturing concern in the world.'

After this establishment of two mutual interests, we settled down to a long chat on cameras — and then, of course, we had to get down to cars. 'What are you going to America for?', he asked. I told him I was going to meet that famous engineer Ed Cole, who was at the time Chief Engineer of General Motors and who was later to become their President. 'I want to see whether I can buy some Cadillac engines to put into my Silverstone cars. I've got special orders from Briggs Cunningham, and would like to go into small production with this engine in place of the Riley. It seems just what I want — very up to date, very light, and very compact for its capacity.'

'Well', he said, 'you're going to see an old pal of mine, and I'll be very happy to get you out to the corner of Detroit where General Motors have their plant. I'll arrange transport for you.

*But'*, he said with considerable emphasis, 'I don't want to disappoint you. I'm practically certain, though, that you won't be able to get hold of the engines you want. Cadillac are so far behind with production of this new engine, which is scheduled for their trucks too, that they can't even keep the truck line supplied. I'm pretty sure they won't agree to the inconvenience — let alone the further hold-ups in their car and truck production — of sidetracking supplies to so small a customer in England.'

'I've got a proposition to make', he said, 'You go off and see Ed Cole. See if you can get engines — and if you fail, come back and have a chat with me. I'd like very much to make a smaller car than the usual run of American cars, and I'd like it to be a sports car — about the size of your Silverstone. So if Ed can't help, come back to me. We can introduce you to my right-hand man, George Romney, and we'll chat about the possibilities of getting together.' A very wonderful man, George Mason was also President of the Hart Foundation, the largest heart-research outfit in the world; as well as being President of a large motor corporation, he managed also to devote much time and energy to the splendid cause of cancer research.

Having found he was right so far as the Cadillac engines were concerned, I got in touch with him and arranged to fly with him in his 10-seater, private aeroplane to his lovely estate in northern Michigan, where he had his own landing-strip, and later to the Nash Motor Corporation's plant in Kenosha, Wisconsin. First, we had discussions with his engineers as to whether their 'Dual Jet-fire' 3.8-litre six-cylinder, o.h.v. Nash engine would be suitable for use in sports cars. There were various snags, among which was its considerable weight. It was one of the heaviest engines I'd ever been associated with; but it was very robust, and I knew it would never break in any conditions it might have to face in so small a car. Another snag was that the gearbox could be supplied only in conjunction with an overdrive in which there was a passage through a free-wheel. I knew from past experience that this was banned by all race organizers. I was certain, though, that my son Geoffrey would find a way round this, and we arranged to ship a supply of units to England, the first arriving early in 1950. They stipulated that on this export-only model we should use every possible production part from their Nash Ambassador cars, including such things as door-handles, wheel-discs, and the radiator grille — which was to pose problems.

Then came the crunch. I had to confess to them that I was in an extremely bad financial position, in debt to the bank to the tune of around £50,000. That may seem only a small amount of money in the world of motor cars, but to me it was a fortune: it meant I was practically bust for my assets would never have covered such a sum. I explained all this to George Romney, and he said: 'Well, don't let that worry you. Let's get together over the practical side of production, shipping, marketing and so on while you're getting on with building the prototype, which we'll pay for. And you can fix up to have the bodies built by whichever coach-builder you may choose.' Naturally I chose Tickford, who had helped so much already, and had produced so many excellent bodies on Healeys.

We eventually came to a wonderful agreement, whereby they paid-off my overdraft, and we were to pay them back in finished motor cars. This was really the turning-point in my career. Without them, I could not have carried on. We had plans for a little sports car; we had plans, too, for the car that was eventually to become the Austin-Healey. But I simply could not afford to build the pro-totypes, or to employ the men to do the work, or even to keep our little place going, on the small profits made by such cars as the Silverstone.

I've gone into some detail in describing this union with the Nash Corporation, as its importance to me can not be over-stressed. They were not building the best car in the States; nor were they producing the engine best suited to my purposes. They were building a thoroughly good, sound, honest car called the Nash Ambassador — and they wanted to get into a smaller, sporting car. George Mason had always held that the American people 'wasted' their huge motor cars; you could see miles and miles of them, commuting each morning into Detroit with one man in each car. Huge monstrosities, he felt, with their massive vee-eight engines doing about 12 miles per gallon — if that — and wasting an awful lot of road too.

At the time I mentioned to George Mason that I was certain my good friends at the Austin Motor Company would co-operate with him in the building of a small car, and, in fact, this 'marriage' did come about. In 1950, George's company produced the prototype NX1 convertible with Austin A40 engine. This American-styled little car was subsequently to be built in quite large numbers by the Austin company in Birmingham, and exported to the States as the Nash Metropolitan — not a particularly handsome car, but quite an effective one.

I returned to England in a very much happier state of mind, and we went ahead with the Nash-Healey prototype. I knew that, for the US market, a convertible top was essential, and that it had to be electrically-operated, self-locking, silent in operation, and with the whole process of raising or lowering the top being effected by the push of a button. A roof of this sort is a real engineering achievement, and there was nothing of its type being produced in England at the time, except for a very few hand-made one-offs for Rolls-Royce by famous, specialist coachbuilders. But the Budd Corporation in America did nothing other than manufacture con-

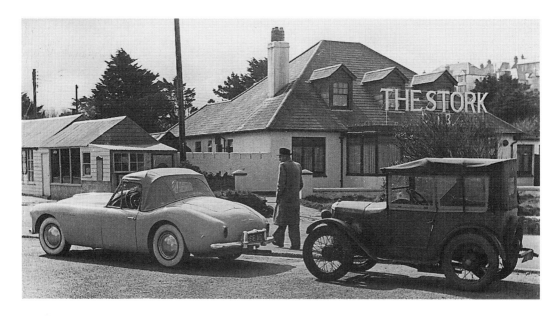

The Nash-Healey prototype, destined for export only, as the left-hand drive suggests — a model that rescued the Healey company, financially. Brian's somewhat humbler Austin Seven lines up astern. (*B. Healey*).

vertible tops of this sort, so we sent them a complete set of coach-builder's drawings of the body, and in a very short space of time they shipped us a prototype top tailor-made for the car, which we sent to Tickfords for fitting.

The final product was not a very beautiful car. As I've said, Nash insisted on our using their radiator grille, which was far too big for the relatively small car. There was a popular comedian of the day called Joe E. Brown, who was famous for his somewhat over-large mouth. It was customary to refer to a certain type of radiator grille as having a 'Joe E. Brown grin', and I have to say that this described the Nash-Healey front precisely. I sent this original prototype across to America. It was not really a running car, being intended merely to show what it would look like as a Tickford convertible. We were not particularly impressed by it, and neither were Nash, so we decided to set about making a straight-forward, open two-seater body with the help of a panel-maker in Coventry. In this form it looked good, except from head-on when the Joe E. Brown front ruined it, I took it over to America on one of the *Queens*.

Nash had laid on a special test track where I could demonstrate the car's performance to the assembled Press of America. To our joy, it seemed to impress them considerably. I am afraid, though, that we weren't particularly skilled at Warwick in the fitting of slid-ing, glass windows, being more accustomed to the old, peg-in, plastic side-curtains. I was going down a straight on the test track at well over 100 m.p.h., demonstrating the car to one of America's leading Press boys, when one of the side-windows blew out with a horrible bang! For me, it was one of my less happy moments.

Undeterred, however, he wrote a glowing report of the car, as did the others, and consequently it went into production back in England.

We had never intended it to be a racing car, and neither did Nash Kelvinator, though they badly wanted to demonstrate it to the public in a big race. As Geoff said on hearing this: 'It's going to be our biggest job yet — making it handle properly with that great, heavy engine in front.' Also, it was going to be none too easy to cover such a great lump of iron with something reasonably aerodynamic. Surprisingly, though, it didn't handle too badly, and Geoff had done a successful job with the overdrive free-wheel, converting it to direct drive. We increased the engine output from a bare 120 b.h.p. to nearly 130 by fitting an aluminium cylinder head, seven-bearing crankshaft, twin SU carburettors, and a special camshaft. We had to find room in the tail for a large fuel tank, as we had no idea what the car would do to a gallon in conditions such as at Le Mans. With a full fuel load, the added weight at the back helped to restore the front/rear balance.

The prototype sports two-seater was completed in April 1950 and, with Nash's co-operation, we decided to run it in that year's Le Mans 24-Hour Race. Before this, however, Geoff and I decided to give it a trial run in the Mille Miglia. Weather conditions were impossible and, like so many others, we were delayed after leaving the road. Despite this, we completed the 1,000-mile course, finishing ninth in the over-two-litre sports car class, and 177th overall out of 383 starters. Not an exciting result, perhaps, but good enough for a prototype; and it confirmed our decision to go ahead with the Le Mans entry.

This was to entail many, many hours' work by Geoff and our people, getting a reasonable fuel consumption, getting enough power out of the engine, with hours of bench-testing, much of the work being done by the Nash engineers — fitting beefed-up connecting rods, locking-up all the many little things that are secure enough on a road car but invariably work loose in a long race, and so on. We enlisted Tony Rolt and Duncan Hamilton as drivers for Le Mans; and when the time came, we were amazed by the car's performance. It lapped consistently at around 90 m.p.h., and by half-distance it had climbed to fourth position. Just as dawn was coming up, greenish over the horizon — that moment of intense relief at Le Mans on the Sunday morning after the long night's racing — a French car shunted the Healey up the rear, and Hamilton left the road. After struggling back again, he found himself able to rejoin the race, and called at the pits for an inspection upon completing the lap. The rear axle and suspension were damaged and displaced, but we decided they should struggle on.

At noon, with only four hours' racing ahead, the two French

Talbots held a very substantial lead and were touring round at reduced speed, with Rolt in the damaged Healey, and a 5-litre Cadillac-Allard, fighting it out for third place. The battle came to a head during the penultimate hour, when the Allard overtook Rolt, who had lapped at 94.3 m.p.h. while trying to hold it off. The Healey took fourth place overall, covering 2,103 miles at 87.6 m.p.h. — a new distance record for the class.

Nash, of course, were absolutely delighted at this, and we started a small production run of this model, eventually getting up to around 20 cars a week, all of which were exported to the States. The bodies were built by Abbey Panels of Coventry, and assembled in our little works in Warwick. The engines and transmissions were shipped over from the States in huge wooden crates containing six sets at a time. It infuriated our English coachbuilders to see so much beautiful timber, which was almost unobtainable at the time, being used for such a purpose.

During the summer of 1950, with our order books now in a really healthy state at last, we stopped building all Riley-engined cars for a while, to concentrate our entire output on the Nash-Healey. It was no comfort to us — at least so far as our British friends were concerned — that at the 1950 Paris and London shows, where the new model was introduced, we had to use windscreen stickers saying 'Export Only'. In those dollar-starved days, though, it was quite a source of pride that our entire output should be dollar-earning, the first British manufacturer ever to have been in such a situation. The production bodies, built by Abbey Panels, had three-abreast seating on a single bench-seat, which was popular in the States, being considered 'neighbourly'. Though some 3 cwt

Geoff and I drove a production model Nash-Healey in the 1951 Mille Miglia and finished 30th overall. (*B. Healey*).

heavier than the Silverstone cars upon which it was based, the Nash-Healey — at 21½ cwt — had a top speed of 110 m.p.h. and brisk acceleration to match.

With Nash now thoroughly enthusiastic about publicising the cars in sporting events, especially the Mille Miglia and Le Mans, we entered a production-bodied car for the Mille Miglia in 1951, driven again by Geoffrey and myself, our fourth appearance in this event at the wheel of one of our cars. Again, the weather was appalling, but again we finished the course, with 30th place in the general classification and fourth in our class. For Le Mans we built a special-bodied coupe, panelled in aluminium on a lightweight steel frame. Again, Tony Rolt and Duncan Hamilton were our drivers, and again they crept up to fourth position overall, though eventually this position was taken from them by a Cunningham. And, as in 1950, Rolt and Hamilton were hotly challenged during the final hours, this time by an Aston Martin. The Nash-Healey finished sixth in the general placings, and fourth in class. Though not outstanding, this result, won against the very best of the world's racing-sports cars, was good enough, and Nash were delighted.

We knew that this three-abreast 'two-seater' was not to be the final bodywork for the car and, after long discussions with Nash, we approached Pinin Farina, the famous Italian coachbuilder, to build us a body. He produced us a really beautiful little two-seater on the modified Silverstone chassis we were still using. This company had a very happy way of panelling their one-off, hand-built bodies in steel, as distinct from our English one-offs which were always in aluminium. The result was a much more robust body. We had already learned, from our lightweight aluminium bodies, how vulnerable this material can be.

The Pinin Farina body turned out to be very expensive — anything made by Pinin Farina in those days was expensive — and the car was to sell at some unheard of figure, more than double its price with the standard Healey body, I think. It ended up somewhere around $10,000, which in those days was an impossible price. Yet, in February of 1952, it was announced that in future the alternative, and certainly very pretty, hand-made Pinin Farina bodies would be available. These cars had engines with the cylinder bores increased to give a swept volume of 4,138 cc.; and, by increasing the compression ratio slightly and using Carter horizontal carburettors in place of the twin SUs, there was an increase in power output. It was a real pioneer example of international co-operation in sports car production, with the American engines and transmissions shipped to us at Warwick, installed by us into the Healey chassis, which were then sent off to Italy to be fitted with the bodywork, the complete cars finally being shipped back to the States to be sold by Nash Kelvinator.

In 1952 we again entered works cars for the Mille Miglia and Le Mans, now with the added, very strong opposition from the superb new sports-racing cars produced and raced by Mercedes-Benz. In the Mille Miglia we ran the 1951 Le Mans coupé, driven by Geoff and myself, with Leslie Johnson and journalist Bill McKenzie in a second car. Unfortunately, Geoff's and my car was involved in a serious crash when a tyre burst on a fast bend — luckily without injury to either of us. The second car went on to take seventh place overall, and fourth in class behind a Ferrari (the outright winner) and two works Mercedes-Benz.

At Le Mans we also ran two cars, one of them the 1951 coupé, rebodied as an open two-seater and driven by Leslie Johnson and Tommy Wisdom. The second was the much-raced 1950 prototype, driven by Frenchmen Giraud-Cabantous and Veyron. By now, the engine output had been increased to almost 200 b.h.p. but at the cost of reliability, probably, for it retired with engine trouble after 15 hours. The Johnson-Wisdom car, however, finished a magnificent third overall behind two Mercedes-Benz — a very satisfactory showing when one considers the vast resources of Daimler-Benz which had been devoted to producing and developing their racing-sports cars. There was an amusing sequel to this, when the time came for the *Motor* magazine to award its annual Trophy for the best-placed British car. At first, they argued that a multi-national, American/British/Italian effort such as the Nash-Healey could in no way qualify as a British car. Eventually, though, they decided that, being British-built and conceived, it was more

Celebrating our third place overall in the 1952 Le Mans 24 Hours. Left to right: Harry Costley of Nash, Stanley Barnes of the RAC, DMH, and Duncan Hamilton and Tony Rolt, and their wives, Lois and Angela.

For the 1952 Mille Miglia we plumped for a closed-bodied Nash-Healey, but crashed heavily into the parapet of a bridge after bursting a tyre. Miraculously, neither of us was hurt. (*B. Healey*).

British than anything else, and we won the Trophy, which we were to do on several more occasions with the Austin-Healeys.

This achievement brought tremendous publicity for our little concern at Warwick, and, of course, for Nash in America, where the Le Mans 24-Hour Race means even more, perhaps, than it does in England. Not only had the car already completed one Le Mans race, but it had raced against, and overcome, the full factory teams of Aston Martin, Ferrari, Jaguar and Cunningham. In the Mille Miglia, too, we had established a great reputation for ourselves; and, during the six consecutive years in which we were eventually to have competed in this event, we performed more consistently and more successfully than any other British make, before or since. The final Mille Miglia outing for the Nash-Healey was in 1953, when John Fitch and Ray Willday ran a special-bodied, streamlined, 4.1-litre car. Unfortunately, though, their race was short-lived, for a brake pipe fractured on the first stage and they had to retire.

The last of the Nash-Healeys was delivered to the States in August 1954, after which recession came to America and there was no further future for a car of this type. Very, very sadly, my happy association with Nash Kelvinator, along with my good friends George Mason and George Romney who, as Governor of the State of Michigan, was later to run as a candidate for the Presidency of the United States, came to an end. In 1954, George Mason's Nash Kelvinator was to combine forces with the Hudson Corporation, and become the American Motors Corporation, also of Kenosha, Wisconsin.

# 7

# From Healey to Austin-Healey: the 100

Towards the end of 1951, when Nash were negotiating with Pinin Farina to build us a special body for the Nash-Healey, I could see that the price of these cars was going to be far too high for the American market, and that sales must inevitably drop. Also, I had to accept that there was no real, long-term future for the cars. The engine was far too heavy, as I have said; and although it had done some wonderful things in competition, and was to do yet more, it was not really suited to a sports car. So — with strong feelings of guilt at the tremendous debt owed to my friends at Nash — I had to look round the British manufacturers to see what I could find as a replacement.

On my visits to the States I had spotted a large, untapped market for a British sports car between the Jaguar XK120 and the MG. I was well aware that to capture this market we would have to produce a car at a very competitive price, and that it would need to be attractive, with a good performance, and economical to maintain — bearing in mind that labour charges in the States were high.

With the use of tried and proven components as the basis for his new car, we would be assured of achieving the right price, comparatively cheap and readily available spares and, if the right manufacturer was approached, the backing of a world market and a full manufacturer's warranty. The Riley engine was getting old and it was heavy; and, for its size, it was somewhat limited in power output. The Healey chassis-frame and suspension were expensive and complicated, and were really suited to a much larger car.

Austin had produced a car named the A90 Atlantic. It wasn't much of a car — the body, which had started life as a design by Graber of Switzerland, had originally been really beautiful. But, as with most car manufacturers, a local 'stylist' always knows better. Graber's design was changed, and the A90 never became a popular car. Austin had adapted for it one of their 4-cylinder units, and were getting somewhere round 90 b.h.p. from 2.6 litres, a figure I knew could be improved by induction manifold and carburettor modifications. I knew, too, that it was available in large quantities, and at a price well below the Riley's which was going out of production. I had a talk with Sir Leonard Lord, chief of the Austin company (which was to merge, in 1952, with Morris and become the British Motor Corporation).

He said they could supply not only all the engines I needed, but the transmissions too, which was important. With my particular way of making motor cars, success is entirely dependent upon getting as many parts as is possible from a standard, production model. It is the tooling for these small bits and pieces that can bite into the profit margin of a limited-production car. The only disappointing part of the A90 was its gearbox, which was not man enough for the job in a sports car, especially on some of the extremely demanding, long-distance rallies; first gear, in the four speed gearbox, had to be removed and, to compensate for this, we felt we could fit the new Laycock-de Normanville overdrive, which could be easily adapted and looked very useable. With overdrive on second and top, we would effectively have a five-speed gearbox.

Early in 1952 Geoffrey, along with Barrie Bilbie, started work on the chassis design while Gerry Coker got on with the body styling. All this had to be undertaken in secret in my own home, because we didn't want to upset our good friends at Nash Kelvinator with the prospect of a new car, aimed principally at the American market, which would do even more to depress sales of the Nash-Healey! Nor, of course, did we want to antagonize the people at Morris (who were still selling us the Riley engines) by letting them know we were proposing to use the A90 engine — the union between Austin and Morris was still in the future at that time, and great rivalry existed between the two companies.

We decided we still needed a simple, straightforward chassis-frame, but an extremely stiff one, so as to give the independent front suspension a chance of working properly. The difficulty with early i.f.s. systems, however good they may have been, was that often they were attached to whippy chassis-frames which flexed, thereby doing part of the suspension's job. While Geoff and his boys were hard at work on the chassis and other fundamentals, Gerry produced some wonderful sketches for the body, which I, as usual, grumbled at, hashed about and modified. Gerry and I had a wonderful working relationship, and unlike most body designers, who can be very pig-headed in this respect, he never complained about any of my suggested modifications. Patiently, he would incorporate my ideas until, finally, he came up with a clay model which was acceptable to both of us.

In this case, it really was something out of the ordinary, and the balance and proportions were lovely. Also, the size of car was just right — exactly what I'd always wanted to build. Our previous cars had had to accommodate the fairly hefty Riley engine and, with their old-fashioned big wheels and tyres, had never been quite what I'd wanted. We decided to have a mock-up body built by Tickfords, who had served us so well making bodies for other Healey chassis. They were co-operative, completing the job in something under two months.

There was a craze in America for fins on the rear wings at the time — jet aircraft were new, and automobile stylists were incorporating all manner of quirks borrowed from the jet-age. The fins did nothing aerodynamically, but, to conform with the times — and against our better judgement — we included them on the mock-up. Thank goodness we removed them — they looked dreadful! We were then faced by the problem of what to do with the radiator grille. As I have already said, I believe strongly that the old, separate radiators were the manufacturer's special, easily identified trademark, or signature. Though contemporary styling prohibited their use on previous Healey cars, I had at least established our own distinctive, shield-shaped design of radiator grille, that had become uniquely associated with the name. It was very reluctantly indeed that I yielded over this — but we had to keep the nose right down, in keeping with the very low lines of the new car.

I also decided that the existing method of folding down the windshield had become so antiquated that we simply had to think up something better. I asked Gerry why we couldn't have a screen that hinged backwards so that, when folded, it conformed with the lines of the car, and improved the airflow, rather than defeating it. After making a number of wooden models that proved the idea would work, he produced the design that finally went on to the Healey 100. Not only did it suggest movement when the car was standing still, but at speed it deflected the wind over one's head even in the folded position — and it turned out to be one of the major sales features of the car.

At that time, of course, we had no idea of any form of tooling, except for the simple hand-pressed, hand-worked aluminium body panels. We had a sample frame made by John Thompson's of Wolverhampton, which was subjected to all the normal torsion tests — loading-up with weights and measuring the distortion — until eventually we decided it was stiff enough for the job. The prototype body was built on to the frame by Tickford's, and so far as we could judge, we were certain we were on to a winner. All that mattered now was to get it ready for its début at the Earls Court Motor Show in October, 1952. Though Tickford's had made a lovely job of the body, it was clearly very much hand-made, and the panels hand-worked. After trying one or two colours on similar, hand-worked sample panels, I found we had to keep right away from dark colours, which seemed to highlight all the minor imperfections and irregularities in the hand-working. At the time there was a new, ice-blue finish, and we tried it out, with wonderful results. Not only did it subdue the imperfections, but it absolutely made the car, emphasizing its low and fast appearance.

I was extremely anxious to have some sort of road test impressions published before the car went on show; so, preparatory to handing it over to the Press, we got it ready for our own high-speed testing. We took it over to the Jabekke Highway in Belgium, where I managed to do more than 110 m.p.h. quite comfortably. Confident, now, that it was not only a pretty car, but had performance too, I arranged with Basil Cardew, of the *Daily Express*, to carry out a short road-test and report on it in his paper. He gave the car a wonderful write-up which, appearing in one of the leading dailies on the opening day of the Show, proved invaluable to us — and it provided something of a 'scoop' for Basil, as things turned out.

Ours was very much a last-minute entry at Earls Court, missing-out on much of the pre-opening day publicity, and when we were hastily arranging our stand I still found myself looking critically and unhappily at the radiator grille. It still wasn't right, and it worried me; especially worrying was the prospect of any head-on views of the car appearing in print. We hit upon the idea of placing the car with its nose close-up to a vast, concrete pillar, so that only three-quarter front views were possible. As things turned out, the advantages were twofold. As one motoring journal reported, it was fortunate for us that the car was protected by the pillar from the thousands of people who swarmed round it!

From the moment the Show opened it was a sensation — we didn't know how to keep people away from it. Manufacturers' executives flocked to our little stand and, within a few hours of the Show's opening, I'd had approaches from two of Britain's leading manufacturers with offers of co-operation in a joint effort. I had to explain that it had been done in conjunction with Sir Leonard Lord and that there was no possibility whatever of anyone else becoming associated with the car. Sir Leonard himself was delighted — not only with the car, but at the effect it was so obviously having upon the sporting public. He completely fell for it, and hurriedly brought along Lord Nuffield and George Harriman. They, too, agreed it was a winner. Sir Leonard asked me to go along to his hotel that evening so that we could have a chat in private, and perhaps come to an agreement over what we might be able to do with it as a joint effort. 'If we can come to some sort of gentleman's agreement', he said, 'we can build probably 200 cars a week at Longbridge, whereas at best you can't do more than 20 a week at Warwick. It will be a far better deal for you financially, and it will suit us well to have a car that'll carry our name into the sporting field.'

That evening, after a few hours' talking, we reached an agreement. Sir Leonard would take on the manufacture of the cars at the Austin works, paying me a small royalty on each car for the

With Leonard — later Sir Leonard — Lord and the new Austin-Healey 100, March 1953. (*J. Wheatley*).

work we'd already done, and would still have to do. I insisted that the car went through unchanged, except for the radiator grille and one or two small modifications Geoff made to cater for the American market. Sir Leonard was pretty keen about this too, having already had the unfortunate experience with his A90 Atlantic, when the Austin company had decided to play about with Graber's design; and I personally had seen far too much of the drawing office attitude around the British motor industry's design departments ('But it wasn't designed here'). I was thankful for his agreement to leave our design alone and, to confirm this, he issued an order immediately to his design people, who would have to make production drawings of the parts, that nothing was to be altered and that every drawing had first to be approved by my people. In fact, right through until the end of our association with Austin, most of the drawings were ours, overstamped 'Austin Motor Company'. Sir Leonard stuck to his promise, though I do know that the considerable delay before they started production was due to this curious anti-outsider feeling in the industry.

On the opening day of the Show, the car had been styled the Healey 100, with its pretty little badge, depicting two wings with 'Healey 100' in the centre designed by Gerry Coker. 'Now we must change the badge', Sir Leonard said — and overnight it was redesigned, and a convincing stop-gap produced and mounted. On the later days of the Show, it was the Austin-Healey 100 — just like that!

We received a tremendous Press — not only worldwide, but in

a great many small, local, British newspapers that wouldn't normally have given coverage to the Motor Show. In consequence, I was particularly anxious to get a few cars into Austin dealers' showrooms as quickly as possible, particularly in America, where I knew our greatest sales would be. As I have mentioned, we were a little slow in getting into production at Longbridge, problems arising over the bodies, which had to be made elsewhere as Austin had no facilities for what, to them, was small-production panelling; and we had laid down the stipulation of 200 cars a week in our agreement. At the time, my old friends the Jensen brothers had been building a prototype body for a semi-sporting Austin, using very similar components. I negotiated with them on Austin's behalf to take over our body-building, the assembly of the cars to be carried out on a small production line at Longbridge. Incidentally, the man in charge of this line was Sir Herbert Austin's brother, Harry, and he put tremendous enthusiasm into the job, getting the line going much quicker than would otherwise have been possible.

In fact, series production started at Longbridge in May 1953, and in the meantime we set about building 25 hand-made cars at Warwick as quickly as possible. I took six cars to America, shipping them to Austin dealers in various parts of the country. I started off with New York, and then went across the States to San Francisco, as it was on the West Coast that I knew the cars would have the greatest appeal. As things turned out, my forecast wasn't far wrong: of the 200 cars a week produced at Longbridge when the

Los Angeles. The 1946 Westland Roadster, DMH and the 1956 100M. Both cars are owned by Fred Cohen (*Hans Nohr*).

Donald Healey

line got going, 80 per cent were shipped either to the States or to American forces in Europe, and of this, 60 per cent went direct to the West Coast.

At that stage I had never employed a PRO, or even a public relations adviser, chiefly because I had so many good friends among the Press and they gave me more publicity than even a professional PRO could have drummed up. Also — and I hate to sound boastful — during my long years of active participation in motor sport I had built-up a very wide circle of good friends all over the world; people who, I knew, would appreciate the little Austin-Healey almost as much as I did myself, and, more important, people whose recommendations would carry far more weight than those of a professional PRO. Nobody could be more conscious than I of Rupert Brook's famous line, 'Gone proudly friended'. As one old-stager told me, 'You don't want a PRO — you're doing the job yourself.'

So I carried on with it. I loved going to America anyway, and still do; for the next 30 years or so I was to cross the Atlantic many times a year. The car was first shown (but not raced) in America at the 1953 Sebring Twelve-Hour Grand Prix of Endurance in March 1953, the first qualifying event for the sports car championship. This was followed by the World's Fair at Miami, where they ran the biggest sports car show in the States. Here it won several trophies, including the premier award for the best car at

# Donald Healey

the show. After that, I took it up to the New York Show in April, where we again won the premier award, John Bentley reporting in *The Autocar*: 'Focal point of the Austin exhibits is the new Austin-Healey 100, gyrating slowly so that the eye may feast on its sleek lines, fine detail finish and attractive metallic blue paintwork. At under $3,000 there will doubtless be long queues of enthusiasts forming up at daybreak with the cash in their perspiring little palms.'

There were, too. Within a very short time of the Longbridge production line getting going, 3,000 cars had been sold, representing $7,000,000 worth of business. UK price at the time was £750 (a reduction by Sir Leonard Lord of £100 on our original price), British Purchase Tax (at £313 12s 6d) bringing the total up to £1,063 12. 6d.

Although production had been entirely removed from Warwick to Longbridge, part of the agreement was that we should continue with all development work on future Austin-Healeys, and that we should take care of the preparation and running of all factory-entered competition cars, as well as sales. My PRO instincts told me that the real publicity lay in matching the car — successfully, we hoped — against our several limited-production, far more expensive, British and Continental rivals. This posed quite a problem, because we knew very little about the engine's potential, and the only way we could find out was the hard way — by entering races, with the extreme high-speed development they provided. We took the car to the Motor Industry Research Association's proving ground at Lindley, near Nuneaton, where we put in a considerable number of laps on their high-speed, banked track and where we had no trouble. Just before the car's announcement at the 1952 London Show, we had taken a car to Belgium recording a two-way maximum of 113 m.p.h. on the Jabbeke highway — establishing new Belgian class records for the flying kilometre and flying mile, at 111.7 and 110.9 m.p.h. respectively. In a road test carried out by *The Autocar*, a one-way maximum of 119 was recorded, with a two-way mean of 111. These figures, however, are slightly misleading as they were achieved by Warwick-built cars which were a little lighter than those off the Longbridge production line.

In September 1953 we took two cars to the Bonneville Salt Flats at Utah, one of them using a specially-tuned engine for international records, and the other a standard car, selected by the American Automobile Association from dealers' stocks in the States; drivers were George Eyston, Roy Jackson-Moore, Jackie Cooper, John Gordon Bennett and myself. The tuned car achieved a two-way best of 146.626 m.p.h. The other car took all US stock car records from five to 3,000 miles, and from one to 24 hours — the long-distance run being completed at an average of over 104 m.p.h. Particularly satisfying was the standard car's fuel consumption of over 21 m.p.g. throughout the record runs. We made an attempt on the international 24-hour record with the tuned car, but had to give up after 18 hours, when rain and storms set in; by then we had averaged over 120 m.p.h. During this run, when the surface became treacherous, George Eyston skidded for nearly 300 yards. One wheel was nearly torn off, and it says much for the car's stability that it didn't capsize. There was no other damage, and, after the wheel had been changed, we carried on.

Encouraging though these demonstrations of high-speed reliability may have been, the Austin-Healey 100's competition work was at first dogged by misfortune. In March 1953 we lent one of the early, Warwick-built prototypes to Peter Reece and Gregor Grant — both, sadly, no longer with us — for the Lyons-Charbonnières Rally, in which it made its competition début. When all was going well, they were confronted at high speed by a cavernous pot-hole. Unable to dodge, they crashed over it and a rear damper mounting snapped off. With the unattached spring boring its way through the bodywork, they carried on and finished the event, but without success.

For our old friend the Mille Miglia, we entered two cars, preparing them at Warwick, for Hadley and Mercer, Lockett and Reid. Both suffered a build-up of pressure in the gearbox, forcing oil through to the clutch; and both cars were held up by troubles with the throttle linkage. In consequence, the Hadley-Mercer car retired on the first stage to Ravenna; Lockett and Reid managed to get through to within 20-odd miles of the finish, having completed almost 1,000 miles of racing, but then they too had to retire. We had learned some extremely valuable lessons, though, and quickly modified these components in time for the Le Mans 24 Hours for which we entered two cars, to be driven by Marcel Becquart and Gordon Wilkins, and Johnny Lockett and Maurice Gatsonides. Ken Rudd was our reserve driver.

Again, luck was scarcely on our side, though the cars did all that was asked of them. During practice, food poisoning and consequent tummy troubles beset our people, including the drivers; and, worse still, one of the race cars was badly damaged in an accident on its way back from the circuit to the garage, on the evening before the race. Though I did my best to persuade them, the Automobile Club de l'Ouest officials would not allow me to run our spare car, so the mechanics embarked on an all-night task of repairing the damage.

Both cars lined-up for the start, looking very standard with their bumpers and tonneau covers; the only visible difference from the production cars was the small aero-screen in place of the wide, folding version. We had, however, taken full advantage of the modifications permitted by the regulations, using higher axle ratios and modified overdrive ratios to spare the engines on the long, flat-out Mulsanne Straight; we had also fitted high-lift camshafts and improved inlet manifolds, and modified the braking system. The result was an output of over 100 b.h.p., instead of the production 90, and a top speed of 119 m.p.h.

We had a completely trouble-free 24 hours, without incident and without anxiety. Gatsonides and Lockett finished twelfth, and Becquart and Wilkins fourteenth. Ahead of the Gatsonides-Lockett car, in eleventh place, came the 4,143 cc Nash-Healey driven by Johnson and Hadley — and ahead of them a host of Jaguars, Ferraris, and Cunninghams.

For what came to be known as 'the cheapest 100-m.p.h. sports car' 1953 was no bad start; Longbridge advertised it as 'the fastest under-3-litre production car in the world'. In this original form it bore the Austin Drawing Office code-name BN1 — but, like the Phantom 1 Rolls-Royce, which never existed until the Phantom 2 came along, it was seldom referred to by this name until, in August 1955, the modified BN2 was announced. On this revised model, the BMC C-type four-speed gearbox replaced the A90's (with its first gear removed, and overdrive on second and top), and a hypoid final drive replaced the former spiral-bevel. Improvements were made to the brakes, giving a greater rubbed area, and longer springs were fitted to the independent front suspension.

# The Longbridge years...
## and the bitter end

With Len Lord's takeover of pretty well all our production worries, I could see ourselves at last with some useful spare time on our hands. The arrangement was that we, at Warwick, should work on all future Austin-Healey prototype models, at the same time preparing all race and record-breaking cars, with my son Geoffrey in control of this side of the business. We still set a very high value on regular race appearances in such events as the Mille Miglia, Le Mans, Targa Florio, Sebring 12 Hours and one or two others, while fairly regular record-breaking runs at Utah had a tremendous influence on our sales in the States.

Part of the Austin deal was that we should have the sale concession in the UK for Austin-Healey cars, that we alone should sell the first batch. As well as the small showroom-cum-drawing office we had built at The Cape, Warwick, we opened a showroom at the Austin service centre, Holland Park, in West London. There was so much pressure from the big Austin distributors, however, that Austin finally persuaded us to allow the Austin-Healey to go out through their normal Austin outlets, in return for which they gave us an Austin franchise. My son Brian took over the retail side,

1955: 100S overtakes Ford Thunderbird at Sebring. Six 100S cars competed that year, taking 1st, 2nd and 3rd places in class, as well as 6th overall. (*R.M. Mottar*).

109

# Donald Healey

1954: With Geoff (right) and Roger Menadue in thoughtful mood before some high-speed runs at Bonneville. (*R.M. Mottar*).

1954: 192.6 mph on Bonneville Salt-Flats, Utah, with the supercharged Austin-Healey 100S special streamliner. (*B. Healey*).

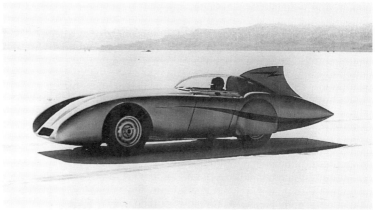

1956: The streamliner at over 200 mph on Bonneville Salt-Flats, with DMH at the wheel. (*B. Healey*).

The 100-Six record-breaker in pride of place on the Austin-Healey stand at the 1956 Earls Court Show. (*B. Healey*).

and is largely responsible for the remainder of this chapter. His appointment with the Donald Healey Motor Company was not quite the 'pierhead jump' it sounds, because he had already gained experience as a sales representative with the Truro Austin distributors, HTP Motors. Brian writes:

'DMH had phoned me following the début of the car at Earls Court and suggested I might like to join him at Warwick, as he was going to be a little short-staffed on the sales side. We sold our home in Cornwall and departed to the Midlands, where I became an employee of the Donald Healey Motor Company — with, once again, no new cars to sell! Cars were in very short supply in the early fifties and, unless you were a doctor, farmer or some other priority user, you stood little chance of getting a new car.

'I think I had been with the company about a week when "The Skipper" called me into his office and said: "Boy — I've had a call from Buckingham Palace, and Prince Philip wants to try a Healey! I think you should take one down." I had never driven in London, and hadn't a clue where Buckingham Palace was, but I set off and got there in one piece. What's more, I think I can lay claim to being one of the very few people who have washed a car with bucket and sponge across the road from the Palace, possibly under the astonished eye of Royalty!

'This was typical of DMH's belief that anybody should be able to complete the most demanding, or menial, task without hesitation. I vividly recall a dream — or nightmare — when the Healey

111

team was record-breaking at Utah, in the States. DMH had broken his ankle and had cabled me to fly over and drive the streamliner in his place. A dream, certainly; but if it had happened in reality I would have taken on the job, as would anybody at Warwick, such was the loyalty he generated. It was certainly nothing to do with the wages he paid us!

'Very soon indeed we started receiving enquiries from United States servicemen in the UK who had heard of our sports car, which was winning excellence awards at various auto shows in their home country. It all began when a Colonel Thorington called me one morning at Warwick, saying he wished to buy an Austin-Healey. Pat Thorington was on the staff of HQ 3rd Air at Ruislip, and I subsequently grew to know him, and his wife Iola, with her charming southern drawl, extremely well. I often used to call at their home in Harrow, on my way back from London to Warwick. It was through Pat that we were introduced to General Griswold, who was to prove so helpful to DMH during a record-breaking trip to Utah, described earlier in this book.

'Pat wanted to buy "one of those little Austin-Healey things", and asked how he should go about it. I hadn't the faintest idea, so I 'phoned Austin, explained the position, and asked their advice. "No idea" was their reply. I tried the Customs and Excise office at King's Beam house in London, and spoke to an extremely helpful young man named Melling. "Well" he said, "that's straightforward enough. We send you some forms which you and the customer complete and return to us. We issue you with a TF (tax-free) number which will enable your customer to buy his car free of Purchase Tax and use it in this country for a period of three years." This was fine; we fixed-up Pat Thorington with his car, collected it from the factory and delivered it to Ruislip.

'From that moment on, we were inundated by enquiries from US generals, colonels, Airmen First, and the rest, black and white, all wanting to get their hands on an Austin-Healey. The Austin dealers had not the slightest idea how to go about selling a car to these privileged customers, and we obtained a sole concession to cover the US forces in the UK. In addition to the air force and the army, we established contact with the US 6th Fleet in the Mediterranean, who purchased cars, not for use in Europe, but for delivery in the States to await their arrival home from overseas service.

'We built up such a wonderful rapport and understanding with the American forces that when we wanted to test the 100S record-breaker, the commanding officer at Brize Norton invited us to use their exceptionally long runway, where they laid on ambulances, crash trucks, fire engines and everything we needed; and they closed the runways for us. We could never thank them enough for their help, hospitality and co-operation. So many names come

back through the years: there was General Stevenson at Sculthorpe, who became a close friend; Colonel Van Sickle who, I believe, was later killed whilst flying up the Potomac River valley in Washington; there was Sergeant Ralph Merritt, who appeared to run Brize Norton and who was instrumental in laying on the test runs; and Major Crombie at their Burtonwood base, who was on weather flights up to Iceland or Greenland, where there was a big base. He used to return with magnificent steaks at a time when we'd forgotten what they were. Lovely people, all of them; and always ready to help us. At one time we badly needed a particular Chevrolet power unit, as DMH had bought a Jensen 541 which didn't perform to his liking with the standard Austin 3-litre unit. The Chevrolet engine was unobtainable in this

Brian Healey and Tom Wisdom (centre) discuss things, while I prepare to take off upon a high-speed run at the US Air Force base at Brize Norton. The USAF were extremely helpful in providing test facilities (complete with ambulances and fire engines), as well as some great social occasions. (*B. Healey*).

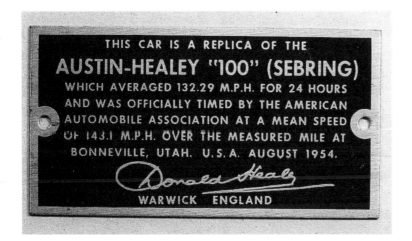

THIS CAR IS A REPLICA OF THE
**AUSTIN-HEALEY "100" (SEBRING)**
WHICH AVERAGED 132.29 M.P.H. FOR 24 HOURS AND WAS OFFICIALLY TIMED BY THE AMERICAN AUTOMOBILE ASSOCIATION AT A MEAN SPEED OF 143.1 M.P.H. OVER THE MEASURED MILE AT BONNEVILLE, UTAH. U.S.A. AUGUST 1954.

*Donald Healey*

WARWICK   ENGLAND

Each of the 52 Austin-Healey 100S cars that we produced was fitted with this plaque on the instrument panel. (*B. Healey*).

My last competitive outing was at the wheel of a 100S with Jim Cashmore in the 1955 Mille Miglia. We failed to finish, but George Abecassis, in another 100S, finished best of the British entries and 11th overall. (B. Healey).

country, but a quick phone call secured the purchase of an engine in the States, which was delivered to us aboard a UK-bound aircraft of the USAF. The resulting combination produced a very pleasant car and provided DMH with a lot of fun.

'A Major Dodd rang me one day from Fairford, near Cirencester, where a new Wing had arrived directly from the States, and had greatly admired his Austin-Healey. "Could you get one of your sales lads here right away?", he asked, "I think we've got 15 firm sales for you." Without delay I despatched Andy Wilson-Gunn and Pete Gosling, both Cornishmen who were with us specifically to handle the US market. Sure enough, they returned with 15 orders. We obtained the cars from Longbridge and the 15 men came up to Warwick in a United States Air Force bus to collect their cars. Some weeks later, at the invitation of a Lieutenant Don Beck, Andy went down to Fairford and was given a ride in one of their high-performance jet fighters. I shall never forget General Griswold's generosity in offering to put at our disposal his specially allocated, personal Dakota aircraft for several of our sorties to Le Mans. There could have been no more convenient way of getting our drivers, mechanics, spares and so on to the race, but it seemed to us almost too open-hearted an offer, and we never took him up on it.

'The retail side of the company continued to expand and, as it was located on an industrial site, we discussed the feasibility of moving the entire operation to premises (provided they could be found) somewhat closer to civilization. The marine business (of which more, in a separate chapter) had been running alongside the retail car business, and we knew that if a move were to take place, we would inevitably have to reduce the manufacturing sector, including boat-building, as this particular aspect was beginning to absorb far too much of the company's resources and finance. It was regretfully decided, in the event of a move, that Healey Marine would have to be wound-up.

'DMH and my mother lived next door to us in Leamington Spa and, as I drove him to work one morning, his ever-alert eye spotted a "For Sale" sign outside the disused Warwick Cinema As soon as the selling agents were open he rang them, and arranged an appointment to view the premises. Within days the deal had been arranged; we signed an agreement to purchase the old cinema, and the premises at The Cape, Warwick, were sold by auction.

'The cinema, as might be expected, had plenty of parking space. It was situated on the main road between Warwick and Leamington Spa and, as a result, was very much in the public eye and ideal as a car showroom. At the rear there was plenty of space for brother Geoff to build himself a workshop away from the public; and, since the auditorium had a very high ceiling, it was no problem to install an additional floor to accommodate the stores and extra offices. DMH set up shop in the projection room and Geoff's office was in the film store. The sales department was

Cinema architecture of the '30s at its classic best — the 'Old Cinema', as we called it, at Warwick. The boys changed the name to 'Donald Healey' as they reckoned it held more appeal than 'Sports Car'. The record-breaking Sprite is in the foreground. (B. Healey).

The showroom, built out in front of the old cinema at Warwick, looked very impressive at night. (*B. Healey*).

located in the foyer and ticket office, and a fine showroom was built on to the front of the impressive brick-built building.

'We opened the new showrooms on 3 July 1961, DMH's 65th birthday, and we asked his old friend Alec Issigonis to perform the opening ceremony, which was attended by the Mayor of Warwick and many of DMH's friends in the motor industry. He had negotiated an agency with Rolls-Royce, and "Doc" Llewellyn Smith and Fred Grylls (another Cornishman) attended from that company, together with Dick Graves, their outside representative, who was later to become sales director of Jensen. Early photographs show the name above the front doors as the "International Sports Car Centre", with agencies for both Austin-Healey and MG. But it soon became clear that the name of the proprietor would carry more weight, and it was changed simply to "Donald Healey" — despite strong protests from the man himself that this move could be misconstrued as boastful.

'DMH's decision to purchase the old cinema quickly proved to have been the right one. There was a dramatic increase in the sales of cars to the public, and the "Base" business, as we referred to the American forces market, continued to prosper. We were not too happy about the Rolls-Royce agency, selling only four Shadows. They kept us desperately short of cars — so much so that it was not long before, along with a number of equally small dealers, we were relieved of the agency.

'All sorts of people, of all nationalities, were getting themselves involved in the lucrative market that existed among US servicemen at the time. We were approached by a Dutchman, living in Spain, who had good connections with the 6th Fleet in the Mediterranean, and whose activities embraced the 7th Fleet in the Far

East. Hans van Capellan was his name, and his company was called Navy Auto Sales; with his perfect English, he sold a lot of cars. I became very close friends with Hans, having come to an arrangement with the factory whereby he worked as our agent, selling both MG and Austin-Healey cars for shipment to the States. The dealer in the US was very happy, as he was receiving a pre-delivery allowance and no doubt made a little on port-clearance charges. In any event, every car shipped to him by this scheme was additional to his allocation, and such cars he would proba-bly not otherwise have sold. Hans located his office in Barcelona, and he employed a team of men world-wide, selling cars. Some of the European distributors were a little put out at our poaching on their preserves, as they put it, but the business had been there for the taking; and, in many instances, they wanted it only when somebody else had gone out and done the spadework.

'Sadly, Hans was killed in a road accident just outside Barce-lona two weeks after he had entertained all his suppliers and their wives to a week's holiday in Barcelona. He drove a massive Chev-rolet convertible, but even this folded under the impact of a car coming down the highway on the wrong side of the central reser-vation. Despite efforts by members of his staff to keep the com-pany going, they could not agree who was boss, and fell out amongst themselves, the company eventually disappearing from the scene. It is interesting to recall the various cars we sold to the US Fleet boys. These included E-type Jaguars, supplied through Tony Mashek at Jaguar, Coventry, with the blessing of his Sales Director, John Morgan; and even an Aston Martin, purchased by a US Navy Pilot who had served a long stretch in the Vietnam war.

'One interesting character who set himself up as one of our "self-appointed" agents was a White Russian by the name of Boris de Vedetski; he had originally been in the business of selling bibles to the sailors, so he knew a bit about them. I shall never forget his notepaper, which was headed "Boris de Vedetski. My motto is Efficiency and No Cock-Ups". Boris was a delightful character who was very happy wandering about the Mediterranean in pur-suit of the US Navy and their ships.

'Because of our close relationship with the American forces, our paths seemed often to cross those of General Griswold, and through him we became associated with the rebuilding of St Cle-ment Danes church in London's Strand. The Americans had, extremely generously, undertaken to finance the rebuilding, fol-lowing its severe damage during the Blitz, as a memorial to mem-bers of the Royal Air Force who had given their lives. When we were approached, DMH contributed a Sprite Mark 2, which was raffled and raised a lot of money.

'The Holland Park set-up didn't last long, as we badly needed a more central showroom in London's West End, so we moved

Donald Healey

in to Grosvenor Street, just around the corner from the US Embassy. During the time that we had the sole concession for Austin-Healey cars, we ran an entirely separate stand at Earls Court during Motor Show time, manned by our own personnel. The Society of Motor Manufacturers and Traders never really approved of this arrangement, maintaining that we were not a separate marque, but a part of Austin, and that we should share one of the Austin company's stands. With the sole concession, however, and with SMMT not caring to do battle with the vast Austin empire, there wasn't a lot they could do about it, even though the cars were prepared, and the stand paid for, by Austin. When we finally relinquished this sole concession at the request of Sir Leonard Lord, we continued with this happy arrangement right through until the end of the marque in 1967.

'I must have attended some 21 Motor Shows in London, but DMH had a record far in excess of this; he attended all the pre-war Shows, and did not miss one until it was transferred to the NEC at Birmingham, becoming a biennial show and alternating with the Motor Fair at Earls Court. It was during the days of the Earls Court shows that we really appreciated DMH's fantastic stamina. He chatted happily with people all day, keeping his vocal cords lubricated with gin-and-tonic, and sending them away feeling that he had really enjoyed speaking with them; and when the Show closed, he would be "out on the town" with friends until the small hours. Yet he was always on the stand next morning before anyone else, a little after 8 a.m., and ready to start the daily grind. Immaculate always, he was never without a red rose in his buttonhole during the period of the Show — a tradition he observed daily in Warwick when he was able to pick a bud in his own, or sometimes my, garden. At no time during that dreadfully stuffy week at Earls Court did I hear him complain of a hangover, although we staff members were often ready to crawl into the office and recover.

'For us, Showtime was always a real occasion — almost always with the possibility of a visit from the Royal Family, usually a little before opening time, so that these busy people could be spared the crush that their visits invariably generated. I recall the year that Pat Moss and Anne Wisdom, driving an Austin-Healey, had triumphed in the Liège-Rome-Liège Rally, the first British crew — male or female — to win this toughest-of-all events. I was asked by the SMMT to arrange for the two girls to be on the stand at 10 a.m., as HRH Princess Margaret had said she would like to meet them; so it fell to me to present the girls to the Princess. She was charming, immediately putting us all completely at our ease and asking Pat and Anne about their driving and resting arrangements, what they ate during the four days and nights of continuous driving, and so on. She was very surprised when she

Earls Court Motor Show, 1956: Sir Leonard Lord, and Sir Anthony Eden (Member of Parliament for Warwick and Leamington, and later Prime Minister) discuss the new 100-Six with me. (*Central Press Photos*).

learned that Anne was car-sick during those rallies. I spoke too to Lord Snowden who, though equally charming, had not done his homework as the Princess had done, and asked me whether it had been an all-ladies rally that the girls had just won.

'Visits by members of the Royal Family, and other celebrities too, were always a highlight of the Show; but I am thankful that our Show days came before the era of the pop idols, as I fear I would have had difficulty being polite to these entertainers.

'We were fortunate that with the phasing-out of the "Big" Healey, we still had the MG franchise to help us out; and the MGB and BGT were selling very well. BMC had set up a Personal Exports Division in Piccadilly and it was through this office that all our orders were accepted and processed. By this time, the Division had got wise to the existence of the "Base" market and the US customers, and had the audacity to actually compete with us through their dealer network! They were still getting scores of orders from Healey in Warwick, however, and we were not going to surrender our very personal market, which we had struggled so hard to cultivate.

'There were around 15 people looking after us at PED Piccadilly, and look after us they certainly did. The majority of them never really knew the person with whom they were dealing; and, in order to show our appreciation of the many favours they did us, I made it an annual event to take them out to lunch, supported by the three sales boys and Joe Cooper, our Company Secretary. The Martinez, in Swallow Street, was chosen for these lunches, just around the corner. With the approval, rather grudgingly given at times I felt, of Denis Gale, Export Manager (who, incidentally, would never join in), we gave them a super meal, drinks and cigars before dispatching them back to their office, full of goodwill towards us for another year — and all for £50-60 in those days. Should any of those kind people ever read this, we really were not trying to bribe you!

'Meanwhile, Geoffrey and his team of mechanics carried out an annual programme of competitions, taking part in prestige races throughout the world. I need not dwell upon this side of the business, because Geoffrey himself has recorded it at length in his various books. There is no doubt, though, that any race or rally in which we, as a works team, competed was followed with great interest by owners, especially Americans. Following the several Utah runs in which the Healey team took part, led by DMH and supported by Carroll Shelby, Jackie Cooper, John Gordon Bennett and others, Austin America produced some wonderful films covering our record-breaking achievements. These were much in demand by clubs and other motoring organizations all over the world.

'We continued to sell MG cars around the US bases right up

until the introduction of the Jensen-Healey, when we diverted our sales effort to selling the new cars. Despite their mechanical problems and their poor paintwork, they sold steadily; but we never handed over the keys to a customer with the same feelings of confidence as we did with an Austin-Healey or MG, which we would never see again until they came in for routine servicing (or accident damage, of which there was plenty).

'Many of our American customers had never before encountered "stick-shift", or non-power-assisted steering, so much a feature of the true-blue sporting cars of those days. It was felt that power-assistance removed much of the "feel" of the steering, and therefore the response — and, ultimately, one's control.

'Also, many of them insisted upon driving on the right-hand side of the road, despite being in the UK. I recall handing over a brand new 100-Four to a Colonel Ivan McIllroy one Sunday morning at the office in Warwick. As part of the service, and more perhaps out of consideration for other road-users, it was our custom to take these new owners for a short "training" run around Warwick, and this was the case with the Colonel.

'Out of Warwick and on to the Banbury road we drove. "That's the gear-shift", I explained, "with the overdrive switch. And don't saw at the wheel with both hands grasping the top of it. Hold it lightly in your fingers and thumbs — and at the sides." Back into Warwick, and approaching the roundabout outside Warwick Castle, my feet had already caused severe distortion of the metal foot-well when, to my horror, the Colonel made the unusual decision to circumnavigate the island American-style, anticlockwise. This might have come off, but a substantial truck was approaching down the hill, minding its own business and complying with UK traffic law. Fortunately, the driver was not one of those "Press on and bugger the consequences" types and he had the decency and presence of mind to take evasive action; he executed a hard left-turn and vanished down a one-way street. But for that, it is unlikely that I would be here to write the tale, or the Colonel able to continue with his military career.

'Such incidents aside, though, I did meet some superb characters during my visits to the US bases. I attended flight-crew briefings, control towers and, on one occasion, having been locked out of my hotel bedroom at Bury St Edmunds after giving a film-show at the Bentwaters Base, I returned to the base and the duty officer found me a room in the bachelor officers' quarters. In great comfort I had a shower next morning, followed by a wonderful breakfast. Oddly enough, the duty officer that night was a Lieutenant Kirk who had bought from us a 100-Four, finished, to his special instructions, in a rich and very handsome burgundy colour. It really showed off the car's lines superbly and we would willingly have added it to our standard range of colours, but there were fade problems in those days with dark red finishes.

'The salesmen on the US bases in those early days became our good friends, although they would readily cut each others' throats for a deal. But, come Christmas time, we would all foregather for a monumental celebration. On one occasion it was at the Bull, at Barton Mills near Newmarket, where we used to stay overnight when in the area. For some reason I had been placed alongside a most attractive coloured lady — a real sports-car fan, who turned out to be a doctor. When the wine waiter came round and enquired whether she would care for red or white wine, she replied "Man — red's for sleep and white's for sex. I'm having white!" I never actually established whether white lived up to its reputation on that occasion.

'Another little gimmick that tickled the fancy of our crazy Yank customers (and I use that expression with deep affection) was to change the original-equipment speedometer for one geared to suit the non-standard but optional 3.9-to-1 axle ratio. The result was a reading of 120-plus m.p.h. in second gear!'

These happy, flourishing days, when the world seemed our oyster, could not go on for ever, and there were two main factors that brought about the end of the Austin-Healey in its final 'Big' Healey form. One was the door specification which, as the result of Ralph Nader's safety campaign, was one of the items in a book of requirements that was as large as the Bible. In simple terms, the doors had to be able to withstand a side-impact which was clearly defined: an absolute impossibility with an open two-seater such as ours. There has been a slight easing of these safety requirements since then, but they were extremely strict and demanding in those days. The other factor was in connection with the environmental pollution laws, and demanded a catalyst box in the exhaust system — the final step in the removal of pollution by exhaust gases. The Austin-Healey exhaust system was already low enough, and there simply was not room to install the required box, without redesigning the entire car.

To meet these requirements, and others involving seat-width and the space between them, we built the Rolls-Healey, commonly called the 4000, using the existing six-cylinder Austin 3-litre 'R' engine built by Rolls-Royce. The car was virtually an Austin-Healey 3000 sliced down the long axis, with an extra 6 inches' width let in, and greater ground clearance. It turned out to be a very beautiful car, not only in looks but in handling too. It had marvellous road-holding and handling thanks to the greater width and the redesigned suspension with roll-bars, radius arms and so on. Dr Llewellyn-Smith of Rolls-Royce gave us permission to fit the 'Powered by Rolls-Royce' badge, similar to those fitted to the

One that might so easily have been... The Rolls-Royce-powered Healey, built at Trebah after Lord Stokes had dispensed with my services. (*B. Healey*).

engines of most airliners. Austin had placed a large order with Rolls-Royce for engines to be installed in the Princess R, but this car did not sell in the numbers anticipated. At that stage it began to look as though they were going to experience difficulty in cancelling the order for engines without having to accept a heavy cancellation charge. On reflection it certainly was a pity, so far as my company was concerned, that Austin managed to extricate themselves from this order at no great expense as the 4000 was a fine road car, smooth, a good performer and with considerably more room in the cockpit than the 3000. With a little more development and refinement we would have had a car to equal anything on the road at that time.

Three of these cars were built, one of them entirely at my home near Mawnan Smith in Cornwall, and today they have become the world's most sought-after Healey cars. Rolls-Royce even made a one-off twin-overhead-camshaft cylinder head for this engine — you can imagine what it must have cost them! With this specification the car would have been a world-beater, but it had come too late. Lord Stokes, upon the formation of the British Leyland Motor Corporation, as it was then termed, had decided to kill off the names of Healey, MG and Cooper, leaving the sports car field open to his Triumph cars.

The engine, and its beautiful new cylinder head, went to Austin, who installed it in what must have been the most ill-conceived prototype sports car built! The background to this boob was that Pinin Farina had run a coachwork competition for Italian students, the result being a very beautiful little coupé that made its début at the Turin Show, subsequently being shown at Earls Court. Because we were all so impressed by it, George Harriman decided to buy the design and use it for the prototype of a new sports car to be designed at the Austin Drawing Office. Their big mistake was in fitting trailing-arm suspension all-round — an inexplicable miscalculation, when it should have been all too obvious that the rear axle would steer the car.

They enlisted the services of that great engineer-cum-racing-driver-cum-journalist, Paul Frère, and brought him over from Belgium to test-drive the car. After a lap of the circuit, he brought it in saying that it was impossible, and should be cancelled at once. I immediately sent over to Longbridge with the urgent request 'Get hold of that engine!', but it had already gone to the scrap heap. If the Austin-Healey had been allowed to continue, this would have been its engine — and what a car it would have been!

Before this débâcle, Austin had designed at Abingdon a car to replace the Austin-Healey and MGB, which was eventually to appear as the short-lived MGC. In place of the Austin 3-litre engine they used an Australian-designed 2-litre four-cylinder engine, to which had been added two more cylinders, bringing it up to a 3-litre six — and a seven-bearing crankshaft, which completely ruined its performance. The Healey version of this car was to have been a badge-engineered MGC with a Healey radiator grille. I refused to allow my name to be associated with it, and it never went into production.

After they had decided to abandon their near disastrous sports car — for which, incidentally, most of the tooling had been completed at enormous cost — George Harriman decided to put in a stop-gap, extra order for 2,000 3-litre Austin-Healeys for their distributor in Philadelphia, before finally stopping the line. The Sprite and MG Midget continued hand-in-hand for a while, the Austin-Healey Sprite becoming simply the Austin Sprite after the Healey name had been dropped. Finally the Austin Sprite was phased out, so only the Midget remained.

When the end came, I was summoned to Donald Stokes's office at the Standard works in Coventry during 1967. He told me he was going to discontinue MG, together with the payment of royalties to the names associated with what were BLMC cars. This included John Cooper and myself, together with Harry Weslake; and John Thornley, too, was eventually to be retired. He explained that he didn't need the help of all us people to produce a sports car, as his Leyland people were fully capable of doing so themselves. 'I don't think there's any value in names', he said — to which I replied: 'Right then, you don't think there's any value in Mr Chevrolet, Mr Ford, Mr Buick and the rest — or Mr Morris, even' — and I left it at that.

# 9

# The cobbler should stick to his last: Healey Marine

I can not look back upon the Healey boats era with any great sense of pride, and I am not absolutely certain what it was that inspired me to enter this particular field. Brian has probably put his finger on it with his remark: 'The Old Man was down at Nassau for the Speed Week races in 1955 with Stirling Moss and Ken Gregory, and got carried away by a bit of water-skiing.' Anyway, it appears I returned to Warwick and said 'Right! We've got to get down to boats, boy!' With Austin producing the cars, Brian taking care of the marketing, Geoffrey producing the racers and record-breakers, and Abingdon — under Marcus Chambers — attending to the rally cars, it's possible that the 'Old Man' found himself with time on his hands!

I managed to convince everyone that speedboats were the future

Stirling Moss and I were both keen water-skiers, and spent much time relaxing in this way. This shot was taken at Weymouth, when Stirling helped with the press releases for the Ski-Master. (*Fox Photos*).

Stirling Moss and
myself at Weymouth
with Ski-Master in tow,
water-skis in the car,
and a highly
appropriate registration
number. (B. Healey).

play-things of the masses, and it wasn't long before I made contact with a struggling young naval architect, Geoffrey Lord, down at Bridport. He produced drawings for us of a very good-looking plywood ski-boat hull, which we put into production as the Healey Ski-Master. We used engines made by an American firm of outboard engine manufacturers by the name of Scott-Atwater, who made very good motors but were terrible on spare parts. Building them at Pymore Mills, Bridport, we did surprisingly well with these boats, selling nearly 1,000 of them. What's more, we were exporting them to the States.

On a subsequent trip to America I discovered a very nice little ski-boat, and shipped one of these back to Warwick. We took a mould of the underwater section of the hull and used it as the basis for a glassfibre hull, which became the Healey Sprite. Again, we used outboard engines. These and subsequent boats were built at The Cape, Warwick, in an aircraft hangar I'd bought just after the war and which had accommodated the Austin-Healey 100S production line and had been used as a service shop. Again, they sold surprisingly well. With the completion of the 100S build programme, and the phasing-out of the Le Mans conversions on the 100, the space had become available and we decided to transfer the boat production line from Bridport.

Partly because we were becoming more ambitious, but largely because the supply of outboard engines was pretty precarious during the early fifties, we decided to build a larger, 14ft 9in plywood hull, with an inboard engine — a design upon which Geoff had been working during his spare moments. The engine was basically the 1,498 cc B-series BMC unit with twin carburettors, as used in the early versions of the MG series MGA. We called it the 1500 Austin-Healey Marine Engine. Initially we used the Morris Navigator transmission, which was sturdy but had a tendency to 'creep' when in neutral, especially when warming-up. This was subsequently replaced by the Warner Velvet Drive box, hydraulically operated, which proved to be a winner and far superior to anything available in the UK at that time.

In an effort to meet the demand for outboard motors during the fifties — especially for more powerful units — Walter Hassan of Coventry Climax was working on various ideas with the Ministry of Defence, and we co-operated with him by lending him one of our outboard hulls. Wally and Brian had great fun on a lake near Coventry, especially when he brought along the bowler-hatted gentlemen from the Ministry, anxious to see how their money was being spent. Brian could not resist coming up alongside the craft in which his critical 'customers' were being carried at speed — and spinning his steering wheel. They were not at all amused at the drenching they received. All was forgiven when we took them to lunch at a local pub, however.

Healey-Marine, as the company was called, switched wholly to producing the new 14ft 9in inboard hull, which proved as suc-

Nassau 1956: Stirling Moss and (left) Louise King (later, Mrs Peter Collins) in Stirling's Healey Sportsboat. Power was provided by the BMC B-series unit, prepared to MG Series MGA specification and called the Austin-Healey 55. (*B. Healey*).

cessful as the outboards had been; and, with our many contacts in the sports car field, I was able to write to the majority of the bigger Austin distributors world-wide, who quickly provided us with a good market. These craft were shipped to many parts of the world, with the majority going to the States, where they were handled by a firm in New York which had a London office.

One of my happy memories of the boat-building operation was Lord Aylesford's lovely park at Packington, only four or five miles outside Coventry, with its big lake for which, at the time, Lord Aylesford had no particular use. Brian went over to see him one day, the two getting on very well together, with the result that, for the paltry sum of £100 a year, we were given sole use of the lake for testing our boats. We built a chalet for use as a store for equipment, and every weekend during the summer we would take a picnic lunch to this beautiful spot and spend the day testing and water-skiing. Surrounded by trees and sheltered from the wind, it always seemed warm and sunny. We spent many, many happy days in these idyllic surroundings, and some extremely useful days too. This happy state of affairs continued pretty well until we abandoned the boat-building business, which coincided with Lord Aylesford's decision to develop the lake as a source of sand and gravel — considerably more profitable to him than our meagre £100 a year.

As Geoff's competition programme became more and more ambitious, requiring additional space, we began to look for alternative premises for the boat-building 'line', with a view to handing over the aircraft hangar premises at The Cape. We eventually transferred to Yorkshire, to a furniture manufacturer who was going through a very quiet period. These people made an excellent hull, never late on delivery; and the hulls were transported back to Warwick in a furniture truck, six-at-a-time. The machinery was then installed, prior to the final dispersal to their various destinations. Brian had been appointed sales director, and was responsible for the disposal of these wooden-hulled craft, which were coming off the jigs at an almost alarming rate — one of the first instances in the UK of line-production in the marine field.

Though these inboard-engined hulls were doing very well indeed, we were still interested in building the simpler outboard hulls and found that, with the limited availability in this country of powerful outboard engines, and the understandable lack of enthusiasm among importers to supply the Trade, we would have to become importers ourselves.

We had already made approaches to various companies in the States, home of the outboard motor, and we had already purchased many units from Scott Atwater. Though not one of the biggest of the American manufacturers, they were easy to work with, and the product was reliable and competitively priced, so we eventually took on a concession with them. The boom in powered sporting craft had by now become well and truly established world-wide, and it was natural that companies in the UK should investigate the possibility of producing motors, even if they were to be built under licence to American companies. Leslie Johnson's brother was chairman of Grundig UK and, unlike Leslie who had made a name for himself as a first-class racing driver, he devoted his time to boating. Brian and he spent many happy hours together, discussing the possibility of setting up a company to produce, under licence, one of America's more popular outboard ranges. He asked Brian to take over the sales side of the business, which would have slotted-in nicely with his Warwick interests. Unfortunately there was difficulty in tying down the company involved, and the venture came to nothing.

As might be expected, I could not involve myself in anything that was not competitive, and we soon found ourselves entering races with the inboard craft, powered by the MG engine but known, by agreement with BMC, as the Austin-Healey. I entrusted Brian with one of these boats to compete in UK events, and he scored some good wins, including the Lady Brecknock Trophy, held off Poole in Dorset. We were invited to compete in a 24-hour race at Aix-les-Bains, in France, and on this occasion Tommy Wisdom and I shared the driving. We trailed the boat over, and had

At Warwick with the Healey speedboat which Tommy Wisdom and I drove in the 24-hour race at Aix-Les-Bains, in France, winning the trophy for the best-placed British crew. (*B. Healey*).

a great time, finishing well up in the list and bringing home a trophy presented by *Jeunesse de Sport*. It may have been the Chamber of Commerce under another name, who sportingly presented the prize for the greatest consumption of wine during the period of the race!

Our next venture was the *Six Heures de Paris*, for which Brian was entered. Held annually to coincide with the Paris Salon motor show, it was staged up and down the Seine in the heart of Paris — rushing under such bridges as the Pont des Invalides at speeds approaching 60 m.p.h. Brian had Tommy Wisdom as co-driver, and for this event we installed a 2.6-litre Austin-Healey engine with direct drive, which resulted in a truly scintillating performance. Walter and Ethel Hassan came along with our party, which included Geoffrey, and Brian's wife Mary. We stayed at the Baltimore and had lots of fun visiting such spots as Fred Payne's Bar, the Mouton Panurge, and generally admiring Paris, so beautiful in the autumn. Brian and Tommy were new to this event, and that year practising was not permitted — unless you were a Frenchman, of course!

The race itself proved disastrous, principally because, during the road trip across France, the engine's sump had come into heavy contact, via the hull, with the trailer frame, fracturing the sump. With the lack of practice, this didn't become apparent until shortly before the race. Having travelled all that way, and worked so hard on the boat, we couldn't withdraw, so Geoff and Wally managed a temporary repair which they hoped would survive the race. Tommy Wisdom took first stint, closely watching the oil pressure; when it started to cause concern, he very sportingly came into the 'pit', handing over to Brian so that he could have at least a brief spell in this famous race before the engine gave up.

Brian managed two very thrilling laps, dashing between the arches of the bridges, around the Isle de Cygnes — at all times giving a wide berth to the normal river traffic, including those massive barges for which the Seine is noted. It was in the middle of the third lap that the engine decided it had had enough, leaving Brian drifting with the current in the middle of the river, where it flows quickest. With craft roaring past on either side — their drivers, as he prayed, aware that he was *hors de combat* — he managed to steer clear of a bridge and reach the bank, using a canoe paddle provided for such an occasion. For all that, it was fun, and we decided to return the following year.

Walter Hassan, the man who surely was responsible for putting Britain to the fore in post-war Grand Prix racing, with his Coventry Climax engine, suggested we should use one of his engines, a 2-litre developing 180 b.h.p. This engine transformed the boat. Its performance was incredible — but in a straight line, particularly in choppy water, it was unpredictable, to say the least.

We very quickly hit on the cure — fitting a small fin amidships, half-way along the keel. We set off for Paris in high hopes; the vascillating French even permitted practice on the preceding Saturday, though in a different part of the Seine. Brian gave the boat a run, and it proved very stable and very, very fast; in fact, as fast as anything in the race.

Tommy Wisdom leaves the pits area during the Six Heures de Paris, held traditionally in October to coincide with the Paris Motor Show, the Paris Salon. (*B. Healey*).

Our potential must have been spotted because, a matter of hours before the start, the organizers placed a ban on fins — having checked, no doubt, that such a ban would not place any French entries at a disadvantage! Tommy Wisdom was down to drive with, as co-driver, a great Parisian character by the name of Jean-Jacques Bouillant Linet, who provided the team with a magnificent meal the evening before the race, at his restaurant in Montmartre.

The race got under way, with Tommy at the wheel, and it became clear from the outset that the wash from the other competitors' boats was causing him great problems with the handling, precisely as we had anticipated. Nevertheless, Tommy pressed on and, after two hours, was well placed, when tragedy struck. The craft hit a partially-submerged log, which holed it below the water-line. Tommy abandoned ship and struck out for the shore, while our pride and joy disappeared beneath the waves.

Tommy was brought across the river in the rescue boat, wearing red underpants and a Red Cross blanket over his shoulders, and the inevitable monocle in his eye. There was nothing further we could do that day, apart from attending to Tommy's physical welfare and ensuring that he suffered no ill effects from his immersion. The most humane treatment, and the one which appeared to achieve the best results, was milk followed by liberal chasers of Cognac. This form of treatment seemed the least painful, and it gave us the opportunity of sharing it with him. Fortunately he had taken a few transits and cross-bearings and suchlike before abandoning ship, and was able pretty well to pinpoint the boat's position on the bed of the Seine. The following morning a team of divers was called upon to search the murky water. They insisted on penetrating the depths everywhere except where Tommy said they'd find the boat, and we began to wonder whether they were hoping we'd abandon the idea of salvage, allowing them to recover the boat at their leisure without our knowing.

We spurred them on, though, and eventually the boat was salvaged, complete with the log still stuck through the hull. We replaced it on the trailer with the evidence still in place, and set off for home. That evening, over a relaxed meal while we awaited the ferry, Walter let out that the engine was, in fact, a brand new one. It had been sold, and he reckoned the race would have provided the ideal opportunity to run it in! Later, he told me where the engine had gone after being stripped and rebuilt — and, later still, we were delighted to hear that it enjoyed a long and successful racing career, evidently having suffered no ill effects from its sudden quenching, and the water it must have sucked in!

By now we had foresaken wooden hull construction, and had reverted to glass-reinforced plastics. Although I think we all preferred wood, we were ready to accept the many advantages offered by this comparatively new material. As well as the attractive little outboard hull, based upon the American underwater sections (as previously mentioned), we became ever more ambi-

Donald Campbell's ill-fated *Bluebird*, flanked by two Healey boats at Coniston, prior to a trial run. Brian was invited to join the team, and took the two Healeys along as rescue craft. (*B. Healey*).

tious, adding a larger, two-berth, fast day-cruiser with sliding canopy to our repertoire.

The build programme, however, was to change, following a visit to Warwick by Donald Campbell — in fact to complain about heavy steering on his Rolls-Royce. The addition of oil to the reservoir cured this, but not before Donald had invited Bic to join his team at Coniston for the next attempt to break the water-speed record later that year, and to bring a couple of our boats with him to serve as rescue craft. The topic of conversation inevitably got round to boats and he delayed his departure to inspect our line. He had recently been appointed managing director of Dowty Marine, an offshoot of the Dowty Group with headquarters at Arle Court, near Cheltenham. The company had negotiated the rights for Hamilton Jet, a new form of propulsion pioneered in New Zealand, the craft being driven by a water jet generated by a centrifugal pump. They had designed and commissioned a hull, and the power unit was coupled to a Ford Zephyr engine, the craft being made in Cheltenham. Donald was keen to sell this form of propulsion to us, and invited Brian to try one of his boats at their test lake in Fairford, near Cirencester.

To be driven in a speedboat by Donald Campbell was quite an experience and, after a few minutes' warming-up, he decided to demonstrate the full capability of the craft. It went reasonably well, Brian told me, and they set off at high speed across the lake, heading for a narrow spit of land which jutted out into the water. Donald made no attempt to steer around this, and drove straight across, demonstrating that the jet boat, as well as being able to perform in very shallow water, could run happily in no water at all! But, we wondered, who bought a boat for such a purpose? The jet unit certainly had appeal, though, and we adapted the Corvette day-cruiser to this form of propulsion, powered by an Austin-Healey 3000 engine. The craft performed well, although I can't say I ever enjoyed the same degree of confidence that I felt with a traditional propellor. It is interesting that now — some 30 years later — the water-jet is proving ideal for lifeboats, required sometimes to operate close offshore on a shelving beach, and that the Dutch have carried out round-Britain acceptance trials with a 45-foot lifeboat so powered.

Sir William Lyons of Jaguar became one of our first customers for the Corvette — or the 707 as we called it, after the Boeing jet aircraft of the day. Brian spent a pleasant weekend in the Lake District as guest of Norman Buckley, together with 'Lofty' England and Phil Weaver, during which they passed off the boat as being suitable for Sir William. Needless to say, he had specified twin Jaguar engines, in place of the six-cylinder Austin-Healey; and we eventually delivered the boat to Sir William's holiday home at Salcombe in Devon.

During our few years in boat-building, Brian had managed to sell a total of 1,750 boats, to buyers all over the world. At the outset I had written to Austin and MG dealers throughout the world, telling them about our boats, and the majority had ordered two or three. They sold especially well in the USA and France, through a single big distributor in each country. We also had particularly good outlets in the UK — always people who operated close to the water, of course. Notable among these was Bill Jennings, at that time a Rootes distributor in West Cornwall, who sold many of our boats, collecting them in batches from Warwick in a cattle truck; and there was a Mr Burrows at Ambleside, on Lake Windermere, who always kept one handy in the water as a demonstrator.

It was not all that easy to sell boats, because in those days dealers

Cover of the brochure featuring the Healey 707, fitted with the Austin-Healey 6-cylinder 3000 engine and the Dowty Marine Jet unit. (*B Healey*).

Top flight performance

*1up* **40**+MPH

*2up* **39** MPH

*4-6up* **36** MPH

The new **Healey 707**

Made by the designers of the famous Austin-Healey Sports Cars

HEALEY MARINE LTD., THE CAPE, WARWICK, ENGLAND

were not prepared to stock them, or to provide demonstrations, as can so easily be done in the motor trade — not unless, that is, they were situated on the water's edge — which cut down the possibilities very considerably indeed. If a chap comes along and says he wants to try-out a boat, what on earth can you do? We used to try to weed out the genuine enquirers, and then give them a trial run at Packington. But unless we thought we were really on to a sale — as distinct from providing an outing for joy-riders — it wasn't worth the trouble, which, in those days, represented a cost to us of £25 to £30 a time. There was no question of giving casual enquirers a demonstration on the off-chance that they might put their hands in their pockets and buy.

With the new-found use of glass-fibre, there was also the fact that boat-building was going through an extraordinary boom period, with everybody getting on to the band-wagon and turning out boats by the thousand. Some of them were truly terrible products, and they gave the industry a bad name, which rubbed off on those who were building good, sound, seaworthy craft. We were, as I have said, into a market we didn't really understand — and, apart from that, with only 24 hours in a day, we were hopelessly overworked, especially Brian, who was also in charge of the sales of cars to America — a major, time-consuming task.

1961 — Sprite and Sprite: Silver City Airways' Bristol Freighter transported this combination across the Channel *en route* for the South of France for the introduction to the Press of the Mk 2 Sprite. (*B. Healey*).

135

# 10

# People and places

They were amazingly happy times, those early post-war years. As a family, we'd survived intact, despite being pretty much in the thick of it, one way or another, which of course was wonderful, and took a lot of getting used to. There was the pure excitement of producing our own cars, successfully too; and above all, showing them off in international races and rallies. There were the people too; old friendships renewed after those tense years when we'd all gone our separate ways, losing touch with one another and wondering who had come through safely. Of these friendships, the various people who drove for us stand out particularly, with their funny ways, their girlfriends, their personal problems, and, above all, their individual approaches to the serious business of driving as professionals in a works team, many for the first time in their lives. They varied so much in character and attitude — from light-hearted, irresponsible sometimes, to deadly serious and nervous. However brilliant their driving, one could never be certain how their individual make-up would serve them when the pressure was on, during a race — whether they had the restraint to spare the car, or whether they'd throw caution to the winds in their excitement, and break something. The stock-in-trade of a successful racing driver involves a great deal more than the basic ability to drive fast in safety; and the only real way of establishing whether he has these attributes is the expensive way — by entering him in a race, and hoping one's judgement is correct.

Of all the races, — in fact, of all the competitive events in the widest sense, — in which I drove, during something like 30 years of active participation, I really grew to love the Mille Miglia most of all; in the ten races we entered between 1948 and 1957, I drove in eight. It would have been nine if the synthetic rubber tyres of the day had been up to the speed of the first, Riley-engined Healeys. Geoff and I took a Westland roadster out to Brescia in 1947 for the first post-war Mille Miglia, and tried it out on parts of the 1,000-mile route prior to the race; but, as had been shown during testing in England, the synthetic rubber tyres were simply not up to it, throwing treads at anything over 100 m.p.h. We had to content ourselves with driving round the course at touring speeds — and being bitterly disappointed when the fastest race average was only 60.69 m.p.h., well below our race average in the same car the following year: we could have won hands-down with the right tyres. But I'd been bitten by the Mille Miglia bug in the biggest way possible.

There has never been anything else quite like the Mille Miglia in post-war racing; and unless you actually saw those early post-war events, and drove round the route, you can not imagine the fanaticism and warmth of feeling that existed in Italy for this, the last of the town to town, open road races. And, though the race was last held 'in anger' back in 1957, it's pretty much the same today in the Mille Miglia re-enactments. Even during scrutineering, in Brescia's Piazza della Vittoria, the crowds are overwhelming, milling round the cars in their thousands, begging autographs, examining the cars, photographing drivers, with the

Italy's 1,000-mile race — the Mille Miglia — was banned following the tragic crash of de Portago's Ferrari, but a commemorative re-run is staged annually. The two Healey Silverstones shown here competed in the 1986 re-run, and are owned by Edouardo Lazmann, of Argentina, who has owned the car for 22 years, and Rasmussen from Denmark (the white car). (B. Healey).

tall, beautiful buildings as a background.

I loved the race — it was such enormous fun. And I loved Aymo and Camilla Maggi, the Count and Countess who put us up, and entertained us so magnificently, at Casa Maggi, with its vast estates supplying every possible need of the household. I can't describe it without arousing some strong feelings, but it was like going back a century or two to feudal times, with servants galore to bring you breakfast in bed, and wash and press your clothes every morning; a lovely life which has gone for ever in England — rightly, too — but which survives in Italy. Aymo — now, sadly, no longer with us — *was* the Mille Miglia.

The start was unique, with its raised starting ramp, floodlit during the night, the cars coming up at intervals of one minute to be sent off by Renzo Castagneto, traditionally wearing his bowler hat — and the vast, enthusiastic crowds held back by barriers to give us a clear road, at least from the start. One year, before crash-hats became compulsory, Geoff and I wore felt hats to annoy Castagneto! All along the route, even in the remoteness of the Abruzzi mountains, the crowds were there, pressing forward on to the road to see you coming. In towns it was a nightmare, as they'd leave very little room for the cars to get through — yet we were passing them at racing speeds. It was, of course, absurdly dangerous. Yet, somehow, the organizers got away with it until that final race in 1957, when the Marquis de Portago's Ferrari left the road, killing 11 people. Even so, I remember Aymo Maggi telling us that on those 1,000 miles of roads, during a normal weekend, there would have been a similar number of road deaths — without the Mille Miglia. But it could not have been allowed to continue. This was but a warning of what might well have been in store.

In a way it was a mixture of race and rally, which suited my particular temperament. You could take it at any speed you liked, setting your own pace, and I always drove the full distance single-handed, though I always took a passenger, usually Geoff. I've never been a great driver, because I started in big-time events too late in life; and the reason I won the Monte Carlo Rally was not that 'Healey's the best rally driver in Europe', as the Press used to say. I used to do well in this event, and in other rallies, because of the weeks and weeks of preparation beforehand, of the car and myself, and the endless practice I put in before the event.

In 1948, our first year, when we were running second in class, the biggest dog I've ever seen leaped off a hedge into the road, and we hit it square-on at 100 m.p.h., smashing both headlamps. We were delayed half-an-hour, and had to face the trickiest part of the route in darkness, without lights. Luckily, we were running behind Johnny Lurani's Healey Elliott saloon (which had already broken all previous touring car records, despite damaged suspension), so we tucked-in behind him and drove along the Milan-Como autostrada, sometimes running at 100-plus m.p.h., to finish second in the unlimited sports car category and ninth overall. In 1949 I had Geoffrey Price with me, our service manager, whose father was a great character in the industry as sales director with Daimler and responsible for the preparation of the Queen's cars. Price was a marvellous mechanic, and joined us immediately after the war. He'd work on the car incessantly, even when nothing needed doing, and always had the grubbiest, oiliest hands. With these, he'd keep me supplied throughout the race with endless bits of oil-impregnated chocolate, while sitting back, completely relaxed, peeling oranges.

With my son Geoff again as passenger, I drove the prototype Nash-Healey coupé in the 1952 race, when the Italian domination was being challenged by the mighty Mercedes-Benz works team. We weren't doing too badly, ours and the Johnson-McKenzie Healey running high in the general classification, but our race was short-lived. After only 200 miles, while slowing for a narrow bridge in the middle of a bend, the wheels locked and we slithered straight on, into the parapet, wrecking the car — it was a bit of bad driving. Luckily we had introduced a new idea, setting the screen in rubber, without a metal frame. When Geoff's head hit it, which it did with a mighty thump, the screen simply popped out, and neither of us was injured. Leslie Johnson went on to finish seventh overall, and fourth in class behind the winning Ferrari and two works Mercedes.

We had our ups and downs in our ten Mille Miglias; and, after those first two post-war races, I knew we could never beat the highly specialized, limited-production Ferraris, Maseratis, Mercedes-Benz and others. But we were always there with a team, and always well placed in our class and category, with normal, production cars such as people were buying for use on the road. It gave the owners a strong sense of being a part of the 'family', and boosted their enthusiasm and their unwitting role as public relations officers. The event always received good publicity, second only to Le Mans, especially in America.

As I have said, I found the drivers profoundly interesting, from their individual make-up to the effect which, for a fortunate few, world-wide fame and popularity were to have upon them; and I met some wonderful people, among them Enzo Ferrari. Together with those close friends Peter Collins and Mike Hawthorn - both Ferrari works drivers at the time — and 'The Old Lady' as we referred to Ferrari's somewhat domineering wife, I dined with him one evening at Modena, finding him a warm and kindly man, who chose for some reason to hide his true character behind a tough facade. The occasion was shortly after the death in 1956 of his 24-year-old son, Dino, whom he adored and whose loss he never really got over. It was perhaps because of this that he treated his drivers almost as sons, expecting from them the same loyalty and affection; he was quoted at the time as saying that the closest relationship and the greatest affection exist between a father and his son.

Soon after our dinner party, Peter was to marry the charming Louise King, who had made a successful career for herself on the American stage and television. After meeting her briefly in Monte Carlo, Peter called on her a year later, on his way back from racing in Rio. They fell deeply in love and were married within a week or two. I always felt that Ferrari regretted this marriage in some curious way — having lost a 'son', rather than gaining a 'daughter'. In his very revealing memoirs *My Terrible Joys*, he says of Peter that '. . .a change nevertheless became evident in his happy character. He became irritable.' Yet, so far as I could see, it was a wonderfully happy marriage, a perfect match which tragically lasted so short a time, for Peter was killed at the Nürburgring a year or so afterwards. I used to stay sometimes with Peter, Louise and Mike in the house provided for them by Ferrari at Modena. Each visit was an absolute riot from start to finish, and ever since those days Louise has been a very dear friend, whom I visit every time I go to the States. Peter drove for us only once — at Nassau, in a one-off, Ferrari-engined Healey, the engine of which we bought (complete with the car) from the Marquis de Portago. It was not a success.

Many, many drivers come to mind through the years, some of whom have sadly lost their lives subsequently in racing cars, and each recalling some personal characteristic. I must be forgiven if I do not mention them all; they are not forgotten. There was Paul Hawkins, who came to England as an impoverished Australian mechanic to work for us on the cars in the Healey showrooms in London's Grosvenor Street, and slept on one of the benches in the basement. Paul's colourful speech comes to mind, describing driving a Healey in the wet: 'Just like having a bunk-up in a hammock, with roller-skates on'; and when we supplied him with a smart, new suit of overalls: 'Like Westminster Abbey — no ballroom'. And Clive Baker, somewhat undisciplined and unreliable, yet one of our most skilled drivers, and very, very quick in the wet. The finest wet-weather performance I ever saw was Clive's at Sebring, when it started to rain. With his 'bug-eye' Sprite he began to overtake the opposition, including Ferraris, until he was very well placed. We prayed the rain would continue, but unfortunately it stopped.

Tommy Wisdom, motoring-writer-cum-racing-driver, who had already made a considerable name for himself in both fields pre-war, was a very good friend, and one of the most amusing people I've ever driven with — or against, for that matter. He was extremely courageous, remaining cheerful, however adverse the conditions, and I had the greatest confidence in him as a driver. Yet he could be extremely aggressive, and many's the time I've had to lead him away when a punch-up seemed likely — especially with waiters! They were a splendid pair, Tommy and his wife Elsie (or 'Bill', as we used to call her). In fact, Bill was a better driver than her husband, and at one time held the Ladies' Outer Circuit lap record at Brooklands, driving the mighty Leyland-Thomas; she also won the JCC 1,000-mile race in 1932, with Joan Richmond. Tommy was a war correspondent and, as a Wing-Commander in the RAF, went on one or two bombing raids; and his — and my — good friend Courtenay Edwards OBE, a highly respected motoring writer, was also a war correspondent, who accompanied the D-Day landings and went on through Caen with the army. I shall never forget the way these two used to rib each other incessantly about their wartime exploits, each claiming to be the greater hero — Tommy having apparently overcome the entire German Luftwaffe! Bill took to rally driving after the war, accompanying Tommy on several events — and it was, of course, their daughter Anne (or 'Wiz', as we called her) who brought us one of our greatest Austin-Healey victories, when she and Pat Moss scored an outright win in the extremely tough, long, and fast Liège-Rome-Liège race, driving a 3-litre. The exploits of those two are now motoring history — they won the Coupe des Dames in every worthwhile international rally, not once but several times, becoming the Womens' European Rally Championship winners more than once.

We employed some of the 'names' from pre-war days, including the French-turned-Monégasque Louis Chiron, who was said to have been 'spotted' and given his chance by a wealthy guest at the hotel in which he worked, though I never quite fathomed how his motor racing potential could have been apparent. And there was Count 'Johnny' Lurani, a steady, though not all that fast, driver who took an Elliot saloon through the 1948 Targa Florio with Serafini, finishing 13th overall, winning the unlimited touring class, and coming second in the overall touring classification. With the same car, he went straight on to the Mille Miglia, where he drove with Sandri, winning the touring class outright, and setting up a new class record with 90 minutes to spare. There was Norman Black, too, with whom (and Tommy Wisdom) I had competed in my final Monte Carlo Rally in 1937, driving a Triumph. Norman had had a distinguished pre-war career with Alfa Romeo, ERA and MG, winning the 1931 Tourist Trophy on handicap with a 750 cc MG Midget. Together with Wisdom he drove a Westland roadster in the Paris 12-hour race at Montlhéry in 1948 — one of an eight-car British team consisting of Johnson and Haines' Elliot, the Westland, two Aston Martins and four HRGs. They were matched against a French team of Simcas, Gordinis and Delages, and won the contest, though both Healeys retired. Of Johnson, the only thing that sticks in my mind is a — shall we say biassed? — race commentary by his close friend John Eason Gibson at Silverstone: 'So-and So's in the lead — but *Johnson's* in sixth place, going extremely well. Even though he isn't gaining, he certainly isn't falling back... and all against the strongest opposition...', and so on, in his broad Scots accent. I cannot recall the exact details, but it was along those lines.

Tony Rolt drove for us several times, notably at Le Mans, of course, as mentioned in the Nash-Healey chapter. Together with Chiron and Wisdom, he won the Team Prize in the Production Car Race at the BRDC International Trophy Meeting at Silverstone — driving, appropriately, Healey Silverstones against strong Jaguar opposition. Tony had also raced a straight-eight Triumph Dolomite, after production had ceased and before the remaining engines and cars had been taken over by Robert Arbuthnot's High Speed Motors — the sole survivor, as far as I know, of this magnificent folly being named the 'HSM' to this day. I had known Tony for many years, since the days when he and his mother and two lovely sisters used to come and stay at Perranporth as little children pre-war. His wondrous escape plans from Colditz prison during the war, using a home-made glider, are well known, and his riotous exploits with his co-driver-cum-friend Duncan Hamilton are equally well known, and loved. It was a matter of course that hotel managers, when presenting Tony and Duncan with their bills, should attach a second bill for damage to the hotel.

Carroll Shelby and I, with the model of the record-breaking streamliner. (*B. Healey*).

These were always settled in a most gentlemanly manner, without a trace of complaint. It was all part of motor-racing in those less professional days, when the sport had yet to become big business, involving so many people. I am afraid that I do not look upon today's scene as an improvement.

DMH and Briggs Cunningham with the two Cunningham Le Mans cars at Briggs' museum in California (*B. Healey*).

Carroll Shelby was — and still is — a great and very amusing character, driving for us in several of the record runs at Utah, and in the Carrera Panamericana in which he crashed (apologising afterwards that it had been the fault of an attractive Mexican girl, who had caught his eye). When Carroll was planning to build what were to become his very successful Cobra racing-sports cars, he asked me if I could supply him with an Austin-Healey chassis on which to base it. Unfortunately, Austins wouldn't agree, so he used the AC chassis. He was a first class, steady driver, and though I imagine he must by now have become a millionaire, he hasn't changed — always the same Texas cowboy, with his slow, easy drawl.

There were three wealthy men in the States who decided to take up motor racing at more or less the same time. One was Briggs Cunningham, already famous as a yachtsman and for his helmsmanship in one of the America's Cup defenders, together with Jim Kimberley (of Kimberley-Clark Kleenex), and Bill Spear. All three of these started off with Healeys; and I, personally, delivered to Briggs the first of the Silverstones to cross the Atlantic. Not con-

143

tent with the Riley engine's performance, he fitted a 5½-litre Cadillac unit, and did very well indeed with it in the States. What's more, it sowed the seeds of the beautifully engineered and prepared Cunningham cars that were to do so well at Le Mans, bearing the American colours. A very generous man, Briggs later sent me a Cadillac car to try out on the roads of Europe.

George Abecassis, one of our Mille Miglia drivers, was one of the best true amateurs of his time, with great experience of Altas, ERAs and others pre-war, and with HWM, post-war. He was never perturbed, and — minutes before a race — could chat away happily on any subject, when everyone else was in a state of nerves. Ron Flockhart worked for Rubery Owen at the Charles Clark garage in Wolverhampton; they bought a 100S which he raced along with his ERA in many British events, so we decided to give him a drive in the 1955 Mille Miglia. There developed a private battle between Ron and Lance Macklin, both driving 100S cars — Ron, hell-bent on winning, having decided to travel alone and save the extra weight. First Lance got into trouble, when — on a slow corner — he slid on to the straw-bales, the heat of the exhaust setting the straw alight. With the help of the crowds, he got the car clear before any damage was done, and rejoined the race, now with Flockhart close behind. For some time they drove in company, until Lance felt Ron was pressing him, so he waved him through. Then it was Flockhart's turn, when he took a bridge too fast, hit the parapet and jumped clean over it into the river, and disappeared. Lance, who had witnessed all this, stopped, and was thankful to see Flockhart standing safely on the river bank. The crowds, however, thought there had been a passenger in the car, and were busily diving to rescue him, until Lance put them wise.

We were a pretty international lot, one way and another; we had the Dutchman 'Gatso' Gatsonides driving for us at Le Mans with that famous motor cycle racer Johnny Lockett. And there was Frenchman, Marcel Becquart, who drove with the technical journalist Gordon Wilkins, also at Le Mans. I shall never forget one particular event, for which we had painted the Sprite coupés in Dayglo orange for identification purposes. After scrutineering, the organizers called a meeting and ruled that we were giving ourselves an unfair advantage over all our competitors, and banned us from the race! We had to repaint them the day before the race, which, apart from the trouble it caused, added weight that we'd worked so hard to reduce. We had other troubles too, when poor old Gordon crashed one of the cars on the way back to Le Mans, after practice.

Lance Macklin, the son of Noel Macklin whose Invictas I had driven pre-war, drove in several races for us, notably at Sebring and in the Mille Miglia, scoring a number of worthwhile successes.

A somewhat vain fellow, always immaculately turned-out, he is a very old friend. His many love affairs were a feature of those early Healey days. Eventually we heard that, while down in Florida, he had at last found 'Miss Right', and had married her. Where this story originated, I never knew, but I suspect it was from Lance himself. When he got back to England, David Brown gave a party to celebrate his marriage, and we all went along, only to discover that he hadn't been married at all. Lance had a wretched year in 1955, putting an end to his motor racing. First came the terrible accident at Le Mans, in which his Austin-Healey was involved, Lance having a miraculous escape, then came the Tourist Trophy at Dundrod, when seven cars were eliminated from the race in a multiple, fiery accident that cost Jim Mayers' life. One of the cars involved was Lance's Austin-Healey.

John Sprinzel became a well-known driver of Sprites, especially at Sebring; he also worked for us at one time. And there was Andrew Hedges, of whom my main recollection was when the motoring journalist David Benson decided that the two of them should seek sponsorship from Benson and Hedges, the cigarette manufacturers, for an entry at Le Mans. Benson, to whom the pleasures of the table were no strangers, went into the strictest training, a very considerable act of self-sacrifice — only to discover, when he offered them their services, that Benson and Hedges weren't interested in motor racing!

There was young Roger Enever, too, son of Sid who had accompanied Tazio Nuvolari as riding-mechanic in the Tourist Trophy-winning K3 Magnette pre-war. He drove our special, mid-engined Repco-Brabham vee-eight car at the 1970 Le Mans, with Alec Poole as co-driver. They survived for very, very nearly the 24 hours, only to stop with ignition trouble on their final lap, after the winners had crossed the line and the Healey was running-out its last few moments to complete the 24 hours, in sight of the pits. So certain were we, at the pit, that they'd be the first British car home that my son Brian had gone round to the Moët et Chandon marquee to buy some champagne to celebrate. Generously, Moët refused payment, being proud, as they said, to give us three magnums in our hour of triumph, but all to no avail. Instead, they helped us all to drown our sorrows, bless them. All that had happened was the failure of a little resistor in the ignition system.

Prior to this, we had run mid-engined Healey specials — the Healey-Climax SR — at Le Mans in 1968 and 1969, using a vee-eight, 2-litre Coventry Climax engine loaned to us by Leonard Lee and Walter Hassan. In 1968, driven by Clive Baker and Andrew Hedges, it retired with gear selector troubles after only two hours' racing. We ran it again in 1969, in slightly lowered and lightened form, but again we were eliminated. The official reason was a stone through the radiator, but it would be more truthful to say that

145

**Far left** Geoff (left), myself and Brian check progress on the special car being built for the 1968 Le Mans 24-Hours — fitted with a Coventry Climax engine on loan to us at Warwick. (*B. Healey*).

**Below left** The completed SR Le Mans special at Silverstone, with Geoff, Bic and myself standing in front of the car.

**Left** Robert Harrison, of Sydney, Australia, with his two cars. He has owned the 3000 from new, and bought the Le Mans Healey after the race. We had borrowed the Climax engine from Jack Brabham, and it had to be returned. Robert has since fitted a Rover engine and seems well satisfied with the performance. (*B. Healey*).

it was overheating, about which we could do nothing, short of redesigning the air intake and ducting. We had no end of trouble with this car. During practice it proved to be hopelessly over-geared, and Wally Hassan and my son Brian went up to Paris to collect spares which had been flown over for the Hewland gear-box, as used in the Grand Prix cars. They had a terrible time, what with trouble with the Customs at Orly, and a little Renault in the packed, Friday night traffic in Paris. 'This blighter's leaning on us', Wally said to Brian — and proceeded to 'lean' his Jaguar on the Renault, pushing him up against a neighbouring taxi on his other side.

I've left my very good friend Stirling Moss until last — a born driver, and the greatest and most professional that ever drove our cars. He was a marvellous all-rounder too, as were so many of his contemporaries, being able to jump out of a production car into a 500, then into a sports car, and then into a Grand Prix car, all at the same meeting; he was a good rally driver too. I don't think any of our present-day drivers could do all that — they're nothing like so versatile. Stirling was a first-class test-driver too; he could always spot whatever was wrong with a car. His one shortcoming was that he hadn't the technical knowledge to suggest how to put it right, though unfortunately he often thought he had. I have heard it said — and I repeat this with some diffidence — that this was the principal reason why the Drivers' World Championship eluded him so often; and the blame must lie to some extent with Alf Francis, his personal mechanic, who car-

147

ried out his foibles. Even when an engine or car constructor had delivered him the goods in the highest possible state of tune, he would get Alf to mess about with this, that, or the other — the car finally going to the starting line with its power output actually reduced. In his day, though, he was one of Britain's greatest assets; and he remains a close personal friend.

When I eventually decided to employ a public relations officer, I chose Ken Gregory, Stirling's manager. It was Ken who conceived the fantastic gold-plated Austin-Healey Motor Show car, the first of the six-cylinder cars. Everything was gold plated; it had an ivory steering wheel and was upholstered in mink. It was beautifully done — the sort of job that could have been done only in Birmingham. It still exists and, at the time of writing, it had just been sold to America.

I can not close this chapter without mentioning what was perhaps our proudest moment, when my son Brian — or 'Bic', as he is known — was asked to take one of the early Austin-Healeys to Buckingham Palace for the Duke of Edinburgh to try out. Brian arrived at the Palace and was met by Michael Parker, Equerry to the Duke, who told him the car was to be taken to Goodwood, as the Duke was down there. We eventually heard from Freddie Richmond, the Duke of Richmond and Gordon, that he and the Duke of Edinburgh had had great fun driving it round the circuit. While Brian was at the Palace, Michael Parker told him, 'There's another Cornishman here on the staff, whom I'd like you to meet', taking him along a passageway to a room in which General Sir Frederick Browning, GCVO, KBE, CB, DSO, DL, Extra Equerry to the Queen and to the Duke of Edinburgh, was struggling into a pair of thigh-length, leather boots. Interrupting his effort and shaking Brian by the hand, he said 'How would you like to put on these ruddy things every day of your life?' It was a moment Brian will never forget.

# 11

## What looks right...

At intervals throughout this book I have referred to body styling — expounding some strongly-held views on the subject of radiators standing proudly in isolation from wings and headlamps as the manufacturer's trademark; and decrying the spoilers, air-dams and other gimmicks in use today, which have little or no influence on performance or fuel consumption at the speeds permitted on today's roads. These views are largely, though not entirely, personal — beauty being in the eye of the beholder; but they are not unique. And the fact that the original Healey 100 styling, developed almost unchanged through to the last of the 'Big' Healeys, was acclaimed as something outstanding, prompts me to go into the subject in some detail.

Body style, of course, evolved from the necessity to 'clothe' the major mechanical components, as well as the occupants, of the early horseless carriages; and there was quite a lengthy transition period while the influence of horse-drawn vehicles, at first strong, gradually declined, eventually to be lost completely. This period was, of course, unavoidable — the 'stylists' had yet to learn to think in terms of the pure automobile. The human mind has an odd habit of relating anything new or unfamiliar to something it knows well, and there is a strong reluctance to accept anything strange. The public would have been even slower in accepting the horseless carriage if there had not been at least something about it that was already familiar.

As this acceptance came about, there developed a completely new art form, if you like, applied exclusively to the motor car. People learned to relate one car to another car, forming their own opinions as to its merit — or otherwise — in its own, new sphere. They learned, too, to place and appreciate each car in its own particular category, including so-called sports cars, with which I have always been personally concerned. It is interesting to consider for a moment this somewhat nebulous term 'sports car', which so many of today's writers have sought unsuccessfully to define. As a type, it has largely been replaced by the 'grand tourer', with its closed, streamlined body. As the definition of a type, the term 'sports car' was never popular. The late Freddy Gordon Crosby, writing in *The Autocar* in 1922, says:

It is a pity that we have no better recognized term than that of 'sporting' to represent these modern, super-efficiency, and attractive types of speed cars, which are designed and built, sometimes regardless of cost, and in which appearance often takes precedence over practical comfort. A better term than 'sporting car' is wanted, especially now that so many firms are actually supplying standard 'sports' models — which nomenclature is even worse than 'sporting'. . . The demand for speed and efficiency is, of course, at the bottom of this growing attraction of the sporting car, coupled with a certain amount of vanity in possessing a car out of the ordinary.

Perhaps it is as well that nobody can define the term, since nobody seems to have wanted it in the first place!

It stuck, though, for as long as the type existed. And, in its time, the type was unmistakeable, with its long, high bonnet suggesting a long, high, powerful engine and the implied power and speed that went with it. The extremely shallow windscreens often used, or tiny aero-screens when the main windscreen was folded flat, added to this impression, with the two-seat passenger compartment reduced to a bare minimum to make room for all that engine. There was no mistaking the type — it was a 'piece of machinery'. Of course, the builders of some entirely bogus 'sports cars' were quick to latch-on, producing cars that looked the part, though with negligible performance from a small, side-valve, four-cylinder engine lost in the vast bonnet space! Oddly enough, today these sheep-in-wolves'-clothing have become prized classics, changing hands at fantastic prices. One wonders why.

It was from the great sporting cars of the twenties and thirties, with their singularly static lines, by today's standards, that such cars as the Austin-Healey — and, later, the mid-engined, closed sports and GT cars — were to develop, with their flowing lines giving the impression of grace and speed, even when they are standing still. It is fascinating to follow the train of events that so profoundly altered the concept of a sports or sporting car, and the manner in which human nature was moulded to accept the change, having scarcely noticed it.

While still being limited by allocation of space to the engine, passenger and luggage compartments, fuel tank, spare wheel, battery and so on, today's stylists have a very different chassis upon which to build. Now that the beam axle has given way to independent front suspension in its various forms, the engine has moved forward to a position between the front wheels, and passengers are accommodated well within the wheelbase, making room for the boot at the rear. This could still be subject to change if there is an increase in the popularity of mid engines (for two-seaters), but this seems to be sufficiently far ahead not to warrant any serious thought at present. In this respect, incidentally, I have always felt that the Sports Car Championship events, particularly Le Mans, could provide a very useful lead. It would be logical to lay down that cars of up to, say, 1,500 cc (possibly even 1,100 cc) may have two-seater bodies, which would encourage mid engines in this category — a 'natural' for small, production sports cars. Anything over that engine size would be required to carry four-seater bodywork, which would outlaw the mid-engined, two-seater, large-engined projectiles that have very limited practical applications. Le Mans would thus revert to what was intended — a race for production sporting cars.

Compared with their counterparts in the twenties and thirties, today's stylists have a further problem with frontal treatment. In the past, as I have said, the individual radiator stood in front, somewhere above the front axle-beam, or even abaft it. Today this is no longer possible and most cars carry only the vestigeal remains of a manufacturer's trademark. The only requirement is an adequate air intake, the size of which is dictated by the needs of the engine and, possibly, brakes. By suitable radiusing of the edges, this orifice can be quite small, yet still admit as much air as a badly-designed, unsightly grille. The stylist has a choice ranging from the symbolic radiator, serving only as a grille, via the plain (and logically correct) simple air-intake, to the ornate grille, which, apart from any other considerations, increases the weight on the front wheels, whilst efforts are being made to shed weight by using light alloys in the forward-mounted engine.

Nor can the stylist ignore public taste, expecting it to adapt to his latest, outlandish creation, however aesthetically beautiful and balanced it may be, for it will not succeed commercially. It is said that today's revolutionary designs become tomorrow's accepted standards — but they are not accepted overnight, being arrived at only by a succession of small changes through the years. In the late thirties the forerunners of today's all-enveloping, wind-cheating frontal treatments began to appear — the Chrysler Air-flow, Fitzmaurice Singer, Skoda, Steyr, Willys, Cord and others — but we were not certain, then, whether they were forerunners or freaks. It was with some foresight that *The Autocar* in February 1937, predicted: 'It will not be long before the radiator will be a completely forgotten unit, quite lost behind its prison of horizontal or vertical slats. . . The day when each car had its own jealously guarded radiator shape has irretrievably gone. '

No less significant than this fundamental change in front treatment has been the bulging of the body sides, and the consequent increase in passenger space that went with it. It was only a matter of time, and of course the universal acceptance of unitary, body-chassis construction, before the body went full-width, with the merging of the wings into the body panels, eventually producing the completely flush side. Through a lengthy process of evolution, the old, separate wings and running-board had changed from static to flowing lines. At first there had been very similar front and rear wings, linked by a running-board. Mindful of the fact that the shape of the wings could exert a greater influence than any other upon the overall appearance of the complete car, stylists developed the long, sweeping front wings, merging with the running-boards to curve gracefully backwards to the rear wings, sometimes with elegant valences forming a 'hem-line'. Indications of what was to come were further developed on, for example, the Type 55 Bugatti, where the front wing, running-board and rear wing swept in one continuous, graceful, undulating curve from front to rear.

Finally, this curve moved steadily upwards, straightening out until no more than a trace of the original curve remained, and forming the all-important waistline — while the valences moved downwards to form the hem-line. On a closed car, so long as the waistline remains most important, widely differing roof lines — though harmonious, of course — can be used without spoiling the beauty. But as soon as the waistline becomes subservient to any ugly roof-line, the beauty is lost. With an open two-seater sports car, the waistline (and to some extent the hem-line) becomes critically important, for it must stand on its own as the outline, and it was with this thought very much in mind that Gerry Coker and I went about styling the Healey 100. That we managed to hit it off is indicated in the Motor Show Report issue of *The Autocar* in 1954: 'The open example which we picked out and illustrated last year has not been surpassed, though its perfect outline continues unchanged. Even better is its record-breaking, shark-finned sister on the stand, whose lines are so swiftly-flowing that it is hard to believe it is standing still.'

That, of course, is not all. The stylist has also to bear in mind the many basic principles which collectively can prevent him from designing a bad, or inharmonious shape. In this respect, it is unfortunately not true to say 'If it looks right, it is right' — for, with the exception of a few outstanding examples, what looked right in the twenties and thirties can look far from right today. But it is true to say 'If it is right, it'll look right' — and it will also continue to do so. It is the cars that *were* right in the twenties and thirties that look right today.

In coachwork, as in a picture, it is the largest masses and principal colours that first attract one's attention. Details are a minor aspect of the main masses; the line enclosing a mass is what gives it an ugly or unpleasant appearance. The greatest effect is created by the least amount of (apparent) work; and added decoration and embellishment attract attention only when the general lines are too weak to do so. They are, generally speaking, completely superfluous. The rarest shapes in nature — and therefore those to which our eyes are least accustomed — are straight lines, angles (particularly right-angles), circles and segments of circles; anything containing these is unlikely to be pleasing to the eye. Because a car must be made up of a series of curved lines and shapes, these must bear a relationship with one another — they must be harmonious. There are many cars with unhappily contrasted, or blended, curves which, with a little thought, could have been avoided.

If a contrasting line or curve is required for any reason — the rear edge of a long side window, for example — It should contrast, but remain in harmony with the rest of the body; and contrasting lines should be reduced to a minimum, otherwise they lose their impact. There have been a few cases through the years where the stylist has sought to pull-together an inharmonious, unbalanced design by the use of a second colour, but this has seldom worked. All too often the dividing line between the two colours, as produced in the paint-shop, has borne little relationship to the main masses, as defined by the stylist, and the result has been disastrous. If the use of a second colour is at all practicable, the dividing line will become apparent, clearly and obviously, of its own accord.

I have always felt, and it was a principle to which Gerry and I adhered unswervingly in styling the Austin-Healeys, that clean, unadorned, balanced lines, provided they were 'right' in the first place, are virtually ageless; they will look right so long as the motor car survives. If, during the process of development, any embellishments become necessary, they must be no more than purely functional; any attempt to 'style' them will probably detract from the overall design, and help it to become dated long before its time. Without any effort whatever, I can think of several contemporary cars for which the drawing office produced beautiful, clean-cut lines which would have retained their style for many years, but the addition of pointless, decorative swage-lines and other gimmicks into their body-pressings has dated them almost before they went into production; and to these, I would add all non-essential, non-functional spoilers, 'beards', air-dams and the rest. It is these things that date a car more than anything else.

I have no doubt whatever that there will be those among today's trained and highly-qualified stylists who will disagree with my views, as a self-trained 'tyro', on this controversial and very personal subject. I can only reply that, whatever my views, it is still a source of immense pride to me that Triumph cars, during my years with the company, were described by the Press as the 'smartest cars in the land', and that the Healeys should have been given a similarly enthusiastic reception right from their early beginnings through to the end.

# 12

# The Austin-Healey clubs

One of the lasting joys of my involvement in the motor industry
— probably the outstanding joy, which continues undiminished
to this day — has been the world-wide circle of friends that I have
accumulated through our Healey and Austin-Healey cars. These
are not confined to the 82 Healey owners' clubs that exist throughout the world — though they, of course, form the majority — but
are drawn from motor sport in general. For some reason, people
seem to enjoy talking to the old man who created their cars; and
I, in turn, value their affection beyond words. I have been the guest
of Healey clubs in many countries, including Australia, and also
America on many, many occasions, where their welcome, their
warm informality, their hospitality and their unofficial way of
addressing me as Donald never grow less. I find it difficult to write
of this aspect of my life without becoming sentimental.

It all boils down, I suppose, to the fact that we built what were
essentially fun-cars, as distinct from somewhat soul-less,
consumer-durable, everyday transport. The cars gave, and seem
to continue to give, pleasure, though if someone had told me,
more than 30 years ago, that this would be so, I simply would
not have believed him. Perhaps, somehow, one knew instinctively,
as the result of a lifetime spent motoring for pleasure and excitement, what the died-in-the-wool car-lover wanted — which brings
me back to my contention that there is more in designing a car
than cold, computer-controlled engineering.

Much has been written about the Healey clubs by people who
have been more closely involved than I, though I have been
privileged to be their President for many years. In 1955, a group
of enthusiastic Healey owners decided it was time a club was
formed through which they could get together periodically and
have a bit of fun, although there were insufficient cars on the road
in those early days for them to compete with each other in the
form of one-make motor sport. The original idea for the club was
suggested by Peter Cavanagh, who at the time was Britain's — if
not the world's — finest impersonator; he had his own radio
programme, on which he was known as 'The Voice of Them All'.
It always amuses me to meet people who were involved with Peter
in the early days of the Club, and to hear them recalling their meet-

ings. At one moment, the Prime Minister would be in the Chair; at the next, the President of the United States — with other well-known figures assuming the roles of Honorary Secretary and Treasurer. Combined with Peter's amazing sense of humour, these impersonations caused a riot.

Supporting Peter were John Langrishe, a solicitor from Becken-ham in Kent who had a very nice Healey Tickford Saloon; James Watt, who was a director of my company; and 'Mort' Morris-Goodall, who had driven an Elliot Saloon at Le Mans with Nigel Mann, finishing quite well, and who was to become my Compe-titions Manager at Warwick in later years. Together with my son Brian, these people formed the Healey Drivers' Club. They placed an order with Fattorini, the leading badge-makers of the day, for 50 badges. I don't think any more were ever produced, so they have become collectors' items, and one still survives in the Steer-ing Wheel Club in London. The badge featured Warwick Castle and the Union Flag, of course, denoting the cars' British back-ground — more attractive, in my view, than the subsequent badge designed for the Austin-Healey Club, which included a long bridge to indicate the association with Austin and their factory at Long-bridge, just outside Birmingham.

This early club went along well enough, with a satisfactory mem-bership, but there were never enough Healeys on the road to give it real strength. It was not until the Mark 1 Sprite was announced in 1958 (a model of which 48,999 examples were produced dur-ing its three-year run) that the idea of an all-embracing club took off, credit for this being owed to a crowd of enthusiasts in the South of England, headed by Raymond Baxter and Doug Worgan.

The Austin company were persuaded to put literature in all new cars leaving the factory, advising owners that such a club was in existence. Interest became so great that John Thornley, Director and General Manager of the MG Car Company, added official sup-port to the operation by setting-up its headquarters in the office of the long-standing MG Car Club at Abingdon, under its secre-tary Peter Browning. Finance was made available to the Austin-Healey Club, and the glossy publication *Safety Fast* was enlarged to cater for Austin-Healey owners. From then onwards, the club grew steadily and quickly, first under Peter Browning and, later, Les Needham.

In 1961, Chuck Anderson formed the Austin-Healey Club of America; and, thanks again to Peter Browning's enthusiasm, they were brought into close contact with the club headquarters at Abingdon, and much interest was generated in the States. However, when Donald Stokes and Leyland took over BMC, one of the first moves was to advise Abingdon that the MG and Austin-Healey clubs were not, in his view, of any significant value to the new company. The combined club offices were to be closed and

# Donald Healey

The Austin-Healey Club of Great Britain invited me to cut this birthday cake, in celebration of the 25th Birthday of the Sprite. (*B. Healey*).

Brian had an idea to present DMH with a banner on which were mounted Healey Club badges from around the world; this was to have been on 3 July 1988, his 90th birthday. Sadly, Donald did not live to see it, but Brian's daughter Linda produced it and it was shown for the first time at the Donald Healey Memorial Trophy Meeting at Silverstone on 17 September 1988. It will appear at Healey Club events in future, and it is hoped that more Healey clubs will send their embroidered patches to be added to the banner. (*B. Healey*).

publication of the long-standing and popular *Safety Fast* was to cease; all the clubs' records, photographs, regalia, badges and so on were to be disposed of.

Brian received a telephone call from Les Needham, advising him of this top-level decision, and saying that he was very reluctant indeed to dispose of all this historic material. If Brian were to get down to Abingdon the same day, Les said, he would make it all available to him. We sent a van along which was duly loaded with everything concerning the clubs — Warwick then became their temporary home, with Brian their caretaker-secretary, until the various Centres could get together and sort out their future. Having recovered from the shock of seeing their props knocked from beneath them, they created a new club under private ownership, which was even more enthusiastic.

Warwick became the temporary home of the Austin-Healey Club and Bic took over as caretaker secretary whilst the future of the Club was decided. So keen was I to keep the club going that we offered Les a job at Warwick which would have enabled him to continue to run the Club, but he was reluctant to move his family and was offered a position with the Royal Automobile Club Motor Sports Division, where he is to this day. Typically of Les, he is ever-ready to be present at any Austin-Healey function when his commitments allow.

The Midlands Centre of the Club was numerically, and still is, a very strong one, and it listed many Warwick customers amongst its members. John Gott, one of the all-time great Healey competition drivers, and Chief Constable of Northampton, regularly attended the get-togethers in some local hostelry. John was a great character and a great clubman but sadly was killed whilst driving his Healey in a club event.

While Brian was acting as General Secretary, he began to receive a steady flow of letters, cables and telephone calls from Hank Leach in California, owner of a Sprite and early BN1 Austin-Healey 100. He was very keen to re-form the ailing Pacific Centre of the Austin-Healey Club of America; and we, of course, had an enormous amount of club material in store at Warwick, which we were able to make available to him. Through his stout efforts, and the fact that he happened to be a printer by trade, he got the club well and truly off the ground on the West Coast, where the bulk of the exported cars were going. He published a beautiful club magazine, *Healey Highlights*, which continues to this day and is a credit to all concerned.

During 1981, when Brian was in San Francisco staying with Kevin Faughnan, Kevin and his wife Agnes gave a party for Brian to meet some of the officers of the Pacific Coast Centre — and who should be there but Hank Leach himself. Brian was completely overwhelmed to find that Hank had brought along his complete filing system, which included a record of every telephone conversation, a copy of every cable, every letter he had written to Brian, and every reply he had received — which were not quite as numerous as the letters Hank had written! Healey owners on the West Coast owe an enormous debt to Hank. I was delighted,

With Teri Urban, Miss Austin-Healey 1982 at Snowmass, Aspen, California. Teri and her husband Rex hail from Oregon, and he races a Mark 1 Sprite with success. (*B. Healey*).

Donald Healey

**PHILLIPS PETROLEUM COMPANY**

BARTLESVILLE, OKLAHOMA 74004

C. M. KITTRELL
EXECUTIVE VICE-PRESIDENT

The Right Honorable Margaret Thatcher
10 Downing Street
London SW1, England

Dear Madam Prime Minister:

The Austin Healey legend lives not only in the land where it was born, but in the land where it took root. The legend lives because the automobile was a millenation of ..... One of captured imagination. One of blithe spirit.

The Healey family, creator of the exemplary automobile of British excellence, gathered in Snowmass Village near Aspen, Colorado, this past summer to celebrate the legend's 30th anniversary. As you'll see on the following pages, the Healeys were joined by a few intimate friends -- about 1,000 enthusiasts driving more than 400 Austin Healeys. This was but the latest display of America's long association with the marque. Americans bought 80 percent of the Austin Healeys produced between 1952 and 1967.

This one-week celebration was an opportunity to say thanks to the superior craftsmen who fulfilled the American love affair with the automobile. It was an opportunity to see up close how British craftsmanship is cared for in one of your country's former colonies.

This album is my opportunity to acknowledge quality. The quality of a living legend.

Respectfully yours,

*Charles M. Kittrell*

Charles M. Kittrell

CMK:c
Enclosure

**Far left** Snowmass, California, 1982: The Silverstone belonging to Don Barrows is one of three originally purchased by Briggs Cunningham, and has recently passed on to Brian's son, Peter. (*B. Healey*).

**Below left** Some people were impressed that an 84-year-old should still want to travel half-way round the world. This kind of welcome, from Healey buffs, provided the motivation. The guests at Snowmass, California, in 1982 included (left to right) Peter Healey, Ed Bussey, Mary and Bic Healey, Gerry Coker, John Colegate, Margot Healey, John Harris, Fred Horner, DMH, John Gordon Bennett and Geoff Healey. (*B. Healey*).

**Above** A letter to Margaret Thatcher from Charles Kittrell, an American Austin-Healey fan.

when in the States a year or so later, to hear Brian pay a personal tribute to Hank, asking those present — and there must have been 1,200 people, all Healey enthusiasts — to show their appreciation of him, which they did in a fine and enthusiastic manner.

There are, as I write, 82 Austin-Healey clubs and centres throughout the world, the latest being formed in Japan, which I believe has eight members; but it didn't have that 12 months ago, and I very much doubt if there are more than eight of our cars in Japan. During the production years I was unable to take an active interest in the clubs as I was so heavily committed in other ways, though I did attend occasional meetings in America and Australia. It was not until the death of my wife in 1980 that I really came to know the spirit and affection of these far-flung groups of people. There were messages of condolence from all over the world when Ivy died, and invitations to so many places, and from so many people I had never even met but have since been fortunate enough to grow to know as friends.

From that point, my association with the clubs and centres became very personal — not as Donald Healey, boss of the Healey Motor Company and designer of the Austin-Healey, but simply as 'Donald', a kindly approach used by members of all ages. I appreciate this deeply and wouldn't have it any other way. It has kept me young. Perhaps I am the only motor club president who can boast of being flown across the Atlantic in Concorde at the expense of the club. And, as I write this chapter in my middle eighties, I am preparing to set off again for the States as guest of the Austin-Healey Club of America, on a three-month visit with an itinerary that reads like a gazetteer. I have been on such visits to America on many occasions, and to Canada, Australia and New Zealand too, to be welcomed with a warmth that is almost breath-taking. This has been so much appreciated, not only by myself, but by my sons Geoffrey and Brian, and by some of my grand-children.

This shows, I believe, the sort of affection that can develop through the years for the right sort of car, and I am intensely proud to have provided it — a car which people enjoy, which they're proud to own, and on which they're prepared to spend many, many hours of love and attention, not only in restoration to a con-dition far better than when it left the factory, but in maintaining this condition. Long after I grow too old to travel, and join them at their meetings, the Austin-Healey clubs will continue.

If, as a guest, I have imposed too much upon the hospitality of my hosts, I apologize — though it was not without encourage-

With Mark and Nell Donaldson, of the New Zealand Austin-Healey Owners' Club. Their beautifully preserved 3000 is in the back-ground. (*B. Healey*).

ment! My son Brian has this to say about my globe-trotting: 'The only complaints I've ever heard about the Old Man — and these are made most vehemently — concern his capacity for late nights, or early mornings; for keeping people awake until 3 a.m., drinking them under the table, and then insisting that they join him for a swim at 6 a.m. And this was not an isolated occasion — it seems to be a regular habit whenever he's staying at a hotel with a swimming pool. I'm surprised the clubs haven't got wise to this, and stuck him out in the country somewhere, in a hotel that has no pool.'

As I say, I apologize. But I shall do it again, given the chance.

The United States, with its affluence and sports car climate, was always the biggest buyer of Austin-Healeys, and quite naturally it has far more clubs and chapters than any other country. As a result, more meets are held in that country; and, with such a fine road system, travelling vast distances to attend these meets does not present any great problem. The East and West coasts have their annual gatherings and, in addition, there are smaller conclaves in other parts of the continent. Here again the weather can be relied upon to play ball during the summer months and one can

Boston, USA, September 1986, and more hospitality from trans- Atlantic Healey fans. Roland and Sally Prevost, Malcolm and Lottie Terry, and DMH, about to enjoy some Maine lobster. (*B. Healey*).

Encino, California. July 1984: A magnificent restoration by Don Fisher and family of a 1962 Austin-Healey. (*B. Healey*).

plan ahead in the knowledge that any event will be well attended, with upwards of 200 cars. Only recently the US Clubs were making plans to hold a party to celebrate the 30th anniversary of the Sprite, in Hershey, where the chocolate bars come from. Rick Moses formed a club exclusively for Sprites, and was expecting around 200 cars from all over the country. At the same time the UK will be honouring the Sprite with a party organized by John Mead of the South-Western Centre. One doubts if it will be as well supported as its counterpart in the States, although just as much hard work has gone into organizing it. Many owners in the UK take their cars off the road for the greater part of the year; they do not start to emerge again until June, with the long evenings and the best chance of some fine weather. The UK clubs get together every year to organize the International Healey Weekend and this is hosted by the different centres on a rota basis at a new venue every time. IHW is becoming very well supported, especially by overseas visitors. The Dutch club has always been in regular attendance, so have the German, the French, and the Swedish; and recently we have welcomed visitors from such far-away places as Japan and the United States.

Australia has always been a good Healey country, and in fact the Mark 1 Sprite was assembled there some years ago. The climate is absolutely ideal for a sports car, with long, hot summers and no rust problems. I think Australia can claim to own more 100S cars than any other country, and this is owed to the activities of two individuals, Joe Jarick and Alan 'Sebring' Jones, who is unhappily no longer with us having been killed following the sport he loved, motor racing. The Aussies also organize their annual rally on a rota basis, and they literally cross deserts in their cars to attend these annual gatherings. My son Brian was lucky enough to be a guest of the Victoria Club in 1985 when it was hosting the meeting, and he was amazed at the vast distances those enthusiasts covered to be there. Rick Scoular drove his 100S from Brisbane to Melbourne through the night — at, he claimed, a steady 120mph, and with no weather protection. Charlie Mitchell from Perth in Western Australia, in convoy with several other Healeys, drove his 3000 some 2000 miles including crossing the Nullarbor desert, and all he broke was his speedo cable! The Sprite is well catered for in Australia, although the big Healey and its little brother do not mix as well as in other countries. One cannot write about Australia without mentioning John Gray and his long suffering wife Suellen. John's collection includes a Rolls-engined Healey, an ex-Pat Moss rally car, a Clive Baker Sprite and NOJ 392, one of the two Le Mans cars of 1953. In addition he has an old telephone kiosk in his garden, and enough spares to supply the whole of Australia!

Germany has a very strong club with some superb cars, some

of which were purchased in the US and shipped home. Bic was fortunate enough to attend a meeting a few years ago in Kassel which is not far from the East German border, and it rained nearly all that weekend! Wolfgang Bode and Rudiger Robra are joint presidents and regularly attend the UK meets. Whilst attending that meeting they had a barbecue at Wolfgang's hunting lodge in the mountains, and on the Sunday morning the streets of Kassel were closed by order of the police so that the Austin-Healey Club of Germany could hold an uninterrupted drive through that lovely city!

Many club members participate in motor sport with their cars and even after 30 years or more they continue to give a good account of themselves. The calendar is now so full that the individual clubs experience difficulty in booking a circuit for a race meeting, and so we have combined meetings, with several marque clubs being involved. This makes for very keen rivalry and the participants thoroughly enjoy themselves in such events as the six-hour relay at Silverstone, and historic car events.

It is difficult to write about the clubs without mentioning individuals who have devoted much of their spare time towards ensuring their success — whether they are in the US, Australia, Germany or Britain, to name but a few countries. At the same time it is easy to offend by not mentioning everyone, but to do so would be a monumental task and would fill a book. I cannot let the opportunity pass without paying a small tribute to Carolyn Waters and her husband Jack. Carolyn is General Secretary to the Austin-Healey Club Ltd. in the UK and her attention to detail is fantastic. And Joyce and Gordon Pearce, whom I first knew many years ago when they were trying hard to obtain recognition for their New Forest Centre. Today Joyce edits the British club's magazine, *Rev Counter*, and Gordon takes the photographs and assists with the preparation of the magazine; Joe Cox whose father, Peter, owns one of the Rolls-engined cars, and who was Club Chairman for so long; John Chatham — what can one say about him? — always present, always laughing in between swallowing pints of beer, and surely the ultimate in club racers, driving on the limit all the time and providing great entertainment. To Germany and Wolfgang, 'that bloody German' as he calls himself, and his lovely cars. Bert Schaap of Holland; and finally to the United States; to Chuck Anderson for getting the club going originally, Kevin Faughnan, Joe O'Connell and Reid Trummell of the Pacific Centre, and their charming wives and families, Walt Glendenning, alas no longer with us, and Hans Nohr. To all those behind the scenes without whom the clubs could not survive; and finally to Rudy Streng, President of the Austin-Healey Club of America and Joan, and Roland Prevost and Sally, Scotty Aurandt and Tim Flaherty.

163

# 13

# Return to Cornwall

The Midlands fogs were not helping Ivy's general health and I thought it was time we found a retirement home where she could rest more and I could continue to indulge myself in my various hobbies. We looked at properties on the South Coast, but nothing really appealed. I would have liked to retire abroad and enjoy the sunshine, but Ivy was never fond of too much travelling, and did not wish to be parted from the family, which by now included several grandchildren. I went off to the States again in 1963, having temporarily abandoned all thoughts of a move. On my return I was greeted by Bic, who said that he had found the ideal property for us, in Cornwall.

He had sold Freddie Ford, the then owner of Trebah, as it was called, a Land-Rover when he was working for HTP Motors in Truro in the fifties. He had delivered the vehicle and had been smitten with the place on first acquaintance. Very apprehensively I asked him to arrange for us to view the property which we did, at Easter.

I had never been so taken with a place as I was with Trebah. It stood in 26 acres in a valley sweeping down to the Helford River, faced south, had a private beach, and the most glorious show of azaleas, rhododendrons, tree-ferns, and trees which were unique to that valley. The house, which was considerably smaller than the original manor house which had been partially destroyed by fire in the late 1940s, stood at the head of the valley and was now of very manageable size, yet big enough to accommodate the whole family on holiday occasions. Ivy and I had always been keen swimmers, and could not imagine living in a house where we could not get out of bed and straight into the water. Trebah had a patio on the front which was ideal for a pool, and there was an abundance of coach-houses, which could prove eminently suitable for building prototypes and the closed circuit television cameras in which I had become very interested. Another big bonus was that Roger Menadue, who had worked for me for so many years, had retired to Mawnan Smith, and was anxious to keep himself active in the sort of work which I envisaged at Trebah. At that time we had the Rolls-Royce dealership at Warwick, and my Silver Cloud would serve as fast transport, enabling me to

**Above left** Trebah lies at the head of a 26-acre valley where many trees and shrubs flourish which would not survive anywhere else in Britain. (*B. Healey*)

**Left** Our much-loved Trebah from the air. Ivy's 1275 cc Mini-Cooper S stands by the house — a car she handled with great verve! (*Airviews Ltd*).

commute between Cornwall and Warwick on a regular basis.

The staff consisted of a gardener, Jon Petryczenko, and his wife Frances who looked after the house; and they were not anxious to leave. I have always been one for making a quick decision and this was no exception. Within a matter of hours I had agreed to purchase Trebah from Freddie Ford, and it was a decision I never regretted. Ivy was thrilled with the garden and the indigenous hydrangeas, which were a beautiful shade of blue, brought about by the very acid soil. She very quickly became absorbed in the running of the garden, and this interest helped immensely towards the improvement in her health, although we never persuaded her to give up smoking until she was 80, despite her having suffered from breathing problems for many years. I renewed a friendship with Donald Monroe, whom I had not seen since my early trials days when he co-drove with me occasionally, and who ran a very successful business in Covent Garden. Unknown to me, Donald had been a customer of Trebah for many years and was happy to carry on the association with the new owners. We formed a company, Trebah Gardens Ltd, and were soon despatching hydrangeas, agapanthus, belladonna lilies, eucomis and helleborus by rail two or three times a week. It was amusing to visit some of my favourite restaurants in London and to recognize flower arrangements which I knew had emanated from Trebah.

Jon really was a fantastic gardener, knowing every plant by name, and with the 'greenest' fingers of anyone I have ever met, with the possible exception of Ivy. He worked from dawn till dusk, and very seldom took a day off — being afraid, I think, that someone was going to get at his beloved garden in his absence. An Estonian by birth, Jon had escaped from conscription to the Russian army as a boy, and had made his way to England after travelling across Europe. During the period when he was held by the Russians he had taught himself gardening from books. After reaching England he had met and married Frances, an English girl who helped in the house and made the most wonderful sponge cakes. We turned one of the greenhouses into an orchid house and soon Ivy knew every one of these strange blooms by name.

Ivy believed that a cutting taken without the knowledge of the owner of the parent plant invariably made a better plant, and she certainly grew some beauties that way. I don't think she ever regarded this as stealing, but merely as increasing the stock. At least, that is what she used to tell herself at the time of the felony. One amusing incident occurred in the Canary Islands where we were holidaying with friends from Cornwall. When visiting some public gardens, Ivy was very taken with the geraniums, always one of her favourite plants, and she had spotted some which she had not got. Acting on instructions we all took cuttings and concealed them in Ivy's bag. But all was revealed when, on leaving, we were making a fuss of a small monkey. Unknown to us, it had a mate who was removing our ill-gotten gains and chewing them up! Fortunately we were not seen, and did not have to spend the remainder of the holiday languishing in a hot and stuffy gaol.

No house is exactly as one wants it, initially, but Trebah had great potential and with the help of a local builder, Joe Paget, we soon carried out various alterations to make it more to our liking, including the installation of the swimming pool. This we enclosed, to enable us to swim all the year round, and of course it was heated. The heating was a very big expense but we all got so much pleasure and, I believe, benefit from it. I was still travelling abroad frequently, and during my travels I acquired specimens of some of the more exotic tropical plants, all of which Jon nurtured and accommodated around the pool. It was great fun to pick bananas and oranges, and to admire the many colours of hibiscus which we cultivated.

Some months after we first moved to Trebah, we were approached by one of Britain's television companies, who were making a series of hour-long documentaries covering the lives of six Cornish families. We readily agreed to become involved, and the programme included visits to Warwick to feature Geoff and Bic at work, also a day at Silverstone whilst our people were testing one of the Le Mans cars. The cameraman had never been in a race car before, so the boys put him in with Andrew Hedges, who demonstrated to him that race cars were not designed to carry men with cine cameras. The opening sequence to the film was made up of shots of Ivy seated at the kitchen table and demonstrating how to make a true Cornish pasty; and after so many years she could certainly make a good one, and did so every Saturday. Despite her being 100 per cent Cornish, it was extraordinary the number of phone calls she received, criticizing either her method or the ingredients she used. Pasties do vary from region to region in the Duchy.

Bic has always been a keen fisherman, and he kept a dinghy at Trebah for use during his holidays. Of course the TV people wanted to film him with his three children arriving on the beach with a large catch. On this particular day the catch consisted only of some half-dozen bass, and the ensuing half-hour was spent reloading these fish into the boat, going 50 yards off-shore, beaching, unloading and repeating the exercise, until the viewers must have thought that it was impossible for such a small craft to carry such a weight of fish. We spent some time waterskiing in front of the cameras; and a visit to Perranporth ensured that sand-yachting, with my youngest son John at the helm of his craft, was not forgotten, either. John became very skilled in handling fast land-yachts, and was to become European Champion. All in all,

A summer's day on the Helford River — Ivy and me in Brian's boat, with some of the family. (*B. Healey*).

the programme went down very well; and whilst we still have the film in the family, the sound track, which was on tape, never came into our possession.

We spent many happy times at Trebah with the families, none happier than at Christmas when we were all gathered together. Ivy loved Christmas and spent weeks preparing for it. She was in complete control and the menfolk were allocated various tasks. The children, eight in total, were not allowed into the lounge on Christmas morning until the washing-up was finished and 'Granny Fuss', as they knew her, was ready to unlock the door and reveal the presents beneath the Christmas tree, which came from the garden. On one occasion we swam from the beach on Christmas Day, but it never became a habit.

The spring and summer were idyllic at Trebah with the abundance of colour in the garden and the peace and quiet of the beach. This had been used during the weeks before D-Day as a loading point for American Army landing craft with their tanks, jeeps, guns and stores. Lay-bys had been made at regular intervals along the narrow approach roads to these south-coast beaches, and there are many local people who vividly recall the incessant traffic during those days leading up to the invasion of Europe. The beach itself had been ruined by the laying of a nine-inch concrete pad over its entire surface. The pad resembled a gigantic chocolate bar in sections, and was a most uncomfortable thing to walk on. One plus-feature was the jetty, which had been built at the same time and proved invaluable for launching and as a ski take-off point. It seemed to me that whoever had been responsible for desecrating such a lovely beach should be held liable for restoring it to its former state, and I knew that grants had been paid to landowners who had suffered in the same manner. I made a claim to the War Department, and to my surprise was told that I was eligible for such a grant, as no application had been previously made. I engaged Joe Paget to carry out the work and he and his team broke up the concrete. When all this had been taken away, a mass of cut granite was revealed which had been used as hardcore. Joe suggested that he build a boathouse with the granite, which I readily agreed to, and he erected a very impressive building with teak doors, and over the lintel his brother in law, a granite mason, carved my initials, together with the date, in a section of polished granite.

Roger Menadue and I spent hours together in the coach-house which we had now fitted out as a workshop; and we in fact built the first of the three Rolls-Royce-engined prototypes there, as well as the running chassis for the prototype Jensen-Healey.

I had ventured into the radio manufacturing business in the early 1920s, and had retained an interest in both radio and television as they developed. Remote control television fascinated me and so I decided I would build a camera and instal it near the

Trebah: The house can be seen in the distance, up the valley to the left. The beach is being cleared of the vast concrete pad which had been laid by the US Army during the war and which was used for the loading of landing-craft prior to the invasion of Europe. (*B. Healey*).

beach, so that we would be able to see out around the trees to the mouth of the Helford River and watch the shipping from the comparative comfort of the sitting room. With the ingenuity and help of Roger I built a camera, which embodied four interchangeable lenses, which we could control from the armchair and traverse through virtually 360 degrees, all operated by remote control. The whole thing was housed in a 'Dalek'-type building of cedar wood, and it was amusing to see the expressions on people's faces when the top section started to rotate, accompanied by a whirring noise. The neighbouring farmer, Jim Gundry, took a keen interest in this camera and very often would come in and spend an hour viewing the beach and boating activity. I was very amused one day, when Jim was with me, watching our private 'box'. Knowing that his wife and daughter-in-law had gone down to the beach, I switched the camera on and panned it to reveal his wife enjoying her lunchtime pasty! He did not recognise the ladies initially but they turned — and that was enough for Jim. I would have loved to have been a fly on the wall in the Grundry kitchen later that day!

Ivy retained her keen interest in gardening, and was invited to become President of the Falmouth Spring Flower Show. This was an event which Trebah gardeners had entered for many years with considerable success, as the Trebah shrubs were always some days ahead of the opposition, thanks to the warmth and shelter of the valley. She drove a Cooper 1275S with considerable verve, and spent most of her time — whilst hurtling down the middle of the road — complaining about 'that fool' in the approaching car who had had to take avoiding action. Fred Ellis of Lockheed was developing an automatic gearbox for the Mini at that time, and I had what I thought was a bright idea. Why not take a 1300 Princess, which was a much more refined car than the Mini, and install a 1275S unit with one of Fred's gearboxes? Ivy would have a very much more comfortable car, with a performance not far short of her Cooper. Perhaps I should have consulted her, but I failed to, and when the car was ready, Warwick despatched it to Cornwall in the hands of one of the young salesmen, Roger Beard. Roger duly arrived at Trebah and was told in no uncertain manner that there was no way that Ivy was going to be seen in that 'old woman's car' and he may as well take it back. He did take it back, and we have had many a laugh over it since.

Electronic organs were then in their infancy, and I decided I would amuse myself by building one for family use, as I had a readily available 'test driver' in Ivy, who had played the wind-operated organ in Perranporth chapel in her younger days. On one of my visits to the States I made contact with the Schrober people who produced organs and who were very happy to let me have whatever components I needed to build my first prototype. I spent many happy hours with the soldering iron, and in time had assembled something which was worth installing in a cabinet, the first of which was made in Banbury and was built to my dimensions to accommodate the result of my labours. It worked! I was not happy with the noise reproduction and installed larger speakers, which helped, but by this time I was determined to produce a super organ with full keyboards, background instruments and sound production better than anything produced to date. The end result was a massive thing and I enrolled Joe Paget's son John, a very skilled cabinet-maker, who made me a unit which took up far too much space, but nevertheless had excellent sound production. I set myself a target to build two more, so that the boys could have one each. Having done that, I devoted my time to improving the sound of the television set by bypassing the tiny speakers and routeing the sound through a massive speaker, housed in a very large and attractive cabinet, again made by John Paget. I had never been blessed with an ear for music, and whilst I progressed to playing *Home Sweet Home* and *Rock of Ages* with two fingers, I quickly tired of organs, and looked for something else to do.

Lying in bed one night and having knocked the bedside clock on to the floor whilst trying to read the time, I had the idea of making a digital 24-hour clock which, by means of a series of angled mirrors, would project the time on to the ceiling. I had great fun designing this, and it worked. The first one had no means of turning it off when not required, but the next incorporated dimmer and on/off switches. I never pursued this idea any further; of course, today we all have bedside radios with built-in alarms and clocks.

As I have said earlier, Trebah beach was ideal for all forms of boating, and I bought a high-speed inflatable craft made by, of all people, Messerschmitt. It was a super little boat with a 'V' bottom with wooden floors, and served as an ideal water-ski tug. One amusing incident occurred when Wally and Ethel Hassan were spending the weekend with us and I offered Wally a ride in the boat. He jumped at it, and, Wally being of somewhat larger stature than myself, I had difficulty in trimming the craft. Eventually we set off at reasonably high speed and I started demonstrating the manoeuvrability of the unit. Whilst I was executing a full-throttle tight turn, the engine completed a 90-degree shift from vertical to horizontal — due, I must admit, to my failure to tighten the clamps fully. This in itself did not represent too great a problem, as all I had to do was switch off, so I thought, and relocate the motor. Unfortunately the propeller had penetrated the sponson and we found we were sinking fast. We were not far from the beach, and with the help of a paddle we managed to reach the shore without the necessity for Wally to swim, which I don't think he had ever done.

We kept several boats of various types at Trebah. Geoff had a very nice cruiser, fitted with a Coventry Victor engine, keeping it on the moorings in the River Fal as he had a holiday home in Truro. He arrived off Trebah beach one evening, having spent the day fishing off the Manacles, and decided to stop overnight. As is so typical of Cornwall, the wind veered to the south-east within hours, and got up to near gale force. Trebah was sheltered from every wind except the south-east, and before we could get a line to the *Manana*, she had been swept on to the rocks. Bic managed to salvage the engine next morning.

At that time Fairey Marine were building a range of hot-moulded plywood boats, including a clever little craft of about six feet in length, which split in two for ease of stowage. All one had to do was to clip the two halves together against a rubber seal. Bic bought one of these, and the grandchildren had great fun in the 'boat-in-two-halves', as they knew it, on the lake which had been formed when Joe Paget had built a boundary wall to the beach. We stocked this lake with trout, and this provided some fine fishing, although the heron probably caught more than we ever did! A pair of swans visited us every year at breeding time and raised cygnets, which the parents drove away as soon as they were big enough to fend for themselves. Bic was always changing his boats and he had at one time a typical Cornish fishing boat with a single-cylinder Kelvin diesel motor. Across the Helford River from Trebah the family had discovered weedy beaches which harboured masses of prawns. What fun they had catching them and bringing them back in buckets to the beach, where we cooked them in sea water. I have never tasted better.

One interesting story concerns the attempts by odd, and they must be odd, people to cross the Atlantic in the smallest possible boat. An American, Robert Manry, had set out from America in a 13ft 6in open boat in an attempt to beat the record, and we knew he was expected in Falmouth. Bic and the boys were out fishing one afternoon when he saw the Press fleet, which had gone out to meet Manry, just rounding the Lizard. He hurried back at maximum speed, seven knots, and collected Ivy and me from the beach, and off we went to meet this intrepid sailor. I had just returned from the States with the latest gimmick, a Polaroid camera, and Bic was able to get close enough to Manry and *Tinkerbelle*, as his craft was known, to take a photograph of him. On being handed the print, Manry was at a loss to understand how he could be presented with a photograph in mid-ocean. My grandson, Peter, has a copy of the original, which he got Manry to autograph 'on site'.

Trebah was a gem, and we spent ten very happy years there. The family spent their holidays with us and it really was a lovely place for children to grow up in, with its safe bathing and acres

of Cowboy-and-Indian country. The valley abounded with but-
terflies and moths of many different varieties, as well as grass
snakes and lizards. The boys caught some of the latter, and we
built a vivarium into which were placed both lizards and slow
worms (a type of legless lizard). At the end of the holiday these
were duly taken back to Leamington, where they survived for a
long time. The slow worms bred every year, and the young were
released into the wild — within the large conservatory which
housed the swimming pool. They too survived and in turn bred
quite happily

However, time passes and Ivy and I found that not only was
the walk down the valley and back becoming tiring, as the house
was some 200 feet above sea level, but the 26 acres had become
a worry. The flower market, which had previously paid for the
gardeners and much of the overheads, was becoming less profitable with the increases in rail charges, boxes and so on. It was a
little remote from John and Joy, who at that time were the only
members of the family living in Cornwall, and with Ivy's failing
health we thought it wise to move nearer to them. The decision
was made to sell Trebah, and we settled on a modern house at
Pill Creek within a mile of Truro.

Beggar's Roost, as we called it, was a complete contrast to the
other family homes which bore that name over the years. The
house was of split-level construction, with the sitting room upstairs, and enjoyed panoramic views over the creek and Carrick
Roads towards Falmouth. It faced south and we were able to enjoy
the sun, provided it shone, throughout the day. The bedrooms
were all downstairs and, as the sitting room above was built out
on cantilevers, there was an area below and directly in front of
the bedrooms which was simply crying out (in our view) for a
swimming pool. It was to prove very convenient having a heated
pool outside the bedroom door, and we used it daily throughout
the year.

Soon I was looking for something to do, and became very interested in windmills, which appeared to offer a cheap source of
power for the household. Utilizing high capacity alternators from
buses, I coupled these to a propeller-driven shaft and installed
the early prototype on a lattice mast of some 25 feet in height,
in the back garden. Results were encouraging, so much so that
I obtained planning permission to instal a tower on the wartime
airfield at Perranporth, where some wind was always available,
situated as it was on top of the cliffs facing the Atlantic Ocean.

Geoff did the detailed drawings and had various castings made
in the Midlands, which I had machined in Truro. Roger Menadue
had retired again, and I called on Bic to assist me as he, by this
time, had left the motor industry and was growing strawberries
commercially within one mile of our new home. We installed

173

another rig on a Mini Pickup, and I was able to obtain readings with Bic driving at pre-determined speeds up to around 50 mph, having established the actual wind speed before moving off. The results were quite startling at times. On one occasion we were charging down the runway, whilst I was studying the charge rate on the test panel, when there was an explosion and the battery (into which we were transferring the power being generated) disintegrated. This was located between my feet on the floor and, whilst we both got peppered with the contents of the battery, the only damage sustained was to my nylon socks, which fell to pieces.

We did consider going into production with a wind-driven generator for domestic use and in fact there was considerable interest. But strange as it may seem, even in Cornwall, one can never guarantee sufficient breeze to be of any value, especially on the small-diameter propeller which we were using. And whilst

In October 1971 Ivy and I gave a party to celebrate our 50th Wedding Anniversary. (*R. Roskrow*).

it was comparatively simple to generate power, the means of storing it was a problem, as numerous batteries would have been required and the Electricity Board were not prepared to allow the energy to be fed into the grid. I am confident I could have developed my ideas on wind power to a commercial stage, but I did not have the finance available to do so, and, on reflection, I know that my interest still lay primarily in cars and I hoped that one day I would see another Healey on the roads.*

Ivy's health, by now, was causing us all concern, and her breathing problems became more acute, necessitating a supply of oxygen alongside her bed. Despite this she retained her sense of humour, and never complained about her condition, all the time showing a determination to recover which put us all to shame. I must admit to being something of a hypochondriac, and when experiencing a slight pain imagine I am 'on the way out'. Mention it to Ivy, and she would tell me not to be so silly — the pain would disappear within minutes! Despite excellent care from the doctors, her attacks became more frequent and as John and Joy, and Bic and Mary were now living in Perranporth, they persuaded us to buy a bungalow within 30 yards of Bic and Mary, so that

1986: With my youngest great-grandson in the straight-eight Triumph Dolomite at Perranporth — 52 years after the proud day when I first took it down there. (B. Healey).

*Footnote by Brian Healey:* It is interesting to note current interest in alternative sources of power. In Cornwall we have the 'Hot Rocks' project which is being grant-aided by the Government; and as I write this (1988), it has just been announced that the Government is backing a scheme to build several large windmills in North Cornwall, to supply sufficient power to feed quite large communities. Such was the foresight of Donald Healey.

someone would be available at short notice. The latest in the line of Beggar's Roosts was very comfortable, and whilst I toyed with the idea of another pool, Ivy was no longer able to enjoy her morning swim, and it did not really seem worthwhile. I ventured down to the beach with Bic for an early morning dip occasionally, but I too, was not as strong as I had been and found that comparatively small Atlantic waves were knocking me down with comparative ease.

We had been married for 59 years when Ivy passed away in March of 1980. She had grown very fragile and seldom left the house, but she had lived to see the first of her great-grandchildren in the family, and that was truly a major event in her life. I could not have chosen a better wife, and mother to the children. I probably made many decisions and never thought to discuss them with her, but she never queried them and always supported me, even if she had doubts as to whether it was right or wrong. I would marry the same girl again.

*Footnote by Peter Garnier:* At this stage, and with so very little of the story yet to be written, Donald died on 15 January, 1988. What had been his autobiography, therefore, as told to me during the greater part of a year of pleasant, weekly visits to his home at Perranporth, becomes a biography. His second son, Brian (Bic) takes over.

# 14

## Victim of circumstances: the Jensen-Healey

By the time the Jensen-Healey came into being in 1972, the Jensen brothers — Richard and Alan — with their instinctive eye for elegance and line, had been producing striking coachwork and, later, building large, high-performance cars, for something like 45 years. Starting in the mid twenties, they had produced some very handsome sporting bodies for small chassis such as the Austin Seven, Morris Minor, Wolseley Hornet and Standard Nine.

In 1934 they had built the prototype of the first production car to bear the name Jensen, based on a Ford V8. After the war came a succession of large, high-performance Jensen cars, including the PW, 541, C-V8, Interceptor and, in 1972, the four-wheel-drive FF. They had also been using their spare capacity to produce bodies in large numbers for the Healey range, modifying the Sunbeam Alpine to take the bigger 4.2-litre Ford V8 engine (becoming the Sunbeam Tiger in the process), painting and trimming the Volvo P1800 coupé, and similar sub-contract work.

DMH had been a friend of the Jensen brothers long before their names became linked with the Austin-Healey and, subsequently, the short-lived but promising Jensen-Healey. The Healey company in Warwick and the Jensen company in West Bromwich both produced cars in limited numbers, and both used American engines, in the contemporary Interceptor and the Nash-Healey.

DMH had always had a great respect for the Jensen brothers, probably because, like himself, they were triers in a very competitive field, and had no illusions about featuring among Britain's large motor-manufacturing conglomerates. Dick and Alan were both quiet and unassuming and, strictly speaking, had no place in the rough-neck motor industry, but nevertheless they had found their niche and continued to build very worthwhile cars.

During the fifties, with capacity to spare and a very loyal and skilled work-force, they considered introducing a small sports car to their range. This did not materialize, however, and their connection with that type of car was confined to the Austin A40 Sports, which they produced as part of the Austin company's range. It had very limited appeal, unfortunately, as it was not sporting enough in appearance and had an unimpressive performance.

With the birth of the Austin-Healey 100, it was quite obvious that Healey, with their limited factory capacity, were never going to satisfy the demand; and Tickford of Newport Pagnell (now a part of Ford) who had previously built the majority of Healey hand-built bodies (including the prototype body for the Healey 100) similarly lacked space and capacity. Austin had been associated with Jensen for many years, and were currently providing six-cylinder engines for the Interceptor, and discussions had already taken place between the two companies concerning the introduction of a sports car using Austin components. Jensen did, in fact, produce a prototype, but — luckily for us — it did not appeal to the hierarchy at Austin as much as the Healey 100 did. Austin, however, were well aware of Jensen's reputation for quality, and that they had the spare capacity and skilled work-force to go into quantity-production with the bodies. Thus were forged the close links between West Bromwich, Longbridge and Warwick which were to continue for a further 20 years, until the demise of the Healey 3000.

In fact, Jensen produced a total of 71,000 Healey bodies — virtually all, that is, except for a short period when Austin decided that they could make them cheaper and better themselves (and proved themselves wrong!). The cars from West Bromwich were built to a very high standard — which was, of course, to be instrumental in ensuring that the name of Healey should continue, despite the axing of the Austin-Healey 3000 by Donald Stokes, through a link-up with the Jensen brothers.

DMH had met the Norwegian-born arch-salesman, Kjell Qvale, on numerous occasions in the States, as was to be expected since Kjell was selling more Healeys and MGs than any other importer, and DMH had arranged the MG dealership for him in the very early post-war days. The demise of the Austin-Healey 3000 had left Kjell looking for a replacement, so he suggested to DMH that Warwick should design something suitable, adding that he would buy Jensen and they would produce it. Donald returned from the States with his ideas for the new car already firmly taking shape. It should simply be a restyled 3000, he reckoned, without all the faults which it possessed (understandably, as it was nearly 30 years old) and complying in all respects with the severe US safety requirements.

At that time I was representing the company on the smaller car manufacturers' committee, as well as the Council of the Society of Motor Manufacturers and Traders. As a result, I had got to know many of the motor industry bosses, including David Hegland, a charming American who was currently in charge of Vauxhall Motors, the UK component of General Motors. Coincidentally, among the possible power units that my brother Geoffrey had considered for the new car was the Vauxhall 2.3-litre, which was produced in sufficiently large numbers to make the price attractive. DMH, too, was insisting that the car be based on volume-produced components, as in the Austin-Healey. For obvious reasons, we could not turn to British Leyland.

I telephoned Vauxhall at 8.30 one morning, and asked to be put through to David Hegland — and to my amazement, I was! I couldn't help comparing the endless hurdles one had to negotiate when trying to make contact with senior executives at Longbridge — to be told finally that, sorry, but Mr So-and-So was at a meeting. An appointment was made, and we duly presented ourselves at Vauxhall, to be received cordially by David Hegland, John Alden (Chief Engineer) and Wayne Cherry (Chief Stylist). Nothing was too much trouble, and my brother Geoff was introduced to the staff who would work with him, and who had been given instructions that he should be given every possible assistance. It was just like our days with the Austin company under Sir Leonard Lord, and we came away fully convinced that there was to be another Healey — that the name was to continue, using proven Vauxhall components and carrying a full General Motors warranty.

As things were to turn out, the power unit went up in price and down in power output when modified to comply with the American emission regulations. When eventually it did meet these requirements, the unit produced insufficient urge to make the car's performance attractive to world markets. Alternatives had to be sought, and we considered German Ford, BMW and others, but none could promise to meet the anticipated demand.

So far as the rest of the car was concerned, the early styling had been by Hugo Poole, who had worked with Chrysler, and was attractive. But, in the process of modification to accept the Vauxhall unit, the car had lost its squat, purposeful appearance, becoming almost narrow-gutted in looks. Qvale then decided to let Bill Towns have a go — he had previously styled cars for Rover and the Rootes Group, and the handsome-looking Aston Martin DBS. He came up with a design that was in no way distinguished-looking, but was probably the best that could be done within the restrictions imposed by the American crash regulations, which include stipulations on size and positioning of lamps, easily-replaceable body panels to reduce the cost of accident damage repairs in a country where labour costs are high, and several others.

The design team was headed by Kevin Beattie; another ex-Rover name, Gordon Holt, who had previously worked with Jensen, took over the coachwork side; Healey's chief chassis designer, Barrie Bilbie, became Chief Chassis Engineer; Brian Spice looked after the development work on bodies and chassis; and Howard Panton attended to the day-by-day design work. Everything, in fact, was covered except the major problem of finding a suitable engine, for which we needed an output of at least 130 b.h.p.

Kjell Qvale met Colin Chapman of Lotus in 1971 at a time when Lotus were due to introduce a completely new, 4-cylinder, 16-valve, 2-litre engine, built at their Hethel factory and, ironically, using the Vauxhall block — a slant-four Lotus engine design that almost coincided with Vauxhall's introduction of the slant-four Victor engine. Chapman offered this promising unit, which had a potential 240 b.h.p. in fuel-injected, race-tuned form, to Qvale for the new Healey. He quickly became convinced that this was the engine he had been looking for; the dimensions were almost the same as the Vauxhall's, and, clearly, it would put the car in a class of its own, with a scintillating performance. Qvale agreed to buy the Lotus engine — accepting it without a warranty, and completely lacking in development. This, coupled with the fact that Lotus proved to be unable to produce engines when promised, ensured that the Jensen-Healey, upon its debut at the 1972 Geneva Show, appealed to many potential buyers, few of whom could get one. Those early Jensen-Healeys were so disappointing that it was difficult to believe they came from the same factory as the Jensen Interceptor. Forgetting the engine problems, which were numerous, the car was badly finished, despite an expensive new paint plant; and the noise factor was far too high.

There was no excuse whatever for the noise level, and when I was approached by Peter Riley and Paddy Hopkirk with the suggestion that they make up one of their popular Interior Silent Travel kits for the car, I readily agreed, making one of our demonstration cars available to them. When the car was returned the improvement was immediately noticeable; and when I reported back to Peter Riley, he asked if he could offer the kit to Jensen-Healey dealers, quoting me by way of an introduction. Naturally, I had no objections. I had commented on numerous occasions to the factory about the noise-level inside the car, though they steadily refused to accept these criticisms. The IST kit was important to the general future of the car, and it was not expensive.

Within a matter of days I received a telephone call from a very irate Jensen Sales Director, accusing me of making irresponsible statements which could harm Jensen's good name. I remained unrepentant, though, and continued to fit IST kits to all the cars sold by us from Warwick. It is amusing to recall that the factory very quickly took steps to introduce much more efficient sound-deadening than they had been doing — possibly supplied by Peter Riley and Paddy Hopkirk!

We seemed to have built some sort of a jinx into those early cars. When showing a potential customer the car, I dreaded being asked to lower the soft top. The mechanism was completely unacceptable, and the customers let us know it. I could never understand why Kjell, who had insisted that the car must have an easily raised and lowered soft top, should ever have accepted such a finger-trapping contraption. He had, after all, purchased a Fiat 124 Spyder through our contacts at Fiat, because Kjell regarded it as the best soft-top entering the States at the time, and he wanted the one on the Jensen-Healey to be based on it. One can only assume that some pig-headed draughtsman — and there are a few of those about — decided that he was not going to copy some Italian design and that he could do better himself, given the chance.

Adding further impetus to our efforts to improve the car, DMH invited Bill Heynes, of Jaguar fame, to give us the benefit of his vast experience in the motor industry. Since he was retired, but was looking for ways of keeping his very active brain working fully, Bill was pleased to accept. He was of immense help to us, though it is doubtful whether Kjell Qvale ever appreciated just how much this respected veteran of the industry had to offer us. Sid Enever, for many years Chief Engineer of the MG Company, was also engaged on a consultancy basis, and his design for a 'gull-wing' Jensen-Healey reached an advanced stage, before the company eventually collapsed.

By mid-1973, when our high quality-standards were being more or less achieved and the supply of components was improving, production had increased to around 100 cars per week — but this was still a far cry from our intended target of 200-plus. At the same time, Jensen were producing between 25 and 30 Interceptors a week, taking roughly seven weeks per car, compared with ten days for a Jensen-Healey. Small wonder we felt like a poor relation!

The continuing inability to deliver cars helped neither the company finances nor its reputation, and the severe shortage of cars placed it almost in the joke category. The fault lay, in the main, with Lotus, who simply could not make engines available to us as and when required; nor, indeed, as promised in the initial discussions between Colin Chapman and Kjell Qvale. This shortage, coupled with the poor finish on cars that actually reached the customers, didn't exactly get us off to a flying start; and I could never hand over the keys to a car's proud owner with the same degree of confidence associated with an Austin-Healey. Worse still, even the range of standard colours did not flatter the car — when they could so easily have done. It appeared to us that somebody at Jensen had decreed that the standard of finish should be several stages inferior to that of the Interceptor. There was no excuse for dirt in the paint; and even less excusable was the attitude of those in charge of the Sales Department, who would not accept any criticism of the finish, dismissing it as unfair comment!

Next in our mounting list of troubles came the resignation of Jensen's excellent managing director, Alfred Vickers, who moved on to join Keith Duckworth and Mike Costin at Cosworth Engineering. Alfred had been a great asset to the company, brilliant in the fields of production engineering and quality control. He had guided the company through the successful Interceptor years, and the work-force had increased from not much more than 400 to almost 1,000 during his leadership. Kevin Beattie, who had been in charge of the Jensen-Healey team, was invited by Kjell Qvale to take over Alfred's chair — a move that at first seemed good for us, as he had our particular interests at heart. But it was a mantle for which he was not suited, and nor did he want it. Worse still, his health was failing and, sadly, he was to die soon after the demise of Jensen in 1976.

Against all these set-backs, however, the car was turning out

Looking prouder, perhaps, than I was actually feeling — with the Jensen-Healey line-up at West Bromwich. (*Birmingham Post and Mail*).

better than we had expected. The late Maurice Smith, then editor of *Autocar*, had written: 'It is everything a Healey and a British sports car should be, simple in concept, basic in construction, sporty in performance and nimble through curves. It felt like a future classic, the kind of car that one day will become a collectors' item.' Beattie's policy, under the guidance of his marketing man Richard Graves, was to increase his dealership progressively as car production increased, and, by mid-1973, the number had advanced from nine to 52. The marketing operation in the States was controlled by Qvale from his British Motor Car Distributors operation in San Francisco, where he also held the franchise for Rolls-Royce. By 1974, with most of the faults eliminated and production approaching 150 cars per week, things began to look a little brighter.

If the oil crisis had not come along in 1976, precipitating the collapse of Jensen, perhaps the car would have become a worthy successor to the Austin-Healey 3000; but both DMH and Geoffrey would have needed a freer hand in developing the car's obvious potential. The end result could have been a world-beater, like the 3000. The factory had a full order book when Jensen collapsed; but already, those at West Bromwich — with some exceptions — were paying no more than lip-service to the two men whose names were on the car, and the casual observer got the impression, not without reason, that they were no longer required.

In February 1971, a month before the announcement of the Jensen-Healey at the Geneva Show, Rolls-Royce had gone into receivership, rumours having been rife for some time. The intensely patriotic DMH, who at the time was Chairman of Jensen, immediately approached Qvale, who gave a Press conference at which he announced that he was prepared to buy Rolls-Royce in order to keep it in British hands. A tie-up between two of Britain's prestige car manufacturers would have strengthened the position of both companies in the competitive field that existed in those days — and Qvale was probably selling more Rolls-Royce cars in the States than anyone else. Both Sir Donald (later Lord) Stokes (of the nationalized British Leyland) and Aston Martin also announced publicly that they were interested in buying Rolls-Royce, but eventually all these overtures petered out when the company was taken over by the Vickers Group. Happily, the Rolls-Royce car division thrives today under the leadership of Sir David Plastow, who was Managing Director at Crewe at the time of the takeover.

Following his purchase of the Jensen Company, Qvale had issued shares to the Healey family with an assurance that, when the company went public, as planned, they would become wealthy people. It should be remembered in this context that Warwick had been given no option but to surrender a thriving BLMC franchise when Donald was Chairman of Jensen. There was no possible way that this franchise could have competed with the other Healey activities, but the sales directorate at Longbridge could not see it that way. Healey lost not only a thriving home market, but the US Base and 6th Fleet concession too, and quickly negotiated a franchise with Fiat, which compensated in part for the loss. As it transpired, however, Jensen never did go public, eventually going into receivership. The association with Qvale ended unhappily, in certain respects. It might be expected that DMH would have been extremely bitter over this let-down, but not a bit of it. He had had bigger knocks in the past and he was, above all, a fighter. He took it all very philosophically, and determined that he was going to get yet another car on to the road.

We ourselves had probably not been without blame for the failure of the Jensen-Healey. It had certainly been a mistake to allow ourselves to be so influenced by people brought up in the quality car tradition — people who gave the impression at times that they regarded the Healey as an interloper into their hitherto exclusive market, where the majority of customers were household names. Certainly those 'names' had the wherewithal to pay for the cars in the first instance. As we saw it, though, from then on these customers expected everything to be 'on the house', in return for the glamour which, rightly or wrongly, they reckoned brought credit and renown to the company. This was an attitude that we had never encountered in the Healey and Austin-Healey days. Warwick had had its fair share of celebrities, but they had been treated in precisely the same way as the owner who had made sacrifices over the years, scrimping and saving to buy his car. Kjell Qvale, as one of the world's most successful car salesmen, must surely have appreciated the folly of Jensen's philosophy; but, perhaps, by running the company from so many thousands of miles away, he enabled those at West Bromwich to get away with it. Possibly, too, having said on numerous occasions that he would never get involved in manufacturing motor cars, he was beginning to regret having done so.

Surely, though, he was not so naïve as to regard himself as the exception — a man who could make more money by manufacturing cars than by selling them!

So we come to the close of another chapter in the long life of DMH. The Jensen-Healey had promised so much; yet it proved to be a disappointment. It was probably a much better-looking car than we had suspected at the time; certainly, with its clean lines, many, many years will pass before it begins to look dated. Only the day before writing these words I saw one, Easter-visiting on our Cornish roads. So scarce are they nowadays that my first reactions were unfamiliarity and admiration — I wondered what this impressive stranger might be, until I saw the familiar badge!

# 15

# The final lap

With Jensen in the Receiver's hands, and DMH now back in his native Cornwall, he began to think in terms of another car bearing his name. By his standards, he was still a relatively young man — not much over 80 — and the thought of settling down to write his memoirs did not appeal.

Jensen had a very skilled and loyal work-force, and a factory in the heart of the Midlands, where the majority of Britain's cars are made. At the time of their demise, they had a full order-book, and it seemed clear to DMH that the best — and by far the quickest — way of getting production under way again would be to purchase the Jensen assets from the Receiver, with whom he entered into negotiations. It was provisionally agreed that these assets could be purchased, but that DMH would have to raise £1,500,000 to complete the deal.

At that time, the British government was pouring sums far in excess of this into the De Lorean fiasco in Northern Ireland, and, since DMH and his backers were British, it scarcely seemed beyond the realms of possibility that such a relatively small sum would be made available by the same source. But it was not to be. DMH paid a visit to the Department of Trade and Industry; he was received by two civil servants who — despite his very obviously advancing years — could not summon the energy to rise from their seats to welcome him, let alone shake his hand.

They told him that the money was not available. In the mean time, De Lorean continued to draw upon government funds almost ad lib — yet nobody had seen a car at that stage. This refusal came as a particularly bitter blow to my father, and one from which I don't believe he ever recovered.

He was an essentially patriotic man, and he never understood the thinking behind the decision — if, indeed, there ever had been any. Kjell Qvale purchased the Jensen assets from the Receiver, and formed another company. So that door was closed, and the fate of Jensen and Jensen-Healey was finally sealed by the man who had originally purchased the company to manufacture cars. It is somewhat ironic that the same premises are now used by a company which services and renovates Jensens, but whose main income must surely stem from the importing and distribution of

Subaru and Hyundai cars from Japan and Korea.

An approach was received from Canada, from a company interested in building a Healey in that country. The project was an exciting one, as the finished article could have been made available in the States with a minimum delivery charge. There is no doubt that this group had considerable funds available, but they would have had to seek further finance from the Canadian government to enable them to build prototypes, crash-test cars, and set up a production plant. DMH met the principals on a visit to Canada, and was satisfied that they could do the job. However, the government refused to finance the venture, as it was still smarting from the Bricklin disaster which had cost much taxpayers' money, with little in return by way of finished motor cars.

Kjell Qvale had not been entirely generous with the distribution of the Healey in the United States, making sure that his own sales outlets received the lion's share of the cars. In this he was probably doing what other people would have done in a similar situation, but it was not to the liking of other big distributors, who were still suffering from the demise of the 'Big' Healey. In order to keep their businesses working to a maximum benefit, a number had sought franchises in Japan; and one, who had become a close friend of DMH over the years, having been granted the distribution rights for a well known Japanese car, tried to persuade them to produce a sports car under the Healey name, in collaboration with DMH and Geoff. At that time, however, the factory in Japan was working to full capacity on its existing range, and did not wish to consider a sports car.

As can be deduced from this, the Healey name still meant something, and was synonymous with a good sports car. DMH remained confident, despite the many setbacks, that one of these approaches would come to fruition. Particularly encouraging was the fact that he was not having to do all the running, and was actually being courted by those who were anxious to become involved in sports car manufacture and to be linked with a worldwide name. A Ford distributor in the UK with factory space, and, he claimed, the finance for such a project, telephoned DMH frequently for a period, but suddenly went quiet and was heard of no more. It would be interesting to learn just why he had a change of heart so suddenly, as he claimed that he had negotiated with the Ford Company for the supply of power units and other requisite components.

As can be imagined, DMH was encouraged by these approaches, although, on reflection, I think that among the genuine people there was a fair proportion of enthusiasts who wanted to get into sports cars but who did not appreciate what was involved in the way of expertise and finance.

Of recent years we have seen replicas, lookalikes and reproductions of the classic Healey line, but none have captured that purity of line which Gerry Coker and DMH achieved in the first Austin Healey. In fact I think it would be fair to say that the later 100/6 and 3000 never compared in sheer good looks with the earlier 100. Several approaches were made by small manufacturers who wished to use the Healey name and had produced a well finished product, but DMH never agreed to place his name on any of these, although the financial reward was often worthy of consideration. He was never a man to look back, and I have featured a Gerry Coker design for a Healey which never saw the light of day but nevertheless was his ultimate aim. He hated flared wheel-arches — they were for race cars with oversized tyres — and never really cared for anything too effeminate in a man's car, such as 'tarty trim'. I recall drawing his attention to a very well produced looka-like at one of the Austin Healey Club's International Weekends, but he dismissed it as a non-starter, and a step backwards. He was very impressed with a Sprite 'Frogeye' reproduction, which with the passage of time was probably a far better car than the original, but he could not bring himself to accept in as one of his creations, and can one really argue with that opinion? One must remember that DMH never forgave British Leyland for their shabby treatment of both himself and John Cooper, and I do not think that he would ever have considered the use of any Leyland components in any of the cars bearing his name. He never said so, but I am sure that he felt very flattered to think that someone regarded one of his cars in such high esteem that they wished to reproduce it. But the one thing that stood head and shoulders above all of these was his burning ambition to produce another Healey, and its success or failure would have been entirely down to his assessment of the market, and he was a pretty good judge of this.

Gerry Coker's suggestion for the Healey. He produced this at DMH's request in 1986, and it certainly was more attractive than other sports cars on the market at that time.

In 1976, DMH visited Australia for the first time in his long career, as a guest of the Austin-Healey Club of Australia, where he entered into discussion with the British Leyland subsidiary. Between them they progressed a long way towards producing a Healey using an Australian engine. The car would have been manufactured in Australia, and shipped to overseas markets, in some instances in knocked-down form for assembly in the country of final destination. The Australian company was making money, unlike its UK parent at that time; and it had the capital necessary to finance the project. Had the UK company been operating on a more profitable footing, there is little doubt that we would have seen, not an Austin-Healey, but possibly an 'Aussie Healey'. As it transpired, the BL hierarchy in the UK called in funds from the overseas companies, including Australia, and so this very promising plan came to nought.

Possibly the most exciting of all the attempts to get another Healey on the road arose when DMH talked initially to John Edwards, son of one of his oldest friends, Courtenay Edwards, and currently Press and Public relations Officer of SAAB in Britain. SAAB were developing their 9000 range, which included a turbo-charged engine, and DMH felt that this was going to be the type of power unit which would be used in the future by the majority of performance-car manufacturers. John advised his people in Sweden of this interest, and Eric Carlsson, their new projects manager, came to London to attend the first of a series of meetings which were arranged. SAAB were as enthusiastic as DMH over the possibility of a link-up with the two names, and he in turn visited Sweden. I recall his returning to the UK and eulogizing over reindeer meat, which the Swedes eat as we British eat beef. To quote John Edwards 'The project failed to get off the ground because SAAB's engineers were too heavily committed in developing the 9000 range, with its turbocharged engine, and they simply had not the time to do justice to the Healey idea.' SAAB had estimated that to produce a mock-up would have cost $150,000 — and that would have been a long way from a running prototype and pre-production cars, which would have cost far in excess of that figure. The front-wheel-drive configuration would have presented some problems in obtaining a satisfactory bonnet line, but both sides were confident that this could be resolved. A SAAB-Healey would have been an attractive offering to the SAAB dealers in the United States. The saloon sells predominantly on the east coast, where the front-wheel-drive proves invaluable in their severe winters; and a sports car would have pioneered the large market which exists on the west coast, in which SAAB was comparatively little known. To quote John Edwards again: 'The Healey project was abandoned purely as a result of timing, coming as it did when the comparatively small company's resources were fully stretched.'

DMH and Geoff had spent a lot of time scheming and talking with SAAB, and I think this project probably came nearer to reaching fruition than any of the others. DMH purchased the SAAB Press-demonstrator turbo-car for his own use and evaluation purposes, and this was in all probability the last car he drove, for his sight was failing and he was conscious of the fact that his reactions were not as sharp as they had been. Very sensibly he decided that he would drive no more. He became a passenger — and not a 'back seat driver', as at no time did I hear him criticize any of the family, even when we happened to be in a 'press-on' mood. My mother had always been proud of the fact that she had taught Geoff, John and myself to drive.

In the autumn of 1985, Tony Merrick brought the rebuilt Triumph Dolomite down to Perranporth, and we had photographs taken of DMH sitting in the car in exactly the same spot where he had been photographed in the same car 50 years earlier. Needless to say, the sight of this brought memories flooding back, and it would not have taken much to persuade him to take the car over all the old, familiar testing routes of those far-off rally days. It gave him further food for thought, and for weeks following Tony's visit he repeated to me what a fine motor car it was. Although he had designed, built and driven a very wide range of cars over the ensuing years, the Dolomite, was, I think, his all-time favourite — but why, I will never understand! It was a very good-looking car, and it had performance and provided the thrill of real open air motoring; but it could not be compared with the Austin-Healey for comfort, ride, roadholding or weather protection — and the Austin-Healey did not always score maximum marks on any of these fea-

Back in 1935, the functional and beautifully-poised straight-eight, super-charged Triumph Dolomite cost slightly over £1,200. Fifty-two years later, this superb Tony Merrick restoration was sold at Sotheby's for £150,000, after ownership by Tony Rolt, and then a long and chequered career as an 'HSM' after a spell with Robert Arbuthnot and his High Speed Motors. (*Sotheby's*).

tures! In all probability the Dolomite was the car which most reminded him of his successful competition career, and in those days it would have excelled on all those points which we have come to expect as commonplace and without which a car would not today be accepted.

How much he would have loved to have shared that car with others, and we subsequently spent hours talking of the possibility of producing replicas so that the experience of driving such a machine could be enjoyed by those, in his opinion, deprived people! I am afraid that by this time I was not really keen to get back into the motor business, and Geoff was nearing 65 and due to retire from his post as development engineer with Austin Rover. The main reason for our lack of enthusiasm was, I think, that we both knew that the 'Old Man' (as Geoff and I always referred to him between ourselves) was simply not physically strong enough to re-enter the tough world in which he had spent so many years. Age-wise, I think that Geoff and I are normal people, and accept that normal people do not start motor manufacturing in their later years. The problem was that DMH was not one of these normal people, and at times I am sure he regarded us both as old men and himself as the younger one. He would never have been prepared to sit back in a purely consultative capacity and would have been happy only if he was the man in charge.

The question has often been asked as to what DMH would have done if Austin had not entered into the agreement whereby they manufactured the Austin-Healey, following its introduction at the 1952 Motor Show. The car was without question the star of that show, and indeed of subsequent shows in other countries, and its success was assured. The answer is that DMH and his small team would have gone back to Warwick and produced the car in limited numbers, since that was the business they understood and enjoyed. Not many miles down the road, Peter Morgan and his equally small team of enthusiasts were, and still are, producing cars at the rate of eight per week, and boast the longest waiting list in the world. I cannot imagine that DMH would have been happy doing this for long, however. He loved the competition side of the industry, and was happiest when attending or driving in some race or rally somewhere in the world. He also grew attached to the social side of motor sport, and had built up many close and lasting friendships in that field. There was no way that seven or eight cars a week could have supported a competition programme for any length of time. Nor would he have had to travel the world to sell that number — yet travel was something else that he enjoyed. The link-up with Austin had provided him with the opportunity for extensive travel, and Austin had valued his knowledge and personality. They had encouraged him to roam the world as an ambassador, not only for the Austin-Healey but

1973: Donald Healey with Ivy, Geoff and Brian at Buckingham Palace, after being presented with the CBE. (*B. Healey*).

for Austin products too. His almost boyish enthusiasm and his charm endeared him to almost everybody he met, and he must surely rank as one of the most successful salesmen and public relations officers the British motor industry has produced. His reward came in 1973, when he was made a Commander of the Order of the British Empire by Her Majesty Queen Elizabeth at Buckingham Palace — a ceremony which my mother, Geoffrey and I attended.

Whilst he was never a rebel, DMH had little time for committees, and never took any part in the activities of the Society of Motor Manufacturers and Traders, preferring to leave this side of the job to me. Though Austin were actually producing the Austin Healey, my father's company — the Donald Healey Motor Company — was a member of the SMMT, the governing body of the motor industry and organizers of the then Earls Court Motor Show. As such, DMH was entitled to attend meetings of this body, with the chance of being elected president, but this did not appeal to him.

191

# Donald Healey

The Mayor of Warwick offers his congratulations on the CBE, in the grounds of Warwick Castle. The tower in the background is the one which is featured in the original Healey badge. (*Warwick Photo Agency*).

Strictly speaking, since the Donald Healey Motor Company was no longer in the business of manufacturing cars, it was not entitled to a stand of its own at Earls Court — the Austin-Healey exhibits should have shared a stand with Austin. But Austin was a large and powerful company; not even the SMMT was prepared to stand its ground and tell them what cars they could display where. In some odd way, they seemed almost out of touch with some of the industry's affairs. At one show, I mentioned casually to one of their senior executives that father must almost be due for recognition in the New Year's Honours List, only to be asked what he had done to deserve it!

As a Liveryman of the Worshipful Company of Coachmakers and Coach Harness Makers, DMH was a Freeman of the City of London — though, again, he took only a small part in the activities of this ancient and deeply respected body, whose origins go back to 1677. He was also a Friend of the Guild of Motoring Writers, an honour bestowed on a small and very select handful of people in the Motor Industry; he was intensely proud of this — as he was, too, of the medal presented to him by Prince Rainier III of Monaco in 1968 for his successful participation in so many Monte Carlo Rallies.

Politics were never of any great interest to him, although his father had been the Liberal Party agent in Perranporth many years before, when Cornwall returned no fewer than seven members to Parliament — every one a Liberal. I have heard him refer frequently to Margaret Thatcher as 'that woman', as he was a little chauvinistic about the fair sex being involved in what he regarded as a man's domain. But it was never unkindly. At the same time, he held her in extremely high esteem — although never freely admitting it. He had one brief encounter with the well known Labour politician Denis Healey, on a very friendly level. I had produced a sticker for our Le Mans car with the message 'I'm backing Healey' emblazoned over the Union Flag, along with a line-drawing of the car. Denis Healey at the time was Minister of Defence in the Wilson Government, and having seen these stickers he instructed one of his staff to call me at Warwick and ask if he could have some to help him in his election campaign. He expressed the opinion that they would improve his image and, he hoped, would not detract from ours! I believe he planned to use them on his Ford Zephyr, which presumably was his personal transport at the time. We duly sent him some and had a very nice letter of thanks from the man himself.

It was some time later that their paths crossed once again: DMH received an invitation to address a meeting in the United States

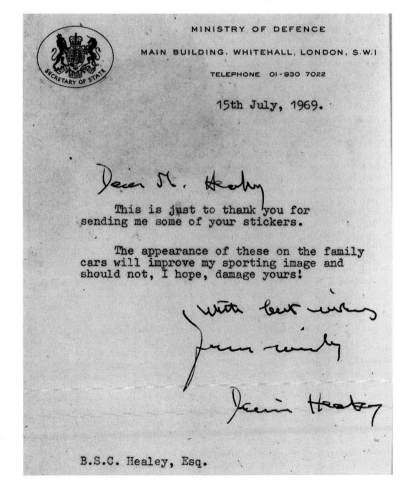

MINISTRY OF DEFENCE

MAIN BUILDING, WHITEHALL, LONDON, S.W.1

TELEPHONE 01-930 7022

15th July, 1969.

Dear Mr. Healey,

    This is just to thank you for sending me some of your stickers.

    The appearance of these on the family cars will improve my sporting image and should not, I hope, damage yours!

With best wishes

yours sincerely

Denis Healey

B.S.C. Healey, Esq.

Denis Healey, then Defence Minister, asked Brian for some of our windscreen stickers — which were duly sent to him. (*B. Healey*).

on the state of the British economy, which he could not understand, as the country's finances were not one of his strongest points! Whilst still pondering over what he should say if, in fact, he decided to accept the invitation, he had a call from Denis Healey to say that he had received an invitation to address a meeting, also in the United States, on the development of the sports car for the American market!

One thing of which DMH was extremely proud was his Cornish ancestry, and whilst he joked about our weather, Cornwall was always home to him. In fact when he returned to his home county after many years in the Midlands, my mother and he were only doing what all Cornish exiles hope to do at the end of their working lives, no matter where in the world their jobs have taken them. In 1955 Cornwall reached the final of the Rugby Union County Championship; their adversaries on the day were Warwickshire and the game was played at Coventry. The home team had the advantage of playing in front of their own crowd, although the Cornish supporters far outnumbered them; and it snowed on the day, giving them a double advantage. We lost by a narrow margin, but the team acquitted themselves admirably. They had been staying near Warwick, and on the day preceding the game DMH hosted them to a magnificent lunch at the Saxon Mill.

Another example of his generosity was when he received a request from the Perranporth Surf Life-Saving Club in 1960 for help in locating a Jeep for use on the beach. He did just that. Having got a member of his staff to find and purchase one, he presented it to the Club painted in the Club colours.

When my brothers and I were boys, father played a little golf, but apart from that he was never actively engaged in any sport, cars occupying the majority of his time. One amusing incident occurred during the early part of the war. DMH had acquired a shotgun with which to shoot rabbits on a friend's farm near Kenilworth, as these provided a welcome meal during the time of severe meat rationing. It was my turn for instruction in the use of firearms, and we were creeping quietly up the side of a hedge when he lifted the gun to his shoulder and blasted off. 'That's how it's done, boy;' he said, and sure enough he had bagged a rabbit. I thrust my arm into the hedge to get hold of the rabbit, but it would not come out. On further investigation it was revealed that the rabbit was already in a snare and presented a sitting target. He never went rabbit shooting again!

For the last six years of his life DMH lived in Perranporth with my brother John and his wife Joy. They had built an annexe on to their house when their children were young, and as they in turn got married and left home, so this became redundant. It proved ideal for DMH as he was getting less mobile, and John and Joy were handy if ever he needed them in the night, which

1960: With the junior members of the Perranporth Surf Life-saving Club, after the presentation of a Jeep to the club. (*B. Healey*).

he frequently did towards the end. He visited Mary and me every Sunday, as we lived within walking distance, but following his last visit to the States, in 1986, even this became too much for him, so we collected him and he would spend the day with us.

The walk to our cottage is along the side of the disused railway bank in Perranporth, and after the closure of the railway, it became very overgrown and the sycamore trees grew without fear of inter-ference. DMH arrived one Sunday in time for his usual gin-and-tonic, and said that he had been giving a lot of thought to the railway embankment. It seemed, he felt, that it would be a pity if such a pleasant stretch should fall into the hands of developers. Why did we not start a fund to buy this and turn it into a walk for those who enjoyed the peace and quiet which it offered? We formed the Perranzabuloe Preservation Society and called a pub-lic meeting. The response of the residents of Perranporth was encouraging, although the asking price of £8,000 was daunting, to say the least. But raise the money we did, through donations ranging from £5 to £1,000, the latter figure coming from the Dis-trict and Parish Councils.

I wrote a letter to Prince Charles, Duke of Cornwall, and he responded with a sizeable cheque, as did Winston Graham, author of the *Poldark* books, and a past resident of Perranporth. Having completed the purchase, we handed the land over to the Perran-porth Gardens Trustees, who agreed to maintain it on behalf of the villagers. The rails had long since been lifted and the stretch along which they ran has been cleared and now makes a very

195

pleasant raised walk with some lovely views across the village. The area has been named the 'Donald Healey Walk' as a tribute to one of Perranporth's more famous sons; and, in fact, it over-looks Woodbine Cottage, where he was born 90 years ago. It is the intention of the Parish Council to erect a memorial seat on the site, so that Perranporth will remember him.

DMH never returned to America following his visit in 1986 when he attended Austin-Healey Club meets both in the Southern states and in Canada. He suffered a heart attack whilst staying with the Schultz family in California, on getting out of the swimming pool. He told his friends in America that the family was not to know, but when I met him off the train at Truro it was obvious to me that he had suffered a major setback in his health, and he then told me what had happened. From that time on his health deteriorated, and life became increasingly more frustrating for him, as he could no longer walk more than a few yards; and crippling arthritis in his hands barred him from playing with his soldering iron and electronics. He became very dependent on the telephone, and enjoyed calls from friends all over the world, who hoped that he would visit them again. I was driving him home one Sunday evening, only a matter of weeks before he was to enter hospital for the last time, when he said to me 'I think I can manage one final trip to the States, boy, and perhaps you should come with me to keep an eye on me. We will go to Texas first' — and then followed the itinerary which he had worked out. It involved travelling thousands of miles — which would have worn me out, let alone him! 'We will not go to Texas', I said, 'it will be too hot for you. We will go to a more central point and I am sure that all your friends will travel to see you' — and I know that they would have gladly done so. I knew that this trip was not to be, but he derived so much fun from working out his itinerary that I would have been the last to discourage him. But I would certainly have taken him if the doctors had permitted it.

Many friends visited him in Perranporth, but Cornwall is a little remote from the Midlands, where the majority of them lived — and he had outlived the majority of those. Duncan Hamilton and his wife called one afternoon and they talked for hours about the Le Mans days, where Duncan had driven the Nash-Healey. He had visitors from Australia, from the United States and Germany, but his most consistent was Roger Menadue, who called every week. If he was well enough, Roger would take him out for a drive and a pub lunch, which he always enjoyed. Roger was a great comfort to him and they spent so many hours talking about the 50 years they had worked together.

Shortly before Christmas 1987, the doctors advised the family that cancer, which he had overcome following an earlier operation, had recurred and there was little that could be done for

DMH. It became clear to us all that he was not going to achieve his cherished target — his 90th birthday. The specialist who was attending him said that an operation in Plymouth might prolong his life by a matter of months; but, being DMH, he thought this did not apply to him and that he would again be cured. By this time he was so weak and requiring constant nursing care that we placed him in the Duchy Hospital in Truro, where everyone was so kind to him.

At 10.15 on the morning of 15 January Mary and I walked through the doors of the Duchy to be met by the Matron, who asked us to wait for a few minutes. We both knew that it was the end and so it proved to be. By a strange coincidence, 250 miles away in Warwick, at 10.15, the bulldozers moved in and started to demolish the old cinema which had been the home of the Donald Healey Motor Company for several years.

Gethin Bradley of Good Relations arranged to let the Press and media know that one of the 'grand old men of motoring' had died, and very soon the family were receiving letters and telephone cables from all around the world.

The tributes came in from far and wide, and I would like to quote extracts from just two letters written in tribute to a man who was a true friend to everyone who met him. Mike Dale joined us at Warwick as a very young man, and on his first day with us managed to 'bend' an Austin-Healey. That was 33 years ago and today Mike is a Vice-President in charge of sales with Jaguar North America. He wrote to DMH on 28 December 1987, and said, in referring to those days at Warwick: 'It was a time of heroes and giants in the auto industry and it was incredibly exciting to be employed by one of them... I don't know if I ever formally said thank you for giving me my first chance in life, if I haven't please accept this letter as a very big thank you... You have accomplished so much and are loved by so many people. I wanted you to know I was one of them.'

The second letter was from Ted Worswick, a great sportsman and a superb driver. He wrote: 'Over his remarkable life DMH had given pleasure to so many people, and provided them with the opportunity to go motor racing, or enjoy the open air in a fun car of his creation, which was above all affordable.'

On reflection I think Ted probably expresses in a few words exactly what DMH set out to do when creating the first car to bear his name. He always enjoyed what he did and those of us who were fortunate enough to be associated with him enjoyed those exciting times just as much.

Tributes and messages of sympathy continued to arrive from around the world for weeks after DMH had died, and the family was approached by the Austin-Healey Club in Britain who wished to arrange a memorial service in Warwick. The idea was to include a parade of cars bearing his name immediately following the service, as it was felt that DMH would have enjoyed such an occasion, and the town of Warwick was keen to be associated with it. Some members of the family felt that a memorial service was not necessary, and the idea was abandoned, although many club members who had been unable to attend the funeral service in Cornwall and who would have liked to pay their last respects were very disappointed.

The Austin-Healey Club has always been closely involved in club circuit racing, a form of motor sport which has provided so much entertainment over the years to those who find formula racing something of a bore and too professional. Several members got together and decided that a fitting tribute to DMH would be a race meeting — preferably at Silverstone, although this very popular circuit, apart form being expensive for a one-marque club, has a full calendar throughout the season. The newly-formed Jaguar Car Club had booked the circuit for 17 September 1988, and thanks to Richard Hassan, a member of the committee and son of Wally Hassan, a great friend of the Healey family, the Austin-Healey Club was invited to arrange two races and to share the programme. So came about the Donald Healey Memorial races for Sprites and Big Healeys.

Another attraction was to be a parade of Healey cars around the Club circuit in between races. This was to be limited to 100 cars and Tony Elshof, the jovial giant of a competition secretary, had even found a 4½-litre low-chassis Invicta to lead the parade, and my brother John and I together with my wife Mary had the doubtful pleasure of riding in this.

After as little as half a lap on the billiard table surface of Silverstone one begins to appreciate just how tough DMH and his crew must have been when they drove such a monster thousands of miles through snow and ice to win the Monte Carlo Rally in 1931. No heater, no headroom, lorry steering and clutch and a very harsh ride all add up to one very sound reason for assuming that those people must have been crazy! We set off very sedately as befits such an elegant old lady, but it was not long before we were being overtaken on both sides by Silverstones, Sprites, 3000s (both modified and in concours condition), and a whole host of Healeys of every conceivable type. What a wonderful turn-out that was, and how DMH would have loved it. Far from a limit of 100 cars it soon became obvious that everyone wished to join in and a conservative estimate put the number of cars on the circuit at one time at over 180! Our 'chauffeur', not to be outdone, did allow the Invicta to 'burble' up to 70-plus and it really was quite enjoyable, but in small doses only!

The British Racing Drivers Club, of which DMH was a member for so many years, allowed the Club the privilege of using its hospitality suite. A superb lunch was enjoyed by a small number of DMH's close friends and the family, and quite understandably the bar facilities were put to good use throughout the day.

Across the Atlantic in America, which DMH often regarded as his second home, the clubs were also making arrangements to commemorate the life of someone who had so actively participated in their meetings and 'conclaves', as they are known in that part of the world. Some close friends in Los Angeles made arrangements for the planting of a number of trees in Israel, and the Austin-Healey clubs in the United States set up a fund to purchase a grove in the Redwood area of California. The money has been raised and the Memorial Grove will be dedicated on 3 July 1989 — which would have been DMH's 91st birthday.

Back home in Perranporth, the Parish Council, as I said in a previous chapter, is erecting a seat in memory of one of its best-known sons, who left Cornwall to become an apprentice to the aircraft industry, who subsequently flew with the Royal Flying Corps during the 1914-18 world war, and following the Second World War set up his own company to manufacture the type of car which he felt the public wanted. Oddly enough in so doing he became one of the few people since that war to build a car which carried the name of the man behind it, and it took a lot of talking to persuade him to do that!

A line-up of Healeys at Old Warden Airfield, Biggleswade, before the 1988 International Healey Week End — at the home of the famous Shuttleworth Collection of historic aircraft. (*B. Healey*).

International Healey weekend at the National Motor Museum, Beaulieu, with Geoff (left) and Brian. (*F. Naylor*).

On the weekend of 23 July 1988, it was the turn of the Eastern Centre of the Austin-Healey Club in Britain to organize the International Healey Weekend meet. On this occasion it was held at Warden Airfield in Bedfordshire, home of the Shuttleworth Collection. This is a small collection of early aircraft, and how DMH would have loved it, as he had flown many of those machines as a young man all those years ago. His eight grandchildren presented the Club with one of DMH's valued desk fittings, to be awarded annually to the Healey Clubman of the year. The first recipient was Carolyn Waters, General Secretary of the Club and a dear friend to DMH.

DMH would never accept that he was in any way an unusual person — either in his World War 1 flying record, which appears now to be almost unique, or in his long years of motoring. He could never accept that his life-story would be of interest to anyone, or that a publisher could be found to take it on. But between us, back in late 1983, Peter Garnier and I persuaded him to collaborate with Peter in writing it. Insisting that it was autobiographical, he reluctantly allowed Peter to coax more than 50,000 words from him — before he reverted to his original, modest opinions, and decided to call it a day.

It was not until two or three years later, when he was in hospital for the last time, that he asked me to get hold of Peter and persuade him to work with me in finishing the book. By a strange coincidence, Peter was in the same hospital, having a hip replacement. I popped into his room on the evening before DMH died, to find him depressed at being unable to get out of bed and visit his old friend. We discussed the book briefly and I told Peter of Father's new-found enthusiasm to get the job finished. At first he offered to give me what he had already written, suggesting I might care to finish it myself — but eventually we agreed to work together upon what little remained to be done. And so, for Peter, began a further series of visits from his home in Newlyn to mine in Perranporth — a series that had started with more than 30 to interview DMH.

Only because we have been obliged to change from autobiography to biography in these final pages, has it been possible to express an opinion of DMH and his achievements. As his son, I may be open to accusations of having overdone it; I have tried not to.

It seemed appropriate, and what Donald himself would have wanted... Brian (at the wheel) and Geoff lead the cortege on the way to the little Methodist chapel at Perranporth in January 1988. Nick Howell's ex-works rally car was also in the funeral procession. (*B. Healey*).

# Endpiece:
# family background

A family prayer book which has been handed down through the years, and was in fact printed in 1766, records in the fly leaf that Henry Healey was born in 1747 and was a resident of Bath in Somerset. Somewhere in the distant past there was an Irish connection, because I recall my grandfather telling me that his grandfather, presumably on the maternal side, was an admiral in the Royal Navy and hailed from County Cork, with the name of Hood. Not many people can claim to have had a battleship named after them!

The Healey family must have found Bath to their liking as they were still there when Edward, who was born in 1825, married and started a family. Edward was a manufacturer of bird cages, but a successful one nevertheless. He named one of his four sons John Frederick and there were two daughters, Sarah and Jane. John Frederick was not very keen on making bird cages for a living and elected to work as a representative covering the West Country for a firm of paper bag manufacturers. One of his regular calls was on Sampson Mitchell, or 'Samp' as he was known, who was the local baker and grocer in a small village, Perranporth, on the north coast of Cornwall. From reports, Samp was a bit of a tyrant, strictly teetotal, the Parish records dated 18 February 1918 stating that 'Mr Sampson Mitchell protested against grain, the people's food, being converted into alcoholic liquor.' Everyone to his own opinion!

Samp was involved in the rocket apparatus which had been invented by a Mr. Henry Trengrouse from 'down west', as the Cornish say, and which consisted of a large rocket to which was attached a stout line. The unit was mobile, being drawn by a team of horses, enabling the crew to get as near as possible to any ship which might get into trouble in winter gales on the notorious open bay of Perranporth. In those early days it was not unusual for a sailing ship to lose its sails in a storm and, if the wind was on-shore, no anchor would hold it once it got into the heavy surf off Perranporth beach. Once aground, the ship would quickly break up and the crew would not be able to swim in such conditions.

The rocket crew would take up station and, on a given signal from the officer in charge, would fire the rocket in the general direction of the stricken vessel after making allowances for the wind. The line, which was very stout and of great length, would straddle the ship; the crew would secure it, and a breeches-buoy would then be hauled out to the ship by a secondary and heavier line. One by one the crew would sit in the 'breeches' and be pulled ashore. This must have been a pretty frightening experience as they would have been thoroughly soaked and freezing cold by the time they reached the beach and safety, but the alternative would have been certain death if they had elected to remain on board and let the ship break up around them. Samp was given a medal by the Board of Trade, who were the governing body in those days, for his long service to the rocket life-saving apparatus. This award was made in 1911, and a very proud man he must have been. I still have it amongst my family heirlooms.

Sampson Mitchell, as well as being the local provision merchant, was a farmer and he was still tending his cattle at 96 years of age. His wife, known by us all as Granny Mitchell, was wonderful at needlework and tapestries, and I can vividly recall her when she was over 90 sewing most intricate works without spectacles, and with the poor light which was available in those days. I have one of her tapestries, of Anne Hathaway's cottage, and whilst it has faded over the years the quality of the workmanship is superb.

The Mitchells had one daughter, Emmie, a very attractive young lady, and John Frederick Healey — J.F. as he became known in the village — courted her and won her hand in marriage. He gave up his job and joined father-in-law in the business in Perranporth. He showed a natural flair for the grocery trade, and with his impeccable manners and dapper dress he quickly became a favourite with the customers. One little detail in his dress, which I readily recall and which one no longer sees, were his spats, which he was never without, and with his polished brogue shoes and well-pressed suit he would have been acceptable anywhere. I am sure that my father must have inherited his flair for 'always looking the part' from J.F.

Sampson Mitchell eventually handed over the business to Emmie and J.F. and devoted the remainder of his long and very full life to his farming interests. J.F. built an entirely new store, using the lovely cut stone from the Wheal Leisure mine engine house which had been demolished; he named it Red House after the famous store in Bath.

The Red House developed into a general store selling groceries, confectionery, clothing and shoes and boasted two floors, the upper one being approached by a magnificent, wide staircase. The smell of freshly ground coffee remains vividly in memory, as does the bacon machine from which was served bacon to the thickness madam required. Chairs were on hand for the ladies whilst placing their orders, and the Red House quickly became *the* place to assemble and to gossip, for anyone that mattered. The canopy with its stained glass which fronted the shop provided all-weather cover, and J.F. ensured that the shop-front exhibited his wares for all to see. Fresh bread and cakes were delivered daily by motor cycle and sidecar, and at one time J.F. and Emmie were employing seven members of the Keast family in the bakehouse as delivery boys, and Bobbie the father as foreman in the building business which he was developing.

At the time of J.F.'s arrival on the scene, Perranporth was a very quiet coastal village with little industry apart from the four pilchard seining companies, which virtually ceased trading when for some inexplicable reason the pilchard changed its migratory route and deserted the coast of Cornwall entirely. The men who operated the seine boats — all pulled by oars, incidentally — were tin and copper miners who supplemented their income by catching the fish and salting them down in hogsheads in which they would keep through the winter and provide regular meals for the poorer families. At that time, 1885, the population of Perranporth had dwindled in 10 years from 3,600 to 2,400 and this was due mainly to the decline of the mining industry, following the emergence of such remote countries as Malaya as suppliers of tin from vast alluvial deposits and cheap labour. The second contributory factor was the free emigration offered at the time to the skilled hard-rock miners of Cornwall.

These men, and their families, sailed to the United States, South Africa, Australia — in fact, to any country where their skills and ability to work hard and under all conditions guaranteed them a good living. Many never returned home, but they prospered; and Cornish communities exist to this day in various parts of the globe. I was fortunate enough to be invited two years ago to the annual rally of the Victoria Austin-Healey Club in Australia, held in Ballarat where there is an excellent reconstruction of an old mining community known as Sovereign Hill. Whilst being led on a conducted tour through the old mine workings, I was thrilled to hear the guide telling the party what great miners the Cornish were and pointing out the tools which they used all those years ago.

In Sovereign Hill there operates a bakery, and the speciality at lunch-time was Cornish pasties! As youngsters we were weaned on pasties, and I had to have one, although it was many years since I had eaten an acceptable commercially-made pasty. This pasty was just perfect and full of meat, and I returned and congratulated the baker, who told me that he had in fact come from good Cornish stock, as does the present Prime Minister of Australia, Bob Hawke. I was accompanied by Joe Jarick of Queensland who is the owner of a beautiful Austin-Healey 100 S and who is a great authority on these rare cars. Joe had had a surplus of

JF and Emmie, on their Golden Wedding day, 1947. (*B. Healey*).

the amber liquid upon which the Aussies thrive, and was suffering as a result. He never knew what he was missing in refusing such a delicacy — probably the finest cure for a hangover known to man!

J.F. and Emmie became parents on 3 July 1898 when my father, Donald Mitchell, was born in Woodbine Cottage, which is still standing despite the concrete jungle around it. He was followed by Edward, who died very shortly after birth, and then by Hugh Frederick some eight years later. By this time J.F. had become part of Perranporth and, as transport was practically non-existent in those days, he seldom returned to Bath. His two brothers Arthur and Archie had emigrated to South Africa, and his youngest brother Henry became a very good photographer and artist, and spent much time in Cornwall.

Truro was the nearest town, or city as it now is, nine miles from Perranporth and very proud of its cathedral. The only form of public transport between Truro and Perranporth, which ran twice weekly, was the horse bus operated by the Mitchell family, also of Perranporth but no relation to Sampson. Leaving Truro on the Perranporth road, one meets a steep hill and at the foot of this all men riding on the bus were requested to get down to give the horses a chance! I am told that the journey took just a little over three hours.

In 1909 the Great Western Railway Co. opened its branch line which linked Truro with Newquay, and this ran through some lovely countryside at a very leisurely pace, stopping at such stations as Chacewater, Blackwater, St Agnes, Mithian, Perranporth (which boasted both a halt and a station), Goonhaven, Shepherds, Trerice, Trewerry and others. This really put Perranporth in touch with the outside world, and the local schoolchildren were given free souvenir tickets on the opening day.

Donald became a regular passenger on this line when he was sent to Newquay College, now the site of the Hotel Bristol, and he quickly showed a flair for all things mechanical. During his holidays he built himself a canoe, which consisted of a wooden frame over which was stretched canvas, heavily painted to make it waterproof. He had a lot of fun with this, although his mother must have lived in fear every time he put to sea in it, as the north Cornish coast is not the sort of place for such a fragile craft. I can imagine how my mother felt many years later when Geoff and I repeated the exercise in a similar craft. Donald was brought up like all youngsters in Cornwall, in the traditions of the Methodists, and this meant going to chapel every Sunday followed by Sunday school in the afternoon. At that time the Boys' Brigade and the Band of Hope provided leisure-time activities.

During the period of my father's education, the motor car was something of a rarity, and a very unreliable one at that. J.F. had one of the first in Cornwall, let alone Perranporth, and this was a 1907 Panhard, on which he broke his arm on one occasion swinging it! The Panhard was followed by a variety of machines, mainly American as it seemed these were more readily available than the home product. He was a true motoring enthusiast and to a great degree he influenced his eldest son into deciding on making engineering his career, as he knew Donald was not interested in becoming a village grocer! There was nowhere in Cornwall to which he could go and learn to be an engineer, as the motor car was still a comparative novelty and few engineering companies engaged apprentices. So in 1914 Donald left school and his father paid £200 to enter him into an apprenticeship with Sopwith Aviation, took him up to Kington-on-Thames, found him some 'digs' with the local minister and his wife, and returned home. My father tells the story in Chapter 1.

My mother's side of the family originated from Bolingey, a small hamlet within one mile of Perranporth, and home of the Chudleigh family. A mining man, Edward Chudleigh had travelled extensively throughout the world, and had married and raised 7 children, the eldest of which, Mary Ellen, was a wiry but tough young lady. Grandpa Chud as we knew him, had spent many years in Kimberley, South Africa, where he had prospered, and he took members of his family with him on occasion. Mary Ellen had visited him as a girl of 10, having travelled by sailing ship from England, unaccompanied, locked in her cabin, and arriving in Cape Town six weeks later, from whence she had completed the journey by ox cart, taking a further three weeks. Living conditions were not really suitable for white children in Africa in those days, so she made only one trip and came home to Cornwall to go to school. Mary Ellen's four brothers all became involved in mining and again travelled to all parts of the globe where Cornish skill and expertise were needed. One brother, Bob, went to the United States for a period and I have a postcard in woven silk from my mother's collection, dated 1907, which was posted on the ill-fated *Lusitania* which was tragically sunk during the Great War.

Grandpa Chudleigh had accumulated a considerable amount of money during his working life and, being a very religious man and a strict Methodist, he spent both time and money on Bolingey Chapel. At that time it was the only Methodist Chapel in the district, Perranporth Chapel not yet having been built. A lovely stone building, the chapel has now been converted into flats, such is the progress of the Church of England into that hitherto Methodist stronghold, Cornwall. Strictly teetotal, he was never known to touch alcohol and even when on his death-bed he was offered brandy, he refused, saying that he was not going to meet his Maker with the smell of alcohol on his lips. He left the bulk of his money to some obscure Docks Commission in the East End of London, and his family could well have benefited from it.

Mary Ellen grew up into a very attractive young lady. A very strict upbringing ensured that Sunday was a day of rest in every respect and it was many years before my mother was able to persuade her that knitting on a Sunday was not really all that sinful, and that Sunday newspapers could be read without invoking the wrath of the Good Lord!

Faithful James was one of a family of 12 brothers who hailed from another small hamlet just to the north of Perranporth with the delightful name of Wheal Frances. There was little work in and around Perranporth, but there was plenty, as I have said before, for skilled hard-rock miners, and especially Cornish miners, overseas. Faithful and several of his brothers went overseas to seek their fortune. He too chose Kimberley, South Africa, although I do not know if he met his future father-in-law there. He worked hard in very difficult conditions, he prospered and purchased property in Cornwall including a small farm and land in Perranporth on which he built a home, which he named Kimberley, and which still stands in a prominent position overlooking the village. During his infrequent visits to England, Faithful courted Mary Ellen and eventually asked her to marry him, and she accepted.

After a short time together enjoying their new home, Faithful again departed for South Africa, delighted in the knowledge that Mary Ellen was going to bear him his first child, although he doubted if he would be home again in time for the big day. Faithful was destined not to come home again. He was some weeks out in the hinterland prospecting when he was taken ill with black-water fever, from which he died. His daughter Ivy was just seven weeks old.

Ivy grew up in Perranporth, was educated at Truro High School and was very gifted at music, playing the violin and organ. She did in fact play the organ in Perranporth Chapel where her mother was a trustee, and where she was subsequently to marry Donald.

At the turn of the century mining in Cornwall enjoyed a temporary boom and a few enterprising people decided to establish a factory for the manufacture of explosives to supply the mines. The Great St George mine at Perranporth had closed down some years earlier, but its isolation and general suitability made it first choice for the enterprise, and so was formed the Cornish Explosive Factory Ltd. Very shortly the company was taken over by the Nobel's Explosive Corporation, and at the outbreak of war the factory was utilized for the filling of hand grenades and the fitting of projectiles for shells. Some 1,000 local people were employed in this very necessary wartime exercise, and situated as it was on top of the cliffs, there was very little fear of damage to the village in the event of an explosion. Ivy James joined the staff of Nobel's, and was appointed as a chargehand. Whilst the work was probably pretty monotonous, I imagine that the employees, who were mostly women, felt that they were doing their bit for the lads in France. Occasionally the routine would be broken by the appearance, reasonably close inshore, of a German submarine on the surface, charging its batteries.

Ivy had never been away from home, apart from holiday jaunts within the county to stay with relatives, so when the opportunity arose to transfer to Bedford on a similar job she jumped at it and quickly settled in to her new and very strange surroundings. She was a great collector, and during the war she gathered together an excellent selection of cap badges from soldiers in the various regiments, including that of the Duke of Cornwall's Light Infantry — to the Cornish, Britain's finest regiment, but regretfully now merged with some junior regiment. She also amassed a considerable collection of postcards, all in albums and a constant source of pleasure to the family, as they were, in the main, posted in and around Cornwall. It is interesting to compare the villages they portray with the apologies for Cornwall that some of the coastal villages have become today.

For much of her life Ivy smoked, and that led to another collection, this time cards of different trades, sportsmen, military uniforms, birds' eggs, cars, wonders of the world, and many more. I am lucky enough to have retained these mementoes, despite several moves around the country.

The war over, Ivy returned to Perranporth to live with her widowed mother. Her time spent filling the grenades and handling explosive materials had left her with very yellow hands, which persisted for some time. Living in their home, Kimberley, she overlooked the village and in particular the Red House, where Donald was living with his parents. Both were readjusting to the slower pace of life and the newly-won peace, and inevitably in such a small community they soon met once again. Donald was becoming very involved with his garage and was building up a very good business. Ivy, with her machine shop experience in Bedford, was able to assist him in many ways, and this common interest brought them closer together, until on 21 October 1921 they were married in Perranporth Methodist Chapel.

# Donald Healey's competition career

| Year | Event | Car | Notes |
|------|-------|-----|-------|
| 1923 | London-Lands End Trial | A.B.C | First major event — wrecked valve gear on Porlock |
| 1924 | London-Lands End Trial | Riley | Car burnt out on way to start |
| | | Substituted A.B.C. | Won first Gold Medal |
| | Lands End-John O'Groats Trial | Ariel 10 | Gold Medal |
| 1925 | London-Lands End | Ariel 10 | Gold Medal |
| | J.C.C. High Speed Trial, Brooklands | Ariel 10 | First outing at Brooklands. Gold Medal |
| | Lands End-John O'Groats-Lands End (officially observed R.A.C. petrol consumption test) | Ariel 10 | Petrol consumption 52 mpg at average speed of 20 mile/h |
| 1926 | London-Lands End | Fiat 7 | Gold Medal |
| 1927 | London-Lands End | Rover 10 | Gold Medal |
| 1928 | London-Lands End | Triumph 7 | Silver Medal |
| | Bournemouth Rally | Triumph 7 | Premier Award, starting from John O'Groats |
| 1929 | Monte Carlo Rally (Riga start) | Triumph 7 | Unable to reach Riga, returned to Berlin and started there. 2 minutes outside time limit |

| Year | Event | Car | Notes |
|------|-------|-----|-------|
| | | | Monte. Won class at Mont des Mules hill climb |
| | London-Lands End | Triumph 7 supercharged | Gold Medal |
| | Brighton Rally | Triumph 7 | Premier award, starting from John O'Groats |
| | Riga-Barcelona | Triumph 7 | Class win, best British car |
| 1930 | Monte Carlo Rally (Tallinn start) | Triumph 7 | Snow and ice all the way. Seventh overall, first British car |
| | London-Lands End | Fiat 10 | Gold Medal |
| | Austria Alpine Trial | Invicta | Won Glacier Cup for penalty free run. Fastest climb of Arlberg Hill |
| 1930 | International Alford Alpine Trial | Invicta | Won Glacier Cup |
| 1931 | Monte Carlo Rally (Stavanger start) | Invicta | Made best time in final test. Won Rally outright |
| | International 10,000 km Trial | Riley 2 litre | Longest trial ever organized traversing 20 countries in 14 days, finishing in Berlin. No marks lost, won First Award |
| 1931 | Paris-Nice | Riley Nine | Class win |
| | La Turbie Hill Climb | Riley Nine | Class win |
| | International Alpine Trial | Invicta | Fastest climb of Galibier. Glacier Cup |
| 1932 | Monte Carlo Rally (Umea start) | Invicta | Second overall, first British car |
| | International Alpine Rally | Invicta | Fastest climb of Stelvio. Won Glacier Cup |

| Year | Event | Car | Notes |
|------|-------|-----|-------|
| | Klausen Hill Climb | Invicta | 2nd in unlimited class |
| | Tourist Trophy Race | Invicta | Seized axle in practice |
| | Brighton Speed Trials | Invicta | Tied for fastest time in class with Kay Petre who borrowed and drove same car |
| | Paris-Nice Rally | Invicta | Won class |
| 1933 | Monte Carlo Rally (Tallinn start) | Invicta | Crashed in Poland |
| | International Alpine Rally | Brooklands Riley | Glacier Cup |
| 1934 | Monte Carlo Rally (Athens start) | Triumph 10 | Third overall. First British car |
| | International Alpine Rally | Triumph 10 | Class fastest on Stelvio. Won Glacier Cup |
| 1935 | Monte Carlo Rally (Umea start) | Triumph Dolomite | Hit train in Denmark — unhurt |
| 1936 | Monte Carlo Rally | Triumph Dolomite | Eighth overall, first British car |
| | International Alpine Rally | Triumph 14 | Won Glacier Cup |
| 1937 | Monte Carlo Rally (Palermo start) | Triumph 12 | Retired with engine trouble |
| 1948 | Mille Miglia | Healey 'Westland' | Ninth overall, first British car |
| | Rally des Alpes | Healey 'Westland' | Lost marks through stopping to aid injured driver |
| 1949 | Mille Miglia | Healey 'Elliott' | Fourth in touring category (Son Geoff won touring category in Roadster) |
| 1949 | Rally des Alpes | Healey 'Silverstone' | Lost one mark through hold up at Level Crossing |

| Year | Event | Car | Notes |
|------|-------|-----|-------|
| 1950 | Mille Miglia | Nash-Healey | Failed to qualify after going into ditch |
| 1951 | Mille Miglia | Nash-Healey | Finished 30th overall |
| 1952 | Mille Miglia | Nash-Healey Saloon | Crashed after bursting tyre |
| 1953 | U.S.A. (Bonneville) Record Breaking | Austin-Healey '100' | International Records from 1,000 km to 5,000 km and 6 hours to 24 hours. American records from 1 km to 5,000 km and 24 hours. American flying mile 142.64 mile/h |
| 1954 | U.S.A. (Bonneville) Record Breaking | Austin-Healey '100-S' | International Records from 5 km to 5,000 km and 1 hour to 24 hours. American records 1 km to 5,000 km and 24 hours. American flying mile 192.62 mile/h |
| 1956 | U.S.A. (Bonneville) Record Breaking | Austin-Healey '100-Six' | Maximum speed reached 203.11 mile/h |

This table is reproduced by kind permission of G.T. Foulis & Co Ltd, from *Healeys and Austin-Healeys* by Peter Browning and Les Needham.

Having achieved the magical 200 miles per hour, Donald decided to call it a day after a competition career covering over 30 years. As a result he never drove a Sprite competitively or participated in the record runs with the streamlined EX 219 at Bonneville in 1969.

# Index